ecpr PRESS

I0094613

economic knowledge in regulation

the use of expertise by independent agencies

Lorna Sarah Schrefler

ecprPRESS

First published by the ECPR Press in 2013

The ECPR Press is the publishing imprint of the European Consortium for Political Research (ECPR), a scholarly association, which supports and encourages the training, research and cross-national cooperation of political scientists in institutions throughout Europe and beyond.

ECPR Press
University of Essex
Wivenhoe Park
Colchester
CO4 3SQ
UK

Typeset by Anvi

Printed and bound by Lightning Source

British Library Cataloguing in Publication Data

A catalogue record for this book is available from the British Library

Paperback ISBN: 978–1–907301–45–2

www.ecpr.eu/ecprpress

ECPR – Monographs
Series Editors:
Dario Castiglione (University of Exeter)
Peter Kennealy (European University Institute)
Alexandra Segerberg (Stockholm University)
Peter Triantafillou (Roskilde University)

The Nordic Voter: Myths of Exceptionalism (ISBN: 9781907301506) Åsa Bengtsson, Kasper M. Hansen, Olafur Þ. Harðarson, Hanne-Marthe Narud and Henrik Oscarsson

Representing Women?: Female Legislators in West European Parliaments (ISBN: 9780954796648) Mercedes Mateo Diaz

The Personalisation of Politics: A Study of Parliamentary Democracies (ISBN: 9781907301032) Lauri Karvonen

The Politics of Income Taxation: A Comparative Analysis (ISBN: 9780954796686) Steffen Ganghof

The Return of the State of War: A Theoretical Analysis of Operation Iraqi Freedom (ISBN: 9780955248856) Dario Battistella

Transnational Policy Innovation: The role of the OECD in the Diffusion of Regulatory Impact Analysis (ISBN:9781907301254) Fabrizio De Francesco

Urban Foreign Policy and Domestic Dilemmas: Insights from Swiss and EU City-regions (ISBN: 9781907301070) Nico van der Heiden

Why Aren't They There? The Political Representation of Women, Ethnic Groups and Issue Positions In Legislatures (ISBN: 9780955820397) Didier Ruedin

Widen the Market, Narrow the Competition: Banker Interests and the Making of a European Capital Market (ISBN: 9781907301087) Daniel Mügge

Please visit www.ecpr.eu/ecprpress for information about new publications.

To Dominik.

To my parents.

| contents

| list of figures and tables

list of abbreviations

21CN	Twenty-first Century Network
2G:	Second generation mobile telephones (*see also* GSM)
3G	Third generation mobile telephones (*see also* UMTS)
BEREC	Body of European Regulators in Electronic Communications
BIS	UK Department for Business, Innovation and Skills
BT	British Telecommunications Plc
C&W	Cable&Wireless
CAT	Competition Appeals Tribunal
CC	Competition Commission
CP	Communication Provider
CPB	Countervailing Buyer Power
CPS	Carrier Pre-Selection
DCMS	UK Department for Culture, Media and Sport
DTI	UK Department for Trade and Industry
ECTA	European Competitive Telecommunications Association
EOI	Equivalence of Input
ERG	European Regulators Group
EU	European Union
EU RF	European Regulatory Framework
FCS	Federation of Communication Services
GSM	Global System for Mobile Communication
IP	Internet Protocol
IRA	Independent Regulatory Agency
ISDN	Integrated Services Digital Network
ISP	Internet Server Provider
ISTPA	International Security Trust & Privacy Alliance
KCOM	Kingston Communications
LRIC	Long Run Incremental Costing
MNO	Mobile Network Operator
MPF	Metallic Path Facility
MTR	Mobile Termination Rates

NAO   National Audit Office
NGAN   Next Generation Access Network
NGN   Next Generation Network
NGNUK   Body set up by Ofcom to oversee NGN deployment in the UK
NRA   National Regulatory Authority
OECD   Organisation for Economic Co-operation and Development
Ofcom   Office of Communications
Ofgem   Office of Gas and Electricity Markets
Oftel   Office of Telecommunications
Ofwat   Office of Water
PTSN   Public Telephone Switched Network
(R)IA   (Regulatory) Impact Assessment
SMP   Significant Market Power
SMPF   Shared Metallic Path Facility (see above MPF)
SSE   Scottish Southern Energy
SSNIP   Small but Significant and Non-Transitory Increase in Price
TDM   Time Division Multiplexing
UKCTA   UK Competitive Telecommunications Association
UMTS   Universal Mobile Telecommunications System
WLR   Wholesale Line Rental

| acknowledgements

I would like to extend my sincere gratitude to all those who have contributed to the completion of this project with their intellectual, personal, and emotional support.

A big thank you goes to the Department of Politics at Exeter University for funding three years of my research and for offering an intellectually stimulating environment. I am particularly grateful to Professor Claudio Radaelli for his intellectual guidance, open mind, and his sharp and valuable comments on my work. I also indebted to Susan Banducci, Stephen Wilks, Claire Dunlop, Bruce Doern, Ian Sanderson and the Anonymous Reviewer for their interest in my research and the precious suggestions they offered along the way.

I would also like to thank all my academic colleagues and friends. Nicole Bolleyer, Theofanis Exadaktylos, Martino Maggetti, and Anne Meuwese deserve a special mention for their intellectual and personal encouragement.

I am particularly grateful to the all the interviewees from Ofcom, the European Commission, industry and academia that accepted to contribute to this research, as well as to the ECPR Press team. Without you, this book would not have seen the light.

I would also like to express my deepest gratitude to my colleagues at the Centre for European Policy Studies in Brussels, and in particular to Andrea Renda, Jacques Pelkmans and the Regulatory Policy team, Can, Consuelo, Federica and Giacomo, for giving me the support, space and time I needed to complete this book.

Last but not least, my deepest and heartfelt gratitude goes to my family and to Dominik.

Lorna S. Schrefler
July 2013

| credits

Figures supplied courtesy of:

- William Gormley, the Centre for European Policy Studies, Ofcom, The OECD (2008) Convergence and Next Generation Networks.
- Ministerial Background Report. Online. Available: DSTI/ICCP/CISP(2007)2/ FINAL http://www.oecd.org/sti/40761101.pdf.
- The National Audit Office for "The creation of Ofcom", page 4 of The creation of Ofcom: wider lessons for public sector mergers of regulatory agencies.
- HC 1175 Session 2005–2006, 5 July 2006. Online. Available: http://www. nao.org.uk/publications/0506/the_creation_of_ofcom_wider_l.aspx.
- "Ofcom's appeal costs" page 32 of The effectiveness of converged regulation. HC 490 Session 2010–20I0,10 November, 2010. Online. Available: http:// www.nao.org.uk/publications/1011/ofcom.aspx, Governance.

chapter one | introduction

Preliminary remarks

The focus of this book is the use[1] of knowledge, and in particular of economic analysis, by Independent Regulatory Agencies (IRAs), the appointed bodies[2] entrusted with regulatory powers in a given policy sector that have become a core feature of the modern regulatory state (Majone 1994, 1997). Examining the role of knowledge in policy-making is particularly relevant in the case of IRAs as, very often, their legitimacy and the justification for their existence are based on the assumption that these organisations will use knowledge to perform their duties (Majone 1996; Vibert 2007). In this respect, the following quotation from the European Commission's operating framework for European Regulatory Agencies is rather telling:

> The independence of their technical and/or scientific assessments is, in fact, their real raison d'être. The main advantage of using the agencies is that their decisions are based on purely technical evaluations of very high quality and are not influenced by political or contingent considerations. (COM 2002 718 final: 5)

Similar views are echoed in the House of Lords' 2007 Report on Economic Regulators in the United Kingdom. In a way, expectations on the fundamental role of expertise[3] in IRAs have become almost institutionalised and taken for granted, without being adequately problematised or questioned. In fact, theoretical and empirical research on the role of knowledge in the decision-making process of these organisations is still scarce.

On the other hand, several scholars (for example, Feldman and March 1981; Heller 1986; Lindquist 1988; Weiss C. H. 1979, 1986; Wittrock 1991) have investigated the role of knowledge in decision-making and, in particular, the impact of policy-relevant research on the actual content of policies adopted by governments. This strand of literature portrays a rather complex link between expertise and policy, where relevant knowledge is not always reflected in policy outcomes and ends up playing several functions besides 'speaking truth to power'

---

1.   In this book, 'use', 'usage' and 'utilisation' are used interchangeably, since instances of knowledge use are also instances of modes of using.

2.   IRAs are formally separated from parent ministries and are not elected or managed by elected officials (Thatcher 2002b: 956). For further details, *see* Chapter Two.

3.   Throughout the book, I employ the terms 'expertise' and 'knowledge' interchangeably.

and facilitating the solution of policy problems. For instance, knowledge can be used by an organisation to gain legitimacy in its policy environment and establish its reputation as a credible actor (Boswell 2009).

These findings put theoretical and normative expectations about the role of knowledge within IRAs in a different perspective and raise a series of new research questions on the input that expertise has in regulatory decision-making. In particular, how do independent regulatory agencies use knowledge? Do they use expertise for other purposes than problem-solving? And, if so, what are possible alternative usages of knowledge and when do they occur? Without an answer to those questions, we will keep facing what regulatees in policy debates call 'the black box' of an agency's decision-making, where expert input enters the agency but results in sometimes unpredictable or questionable regulatory outcomes.

Defining knowledge

Following Boswell (2009: 23–4) 'expert knowledge...refers very loosely to the knowledge produced by academic research'. As pointed out in many instances (e.g. Wilsdon *et al.* 2005), the boundaries between this type of knowledge and more practical and lay expertise are not always clear cut. Against this backdrop, Boswell (2009) puts forward two criteria to distinguish academic knowledge from other types of expertise, including that produced by generalists in the civil service: the method of production and the setting of production. The former indicates that, to be considered as such, research knowledge must conform to a set of standards commonly accepted in most research disciplines, for example, the process and methodology employed for producing the knowledge must be clear and acceptable to most scholars, substance must be coherent theoretically and conceptually and findings should be transparent enough to be replicated by other researchers. As regards the setting (what Boswell calls the 'institutional context') of production, expert knowledge should be generated by people having appropriate qualifications and who are normally affiliated to specific institutions such as academic bodies or dedicated research departments in government and agencies.

An assumption that Boswell (rightly) does not make but that is often implicit, particularly in policy circles (e.g. European Commission 2002; House of Lords 2007), up to the point of becoming a third criterion for some, is that research knowledge is neutral, that is, it portrays reality objectively and without bias. This belief stems from the fact that research knowledge is perceived as being produced in a *super partes* setting, which is relatively immune from the influence of specific interests. As the remainder of this book shows, this assumption is inaccurate for disciplines such as economics and has also been questioned by some (e.g. Abraham and Sheppard 1999; Latour and Woolgar 1979; Montpetit 2011: 518) in the case of natural sciences. Moreover, even if we assume that neutral expertise exists, this does not automatically imply that such neutral knowledge will also be used in a neutral/unbiased way by policy-makers.

Hence, neutrality should not be considered as a criterion for identifying research knowledge, especially in relation to decision-making. In fact, the neutrality label becomes particularly misleading in a public-policy context, in which values are often at stake (Jennings and Hall 2011; Lindblom 1959, 1979), as expertise can be invoked by policy-makers to make truth claims about a preferred course of action that bears no specific relation to the way used knowledge was produced in the first place.

What this book is about

As mentioned, this book addresses the underexplored question of the usage of (economic) knowledge by independent regulatory agencies. My main argument is that, in the context of regulatory policy-making, the traditional depiction of an instrumental/problem-solving use of knowledge[4] as the only approach to expertise in decision-making is inaccurate. This is so even in an ideal setting, such as that of an independent regulator in charge of technical dossiers. Instrumental/problem-solving may be the prevalent usage of expertise for an IRA but it tends to be complemented by other approaches. Specifically, I identify four possible uses of expertise (instrumental/problem-solving, strategic, symbolic, and non-use) and illustrate how each use follows a certain logic and may be (more or less deliberately) selected by an IRA as an appropriate response to a given set of circumstances. Rather than anomalies, these different usages of knowledge appear as a natural feature of the policy process and can at times be beneficial, damaging, or simply the only possible path for a regulator. The book seeks to explain under which scope conditions each use is most likely to occur.

Hence, this book intends to contribute primarily to the literature on knowledge-utilisation by testing some of its main tenets in a setting that offers, *prima facie*, the perfect context for observing patterns of production and use of expert knowledge. In addition, I also put forward a possible solution to one of the core challenges for knowledge-utilisation scholars: the difficulty of operationalising research questions on the role of expertise in policy-making. Knowledge is only one ingredient of the policy process, and disentangling its influence from that of other equally relevant variables is undoubtedly a daunting task. This point is possibly the best explanation for the gradual decrease in the number of publications on the topic after its initial success, with some notable exceptions (e.g. Jennings and Hall 2011; Radaelli 1995; Radaelli and Dente 1996; Weiss C. H. 1999).

While scholarly attention for the issue of knowledge-utilisation may have diminished, its relevance remains unquestionable. In fact, it has become a central topic in recent debates on evidence-based policy-making (Baldwin 2005; European Commission 2001, 2005; Hahn and Tetlock 2008; Jennings and Hall 2011; Meuwese 2008; Nutley *et al.* 2007; Radaelli 2009b; Sanderson 2009) and, more generally, in connection with the administrative reform movements of the

---

4. An instrumental use of knowledge implies that expertise is directly used to solve a policy problem and thus entails a clear connection between knowledge and policy solutions. The different usages of knowledge employed in this book are described in detail in Chapter Two.

last decades (European Commission 2001; OECD 2002; Galli and Pelkmans 2000; Pollitt and Bouckaert 2000; Radaelli and Meuwese 2009). Knowledge and – in particular – specific tools and methods for producing, systematising and connecting expertise to policy-making remain at the core of regulatory-reform initiatives (Radaelli 2005b, 2007) and have increasingly spread to developing countries, thanks to the influence of international organisations (OECD 2002; World Bank 2004). In some cases, the use of evidence in policy-making has become one of the conditions imposed by international donors for granting aid to developing countries (Kirkpatrick and Parker 2007). Therefore, the Pandora's Box of knowledge-utilisation is open again. As in the case of independent regulatory agencies, however, theoretical and normative contributions on the role of expertise abound (e.g. Lambright 2008) but the empirical question of how knowledge is actually used in a policy context remains relatively unexamined.

Exploring how IRAs use knowledge and economic analysis in particular is closely linked to crucial questions in political science: the interaction between politics and bureaucracy (Majone 1996; Pierre and Peters 2004; Radaelli 2009b; Thatcher 2002b, 2005); the control over and accountability of public institutions (McCubbins *et al.* 1987, 1989), especially those with delegated decision-making powers; the effectiveness of the state; and issues of governance, transparency and so on.

Although elusive in nature, the use of knowledge always occurs in a specific context and within a given timeframe: as an intrinsic part of the policy-process it is automatically connected to the explanatory variables commonly used to explain policy outcomes and reconstruct the mechanisms that generated them. While these remarks may appear somewhat obvious, this linkage tends to be overlooked in the knowledge-utilisation literature, due to its deliberate focus on the puzzle of the different uses or non-use of expertise by decision-makers.

Yet the very relevance of this research and of this book lies in a contribution to a better understanding of policy processes. Only a strong anchoring of research questions on knowledge-utilisation to political science debates can improve our understanding of the rationale for the range of attitudes policy-makers have towards expertise. By the same token, this book contributes to the literature on IRAs and adds a missing piece of our picture of the functioning of these organisations. In fact, this book is also an attempt to bridge the gap between two strands of literature whose research questions are often intertwined but which have been treated separately until now.

Before I move on to illustrate in greater detail the scope of this research, it is worth clarifying what this book will not do. My work cannot be inscribed among science and technology studies, as my research questions do not touch upon the ethical issues that are central to this literature. Moreover, I do not concentrate extensively on the production of knowledge, except when it has a bearing on the final usage of a given piece of evidence. In the same vein, I do not directly contribute to current research on the regulation of risk, although the issue of risk and uncertainty in policy decisions inevitably surfaces in the empirical part of the book. However, my focus remains essentially on the policy process and the institutional and political context of regulatory decision-making.

My research questions on the role of expertise in the decision-making process of IRAs will be limited to the case of economics. Economic knowledge, also termed economic analysis/expertise or simply economics in the pages that follow, is intended as the product of economic research performed according to methodological criteria commonly accepted by the discipline and by qualified people affiliated to traditional research settings (that is, academia, think tanks, research units in organisations and specialised government departments).

The choice of economics among the different types of expert knowledge available to policy-makers was driven by three motivations. First, growing attention to the role of the state in the economy, coupled with ongoing discussions on the sustainability of public finances, particularly in the wake of the recent economic and financial crises, have embedded economic reasoning in most policy debates (Furner and Supple 1990; Hall 1989; Revesz and Livermore 2008). Hence, economics, more than other social and natural sciences, has a constant presence in the policy-making process. Secondly, in contrast to other types of academic knowledge such as physics or biology, the basic concepts and tools of economics are widespread beyond academic circles and have increasingly become part of the qualifications required by bureaucracies in modern governments. This trend is reflected, for instance, in the growing emphasis on the value for money of individual policies in political debates. As a consequence, economic expertise offers a better avenue for tackling questions of knowledge-utilisation in policy-making, given that communications between experts, bureaucrats, and politicians faces fewer barriers for this discipline than in other cases.

Finally, the debate on evidence-based policy-making (Nutley *et al.* 2007; Pawson 2002; Sanderson 2002, 2006, 2009) and the growing diffusion among public administrations of policy tools and initiatives based on economic reasoning, such as cost-benefit analysis, regulatory-impact assessments, performance indicators, the quantification of administrative burdens and compliance costs for business, have made economics unavoidable both for governments and for actors wishing to play a role in the policy process. For the former, economic tools are often part of a broader programme of administrative reform (European Commission 2001, 2005; House of Lords 2007; National Audit Office 2007; OECD 1995, 2005; Radaelli 2009b); for the latter they have become additional means to access and influence policy-makers as well as a way to hold state institutions accountable (Meuwese 2008; McCubbins *et al.* 1987, 1989). Regardless of the normative debates surrounding the role of economics in public policy (Ackerman and Heinzerling 2004; Hahn 2005; Posner 2001; Revesz and Livermore 2008), economic expertise has clearly acquired a special status in policy-making. It is thus worthwhile having a closer look at the implications of this state of things with respect to knowledge-utilisation questions.

These remarks are even more appropriate in the case of many independent regulatory agencies and their role in modern states. As stressed by Pierre Larouche (2008), when regulatory functions are separated from operational ones – which is exactly what happened with the liberalisation and privatisation of several network industries (for example, telecommunications, electricity, railways, postal services, gas) in the past few decades – the regulator lets go of the sector to a certain extent. As a result, an independent regulatory agency has less control over the features of the industry than when the state was directly responsible for producing and providing services. Moreover, in a liberalised sector where different players compete on the market, a purely technical knowledge of the industry and its infrastructure is not sufficient to regulate. Under these circumstances, technical aspects become closely connected to broader public policy goals linked to efficiency and the (re)distribution of scarce resources. Hence, the production and use of economic knowledge is not only embedded in general expectations about the legitimacy and the role of the regulatory agency (European Commission 2002; Majone 1996; Vibert 2007); it is also a pivotal instrument for the actual execution of its duties. Such a view is so widely held that authoritative scholars go so far as to claim that economic analysis is 'the tool' for regulatory authorities (De Streel 2008a; Larouche 2008) in many sectors. In this context, understanding how independent regulators function in practice and how they relate to other actors in their policy field inevitably requires an analysis of the role of economic knowledge in such organisations.

While the use of economics is widespread in many policy areas, the empirical chapters of this book will concentrate on the telecommunications sector. Liberalisation and the creation of IRAs in that field occurred more than a decade ago: as a result, the position of independent regulators is clearly established and observable. In addition, the regulation of telecommunications is particularly well suited to the use of economic analysis. It could be argued that other types of knowledge (for example, engineering) are equally relevant for the regulation of telecommunications. While this is certainly true in some cases, economics plays a prominent role in most policy dossiers in this field. This is due to the prevalence in telecoms regulation of classical economic issues such as monopolies, economic bottlenecks and the trade-off between private goals and general public policy objectives over other considerations – such as environmental protection, health and safety and so on. Moreover, the recent evolution of the sector increasingly brings economics to the fore. In particular, the advent of the Internet, path-breaking technological change and the growing convergence between previously separated areas (for example, telephone services and television) have profoundly affected the business models of market players and their respective equilibria. As a result, and much more than in the past, technical and economics aspects are closely related, with economic and commercial choices sometimes driving technological ones, as in the last case study presented in this book. In terms of knowledge-utilisation, this means that telecommunications regulators are faced both with policy problems that are relatively easy to address, and with complex and often intractable questions. In turn, this shows how economics can play a different role within the same organisation, depending on specific circumstances and the type of policy questions under examination.

I will concentrate in particular on the case of the UK Office of Communications (Ofcom) which was among the first IRAs to be established on a global scale and has a proven and traceable track record in the production and use of economic analysis.

The rationale behind my case selection is further explained in Chapter Three. I can, however, mention here that, in many respects, Ofcom is an example of a well functioning independent regulator which has managed to address some of the classical challenges of these organisations through a series of reforms and learning processes since the liberalisation of telecoms in the UK in 1984. Hence, while my findings on knowledge-utilisation cannot be generalised, it is fair to expect that, if non-instrumental usages of knowledge find a place in Ofcom, they are (even more) likely to occur in younger organisations or in regulators with less capacity. As mentioned, the literature on the use of expertise by independent regulators is relatively scarce; however, this is even more evident for European agencies, as most empirically focused publications (e.g. McGarity 1991; Morgenstern 1997; Jennings and Hall 2011) are on US regulators. Focusing on Ofcom allows me to partially fill this gap. I will come back to these points in the course of the book.

Research design and methodology

In terms of research design, this book draws on the methodological device of explanatory typologies (Elman 2005). I apply the core ideas of Colin Elman's approach to derive, describe, and classify a set of causal links, drawn from the findings of the literature on knowledge-utilisation and on independent regulatory agencies respectively. This approach has two advantages: it is fertile ground for gaining empirical insights into the use of expertise, which is traditionally difficult to operationalise. It also allows me to capture, albeit in a simplified manner, some of the central mechanisms that are at work in regulatory policy processes.

Specifically, to explore the role of economic analysis in IRAs, I have selected two explanatory dimensions that reflect both the context and the content of policy: the level of conflict in the policy arena and the degree of tractability of a policy problem. These variables are treated as a continuum in the book so as to reproduce the dynamic nature of policy processes. Although the structure of my explanatory typology is the subject of Chapter Three, I can make anticipatory mention that I will use different combinations of these two dimensions to derive four hypotheses on the possible uses of economic analysis by an IRA: instrumental/problem-solving, strategic, symbolic, and non-use.

The elusive nature of knowledge-utilisation makes the identification and measurement of different uses of expertise highly dependent on an in-depth understanding of the institutional, organisational and political context in which a regulatory decision is taken. I have thus opted for a qualitative approach, based on case studies and process-tracing (Bennett 2010; Brady 2010; Freedman 2010) to appraise the four hypotheses. In a way, my approach, especially for the empirical part of the book and the interpretation of findings, can be described as pragmatic (Sil and Katzenstein 2010).[5] My choice is motivated by the fact that, in the study of the policy process, there are elements that are ontologically subjective, that is,

---

5. The authors term it 'analytic eclecticism'. For further details, *see* Chapter Three.

they exist only as shared representations. However, these ontologically subjective elements can still be captured by an objective epistemology (Jones and McBeth 2010). To illustrate, a narrative of public policy is ontologically subjective. Yet it can be coded, and its effects on public opinion measured. In other words, it can be examined with an objective epistemology.[6] This pragmatic approach should increase our chances of observing causality *in vivo* and help us derive insights into the sequences and causal mechanisms at play in each episode. I have appraised the proposed hypotheses with the help of three case studies on regulatory policy decisions taken by Ofcom between 2005 and 2010.

For the empirical part of the book I performed a qualitative analysis of all the official documents relating to each case study, complemented by 34 interviews with a selection of relevant actors. Given the amount of written material to be examined and the presence of the classical 'thick' descriptions that characterise case-study work, I undertook a qualitative coding of the sources with the NVivo software. This allowed me to systematise my work, record and keep trace of the different stages of analysis, assess potential relationships between variables, identify patterns, and uncover mechanisms and their direction for each episode. Additional details on these aspects are provided in Chapter Three and in the appendix.

Structure of the book

In order to tackle these research questions, I have structured the book as follows. Chapter Two contains a review of the literature and is divided in three parts. The first provides an overview of the contributions on knowledge-utilisation and introduces the taxonomy of the different knowledge usages that I seek to explain in this book. The second part reviews the literature on IRAs from three theoretical perspectives: delegation of powers to independent bodies; organisational theories; and the literature on the policy process. The third part of the chapter discusses what each of these theoretical contributions on IRAs has to say in terms of knowledge-utilisation.

Chapter Three introduces the research design of the book, namely, an explanatory typology and the four hypotheses on the different uses of knowledge. The chapter also illustrates in greater detail my methodological approach and the rationale for the case selection. It concludes with a description of the challenges faced during the fieldwork and the solutions I have adopted in each case.

The empirical part of the book starts with Chapter Four. It describes the agency under examination, the UK Office of Communications (Ofcom), and illustrates the institutional and political context in which the agency operates, thus setting

---

6. When introducing their 'narrative policy framework', Jones and McBeth explain that this approach should not be seen 'as a threat to post-positivist approaches to narrative but rather as an acknowledgment that narratives matter and that by studying them in a systematic empirical manner, positivists and post-positivists can engage in more productive debates over how stories influence public policy' (2010: 330).

the scene for the three case studies of the book. The first case, the regulation of fixed narrowband retail services, is presented in Chapter Five. According to the explanatory typology used in this book, this case appears as an ideal candidate for observing an instrumental/problem-solving use of economic analysis. Chapter Six discusses our hypothesis on strategic usages of knowledge, with a policy episode on the regulation of mobile termination rates. The third and last case study, on Next Generation Networks (NGNs), is presented in Chapter Seven. Covering a policy dossier that stretches between 2005 and 2010, it shows how knowledge usages evolve through time, in line with the dynamic nature of the policy process. In that particular instance, I observe a shift from an instrumental use of knowledge geared towards learning to a symbolic use and a non-use of expertise. Finally, Chapter Eight analyses my empirical findings and concludes.

chapter two | a review of the literature

Knowledge-utilisation: the literature and its role in political science debates

During the late 1970s and 1980s, the apparent contrast between the decoupling of research from policy decisions on the one hand and the increasing emphasis on the importance of expertise for policy-making on the other gradually led to the development of a specific research stream in political science: knowledge-utilisation.

In her seminal work, Carol H. Weiss (1979) suggests a possible explanation for the undeniable disconnection between researchers and policy-makers by going beyond Nathan Caplan's (1979) classical theory of the 'two communities', that is, the existence of a cultural gap, in terms of values and ideologies, between academics and politicians, which severely hampers the transfer of knowledge between the two. While Weiss certainly acknowledges the existence of such a divide, which she partly attributes to researchers and the way they craft and inappropriately communicate knowledge to policy-makers (Weiss 1999),[1] her work points to one of the main weaknesses of the two communities' theory: it only sheds light on the dichotomy between the use and non-use of expertise. This is merely one part of the picture, however, as the use of knowledge is not a monolithic concept corresponding to a linear transfer of research findings into policy-making. As extensively demonstrated by Weiss, knowledge can play several functions in policy; in fact, she identifies six types of possible knowledge usages besides the general role of contributing to the 'intellectual pursuit of a society' (1979: 430). The first type is the knowledge-driven model, which mimics the natural sciences approach, where research discloses some opportunity and, ideally, policy will follow this initial input. Weiss stresses that this type of usage rarely occurs among policy-makers. Conversely, the remaining five models easily find their place in the daily practice of policy-making:

1. the knowledge-driven model where research discloses opportunities;

2. the problem-solving model, in which researchers produce knowledge to solve a given policy question;

3. the interactive model, in which social scientists and other actors pool resources to feed research in the policy process;

---

1. On the 'communication sins' of researchers *see also* Lindblom (1986).

4. the political model, in which research is used as ammunition in support of a predetermined position;

5. the tactical model, in which research is 'used for purposes that have little relation to the substance of the research' (Weiss C.H.1979: 429), such as gaining legitimacy in the eyes external actors; and finally

6. the enlightenment model, in which research has a long-term impact on the way decision-makers interpret the world and the challenges facing them.

Building on this insight, several alternative classifications and explanations of the possible uses of knowledge are provided in the literature (e.g. Boswell 2006, 2009; Lindquist 1988; Hertin et al. 2008; Radaelli 1995; Weiss C. H. 1986, 1999) and show how knowledge can perform different functions, depending on its position in the various phases of the policy cycle. Hence, potential usages by policy-makers will vary accordingly.

Solving the puzzle of the role of expertise in policy-making remains a complex task: how many types of knowledge are available to decision-makers (Albæk 1995; Morgenstern 1997; Weiss C. H. 1991, 1999)? Which conditions facilitate the use of knowledge in policy-making (Owens et al. 2004; Radaelli 1995)? What are the impacts of commissioned research on final policy outcomes (Caplan 1979; Haas 1992; Heller 1986; Lindblom 1959; Lindblom and Cohen 1979; Sabatier and Jenkins-Smith 1993; Weiss C. H. 1979, 1986, 1999)? Does the evaluation of past policies matter for future decisions (Weiss C. H. 1999)? Can policy-makers learn from the knowledge that is produced and transmitted to them (Biegelbauer 2007; Dunlop 2009, 2010; Owens et al. 2004; Radaelli 2009a)?

Although giving a full account of the different answers that scholars have provided to these questions would require a dedicated work, the literature does seem to confirm the initial intuition of the pioneers in the field: knowledge does not often have a direct and recognisable impact on the policy for which it was produced/commissioned (Jennings and Hall 2011; Morgenstern 1997; Premfors 1984, 1991; Weiss C. H. 1986; Wittrock 1991) and – more importantly – knowledge can be used in different ways by policy-makers (Boswell 2006, 2009; Hertin et al. 2008; Radaelli 1995, 2009a; Weiss C. H. 1986, 1999). These findings would, however, benefit from additional empirical research to further dissect implicit theoretical and normative assumptions on the role of expertise in policy-making and bring to the fore under-explored aspects of this research question.[2]

---

2. For example, in their empirical study of the use of scientific evidence in policy-making in the US, Jennings and Hall (2011) point to another problem: evidence may be misused by policy-makers as 'administrators in some fields of practice are less likely to possess the scientific background necessary to properly evaluate the credibility of a piece of evidence with which they are presented'. This happens, for instance, when research findings are used to answer questions falling beyond the actual scope of the original research. Jennings and Hall focus on a broad set of agencies; I only look at IRAs which, in line with common assumptions, tend to possess enough expertise to avoid facing this problem.

The explanandum: a taxonomy of knowledge usages

As mentioned, many classifications of knowledge usages exist in the literature and – whereas labels may vary – one can identify several commonalities between these categorisations by looking at the rationale underpinning each type of use. Although they occur in different contexts, very often, knowledge usages can be ascribed to one of the following three logics: an instrumental/problem-solving logic; a strategic logic; or a logic of appropriateness (March and Olsen 1989), in which knowledge is used to conform to certain expectations. These three logics are the foundations of the classification used here, which I owe to a great extent to Boswell (2006, 2009) and her comprehensive synthesis of previous attempts to describe and categorise existing uses of expertise. While I essentially follow Boswell's taxonomy of knowledge usages, I have adapted her labelling to the specific case of regulatory agencies and their position in the policy arena. From an organisational perspective, the focus of this book is deliberately narrower than Boswell's: IRAs are traditionally in charge of 'technical' dossiers, and thus expected to adhere to a problem-solving use of expertise (Boswell 2009; Weiss C. H. 1999).[3] I wish to explore whether this assumption is warranted and under which circumstances an independent regulator will depart from this type of knowledge usage. This will develop our current theoretical understanding of the functioning of independent agencies and explore normative issues concerning whether departures from an instrumental use of expertise are an anomaly or a logical response to certain features of the policy-making process.

A good starting point for classifying possible uses of knowledge is to consider the dichotomy between the use and non-use of pertinent expertise, that is, the puzzle that originated this stream of research. As noted by Caplan (1979) three decades ago, the resources invested by policy-makers in producing and gathering knowledge are seldom matched by an equal amount of use and impact on final policies. Explaining this mismatch requires an investigation of the rationale for not using available knowledge when it is relevant for a given policy issue.[4]

In the context of IRAs and policy-making, several reasons for not using policy-relevant expertise come to mind: research findings could damage a preferred policy option that has already been chosen or is the only viable one in political terms. Another possibility occurs when the regulatory agency is bound by the electoral commitments of the principal and thus knowledge, although available, does not really play a role in decision-making. Finally, a third explanation could be that pre-existing decision-making patterns and approaches to tackling a given policy issue are so entrenched in an agency that expertise does not really make

---

3. The scope of my research is also narrower in another sense: while Boswell focuses on organisations and their overall *modus operandi* as far as knowledge-utilisation is concerned, the empirical part of this book covers specific episodes and the expertise (in the form of documents) used in each case.

4. It is worth remembering that the question of knowledge-usage is being treated from the perspective of the regulatory agency and not from the perspective of its political principals.

a difference when decisions are taken, particularly when these involve small, incremental changes to existing policies (Hall 1993).

Let us now look at the other side of the coin and introduce the three types of knowledge usages employed in this book and their underlying rationales.

The first type of usage, which I will call instrumental, corresponds to the 'problem-solving' model described by Weiss C. H. (1979) and is the approach commonly referred to in regulatory reform debates (e.g. European Commission 2001, 2005; House of Lords 2007; OECD 2002) and, more broadly, in rational accounts of the policy process (Albæk 1995; Caplan 1979; Torgerson 1986; Weiss C. H. 1979). An instrumental use of knowledge implies a direct connection between research findings and policy solutions/decisions: under this model, expertise is used to perform specific tasks at a given point in time and it is assumed that, once policy problems are identified, knowledge is the means by which to select the best solution for the issue at stake. The instrumental use has both a short- and long-term justification: in the former case, knowledge is used by a regulatory agency to deliver specific outputs in line with the targets the agency has set for itself or that it has been given by its political principals. In the long-run justification, however, knowledge is used to improve the agency's problem-solving capacity (Boswell 2006; Weiss C. H. 1979: 427–8) and increase its understanding of certain policy issues or, in other words, to learn (Radaelli 2009a).

A second type of usage is of a more strategic nature and, while it retains a direct connection with decision-making, this has little to do with identifying the most suitable solution to a given policy problem. In fact, the strategic use of knowledge can perform two functions: political and substantiating. The political strategic use of knowledge is related to the position of the agency in the policy arena and depends on the context and the actors that the agency faces when carrying out its tasks (Sabatier 1999, 2007; Sabatier and Jenkins-Smith 1993). The micro-foundations of this approach can be traced back to an agency's need to respond to oversight mechanisms, such as judicial review, and, in general, to the control of political principals and regulatees. This approach is what Weiss defines as a tactical use of knowledge (Weiss C. H. 1979: 429) and can serve a wide array of purposes, such as increasing the political leverage of the agency, expanding its powers and resources and safeguarding its actions from the potential opposition of the parent ministry.

The substantiating strategic usage (Boswell 2006, 2009) is instead closely linked to the content of policies and less so to the political environment in which these policies are devised. Typically, an agency adopts a strategic substantiating use of knowledge in order to justify and support a predetermined/preferred policy solution (Haas 2004: 573). For example, this happens when a regulatory impact assessment is carried out *ex-post* to justify the adoption of a pre-selected policy option, or when an economic model is deliberately built on certain assumptions so as to obtain a specific result. This substantiating use of knowledge can also serve as ammunition in an adversarial context (Boswell 2006; Sabatier 1999, 2007; Sabatier and Jenkins-Smith 1993). In this case, the agency will select and use knowledge in a manner that supports its preferred approach against the ones favoured by other actors in the policy arena.

Finally, the third type of use is symbolic and is normally driven by a logic of appropriateness (Goffman 1959). In this case, knowledge mainly serves the purpose of gaining legitimacy *vis-à-vis* other policy actors (Boswell 2006): it can help the agency to prove its competence and rationality (Radaelli 1995: 162) and to respond to external expectations and pressures to conform to a specific trend within its policy sector, as depicted in the literature on isomorphism[5] (di Maggio and Powell 1983). If other agencies in the same sector routinely use expertise and research findings to carry out their tasks, a newcomer is pressured to adopt similar behaviour, in order to be accepted as a credible player in the policy arena, and may thus turn to a symbolic use of knowledge whenever it lacks the internal means/resources to produce relevant expertise. This symbolic usage can also have a protective function, when an agency is not acting on a specific policy problem but still wants/needs to signal that something is being done about it (Hertin *et al.* 2008). The difference between this approach and the strategic and instrumental knowledge usages outlined above lies in that the latter are always connected to a specific policy decision, while symbolic uses are generally de-coupled from decisions and merely serve as a means to meet external expectations about the agency's use of expertise, or simply to signal the presence of expert staff in-house. As described in organisational theories and particularly by scholars focusing on a logic of appropriateness (e.g. Boswell 2006, 2009; Brunsson 1989), an adequate response to external expectations is often as important as performing mandated tasks; however, the symbolic use of knowledge is not a viable option for an agency in the long run: it is rather a preliminary form of one of the other types of knowledge uses, or a complement to another type, as no agency can afford to pretend to be doing something for a sustained period of time.[6]

The different uses and their micro-foundations[7] are summarised in Table 2.1.

These are of course ideal types (Weber 1949[1904]) that are not mutually exclusive and can often coexist within the same regulatory agency, depending on the circumstances. Identifying those circumstances and deriving theoretical insights into the impact that such circumstances have on an IRA's approach to (economic) expertise will be the topic of Chapter Three. But let us now turn to the main actors of this book, independent regulatory agencies.

---

5. Powell and di Maggio's concept of isomorphism refers to similarity between institutions in terms of either structures or processes. In the authors' words it is 'a constraining process that forces one unit in a population to resemble other units that face the same set of environmental conditions' (di Maggio and Powell 1983: 146).

6. I am grateful to Claire Dunlop for her suggestions on this point.

7. Developed by economists, the concept of micro-foundations is used by Coleman (1990) in political science to explain the micro-level components of phenomena that are visible at the macro/aggregate level. Maggetti *et al.* (2012: 38) describe it as 'the relationship between an aggregate variable and the individual variables. Individual variables may refer to the single individual as a unit, or to organisations, states, parliaments and so on.'

Table 2.1: Types of knowledge uses and their micro-foundations

Type of knowledge-utilisation	Micro-foundations *A regulatory agency uses knowledge to:*
Instrumental	• Carry out assigned tasks/mandate. • Improve own problem-solving abilities, (e.g. problem-solving in Boswell 2006). • Increase understanding of issue (enlightenment model/ conceptual use: Weiss C. H. 1979: 430 and Weiss 1999: 477) and to learn (Owens *et al.* 2004).
Symbolic	• Gain legitimacy (e.g. prove own rationality and competence: Radaelli 1995:162). • Emulate similar structures and conform to expectations. • Signal political responses to perceived policy problems, in absence of actual measures (Hertin *et al.* 2008).
Strategic *(a) political*	• Respond to control from principal(s), judiciary or regulatees (tactical model: Weiss C. H. 1979: 429). Expand own power/leverage (Weiss' tactical model; Boswell 2006: 7).
(b) substantiating	• Justify a preferred/predetermined policy choice. • Use as ammunition in adversarial context (Weiss 1979: 429).
Non-use	• Avoid undermining preferred policy option. Respect electoral commitment of political principal(s). • Follow established decision-making patterns within agency.

Independent regulatory agencies and the regulatory state

The first step for understanding how independent regulatory agencies (IRAs) use knowledge, and in particular economic analysis, in policy-making is to provide an overview of the reasons behind the creation of these organisations, of their main features and of the internal and external factors that are likely to have an impact on their approach to economics and research findings in general.

The spread of independent regulatory agencies across developed and developing countries is generally linked to the increasing liberalisation of national economies and to the pervasive movement towards what Majone (1994, 1997) terms the 'regulatory state', as opposed to the traditional model of governance provided by the 'positive state' (*see also* Gilardi 2002b; Loughlin and Scott 1997; Maggetti 2007; Vibert 2007).[8] In particular, the growing number of IRAs in North America, Europe and several other countries stems from the liberalisation and privatisation

---

8. Majone (1997:149) provides a detailed comparison of the key features of the two types of states. Essentially the main functions of the positive state are to deal with redistribution and macro-economic stabilisation, while the regulatory state intervenes to address market failures. In turn, the two types of state will have different institutions, policy instruments, areas of political conflict, forms of accountability, and so on. Independent agencies are a typical feature of the regulatory state.

of strategic industries such as utilities, telecommunications (Waverman 1998) and financial markets and, to a certain extent, from the spread of New Public Management doctrines (Peters and Pierre 2001). This shift in the way specific areas of policy-making are managed by the public sector has, among other things, led to the emergence of these new regulatory bodies whose role is to monitor and guarantee the correct functioning of the market(s) falling within their competence, often through the re-regulation of recently privatised sectors (Vogel 1996; Gilardi 2002b, 2007; Jordana and Levi-Faur 2004; Levi-Faur 2006).

In line with national political cultures and administrative traditions, these bodies tend to differ widely from each other in several aspects, namely in their relation with political principals, in their mandate and statutes, and in their capacity, that is, their command of human and financial resources. The specific nature of IRAs is thus difficult to delineate; that said, it is critical at this point to provide a definition of independent regulatory agency that can be used consistently throughout this book. The literature offers several options in this respect; however, a widely accepted definition is provided by Thatcher (2002b: 956): 'an IRA is a body with its own powers and responsibilities given under public law, which is organisationally separated from ministries and is neither directly elected or managed by elected officials'.[9] This definition is particularly suited to the purpose of this book, not only because Thatcher devised it to perform a comparative analysis of regulatory agencies in several European countries but also because it focuses on three crucial features that can be expected to influence an agency's behaviour in general, and knowledge-utilisation in particular: the mandate/responsibilities of the agency; its organisational structure; and its relationship with elected officials.

The existing literature on IRAs tackles these three aspects separately or in a cumulative fashion, as each of them is a determining factor in shaping the role of any agency and its influence on policy-making. Hence, several scholarly contributions address the main reasons that push elected politicians to delegate part of their regulatory power to IRAs (e.g. Thatcher 2002a; Wilks and Bartle 2002); other publications instead analyse the institutional design of IRAs and their ability to perform their task efficiently and effectively. Finally, a whole range of studies focuses on the relationship between agencies and their principals, as well as on the general interaction of these bodies with the broader policy environment and the stakeholders involved in policy-making in a given field.

Against this background, the second part of this chapter is organised along thematic lines that explore how each of these aspects has been viewed and analysed in the literature. The first section focuses on theories of delegation and on the control mechanisms available to political principals and regulatees for monitoring an agency's behaviour once delegation has occurred. Then I provide a brief

---

9. An alternative and broader definition is provided by Majone (2000: 290–1) and follows the United States Administrative Procedure Act, whereby an agency is 'a part of government that is generally independent in the exercise of its functions and that by law has authority to take a final and binding decision affecting the rights and obligations of individuals, particularly by the characteristic procedures of rulemaking and adjudication'.

overview of organisational theories, with the aim of identifying which internal features of the agency play key roles in determining its strategies and ability to perform its duties. This section also discusses how organisations develop internal systems to 'make sense of the world', through a set of frames and narratives (Goffman 1974) that help them interpret events and develop appropriate reactions to different situations (Goffman 1959; March and Olsen 1989). Thirdly, I address research questions on the relationship between the agency and its environment, by drawing on theories of the policy process. Finally, the last part of the chapter draws on some of the tenets of the different theoretical perspectives presented here to develop a set of hypotheses on knowledge-utilisation, thus paving the way for the remainder of this book on the use of economic analysis by IRAs.

Theories of delegation

The delegation of regulatory powers to appointed institutions

As mentioned, the global spread of regulatory agencies in several policy fields is among the most visible results of gradual changes in the nature of modern states. The forceful entry of these new institutional players on the public policy scene is part of a wider process of reallocation of the state's competence as well as an institutional response to the increasing complexity of the policy problems faced by contemporary governments (Bawn 1995; Gilardi 2002b; Maggetti 2007, 2009; Sanderson 2009: 701). As a matter of fact, the shift towards a regulatory mode of governance has visibly affected the supply of policy by the state and increasingly transformed its role of direct producer of goods and services into that of 'enabler' (Barrett 2004: 259) of goods- and services-provision, thus raising new challenges for its traditional structures and modes of functioning. But why is the creation of independent regulatory agencies one of the most common responses to the new challenges facing traditional bureaucratic structures and elected politicians? What are the micro-foundations for delegating powers to an appointed institution?

Those questions are widely analysed in the literature, which points to several reasons behind the increasing delegation of regulatory powers to appointed bodies: the need to make credible commitments; to shift the blame for unpopular policies; to deal with the increased technicalities of regulation; and to comply with international and European legislation, to name but a few.

Building on the US scholarly literature on delegation in the US Congress, Majone (2001b) highlights how delegation to regulatory agencies can indeed follow several logics, depending on the rationale that pushes a political principal to relinquish part of its regulatory powers. However, two reasons seem to be the most prominent drivers of delegation: enhancing efficiency in decision-making and ensuring credible commitments.[10] In the former case, political principals delegate regulatory powers to an independent regulator in order to increase efficiency in

---

10. This second form of delegation is also known as 'fiduciary delegation'.

decision-making by relying on the superior expertise of the agency; in the latter case, instead, agencies are created to signal the principal's commitment to a given policy. The choice between these two types of delegation is driven by an implicit comparison between the present and future policy-preferences of the principal, or between its present preferences and those of its successor(s) (Majone 2001b: 105). If those preferences are stable, the principal will generally delegate for efficiency-enhancing purposes; conversely, when the principal has unstable preferences or wishes to tie the hands of its successor to a given policy option, the second type of delegation will take place.[11] As discussed in greater detail below, the two logics raise different sets of issues once delegation has occurred, particularly as far as the relationship between the principal and its agent is concerned. In his contributions (2001a, 2001b) Majone also addresses the problem of agency independence, a central topic in the delegation literature. To do so, he uses the legal distinction between a trustee and an agent, whereby the trustee is entitled to manage a property for the settlor (owner of the property) himself and hence enjoys the greatest degree of independence. Majone further clarifies that the delegation logic behind the creation of an agency tends to result in different degrees of independence from its political principals. As I will soon explain, the literature clearly distinguishes between formal and *de facto* independence (e.g. Busuioc *et al.* 2011; Maggetti 2007, 2009) and highlights how the actual independence of an agency is the result of a complex combination of factors and of repeated interactions between the agency and its environment (Holburn and Vanden Bergh 2006; Kerwin 2003), which may cause the real level of an agency's autonomy to deviate from the initial intention of the legislator.[12]

The plausibility of Majone's theoretical approach is tested by Fabio Franchino (2002) who devises a set of hypotheses on delegation and statutory constraints and finds evidence that the two logics of delegation identified by Majone pass the empirical test in the case of the European Commission, in spite of some apparently surprising results as far as statutory constraints are concerned.[13] Another empirical application of Majone's delegation model to the case of independent regulatory agencies is provided by Gilardi (2002b) in a comparative analysis of thirty-three regulators from five policy sectors. More specifically, Gilardi focuses on the

---

11. For a thorough discussion of the difference between the problem of time inconsistency (when the principal's present preferences may conflict with its future ones) and issues of political uncertainty (when the principal's preferences may differ from those of its successors), *see* Moe (1990) and Gilardi (2007).

12. Throughout the book, I use the terms 'independence' and 'autonomy' interchangeably, although I am aware of the fact that from a legal perspective 'autonomy' is a more accurate description of reality. As regulatory agencies are statutory creatures, they can enjoy different degrees of autonomy from political principals within the boundaries set by each agency's founding act. Conversely and *stricto sensu*, independence would imply that the link with the political principal is severed, a possibility that is generally absent in systems of representative government (Busuioc *et al.* 2011: 250).

13. Franchino's findings refer exclusively to the case of the European Commission, whose specificities limit the applicability of his work to national IRAs, and thus will not be discussed further here.

frequently under-tested hypothesis of fiduciary delegation, to explore whether this approach can provide an explanation for the observed diversity in the degree of agency independence in his sample. The author derives three observable implications of fiduciary delegation, by linking the credibility goal embedded in this delegation strategy with factors of international interdependence, issue-complexity and features of the decision-making process.[14] Gilardi's empirical findings generally support the main tenets of fiduciary-delegation logic, thus confirming the relevance of this approach among policy-makers facing a policy environment characterised by the pressure of growing international interdependence and by the complexity of public-policy problems (Gilardi 2002b: 875).

The two delegation mechanisms outlined above can be further specified in relation to the national or sectoral context in which delegation occurs. As a matter of fact, the same delegation logic can operate differently depending on the sector of application, as demonstrated by Gilardi (2007) in a comparison between the cases of central banks (on the same topic, *see also* McNamara 2002) and regulatory agencies in other sectors. Moreover, each delegation mechanism will entail different consequences in a federal rather than a unitary state (Doehler 2002) or in various types of parliamentary democracies (Yesilkagit and van Thiel 2011). In this respect, many scholarly contributions are structured around the similarities and differences in delegation along sectoral and national lines, thus shifting the level of analysis from more deductive theories of delegation towards empirical approaches and specific case studies. Other relevant contributions on national or sectoral models of delegation include Doehler's (2002) thorough analysis of the German approach to delegation, which rests on a detailed set of principles limiting administrative discretion. Wilks (2007) instead observes the effects of New Public Management doctrines on the Whitehall model and the emergence of potential new patterns of accountability linked to the increasing 'managerialisation' of administrative structures. Such narrower focus is normally found in what could be termed the post-delegation literature (e.g. Coen 2005; Thatcher and Stone Sweet 2002; Coen and Thatcher 2005), in which issues arising once delegation has occurred are analysed both from a positive and normative perspective. I will come back to these points in the next section.

An alternative theoretical framework to explain the spread of IRAs can be found in neo-institutionalist theories. As pointed out by Thatcher (2002a: 143), purely functionalist and formal institutional accounts of delegation only tell one side of the story and do not fully explain the differences and, in some cases, the striking similarities, in the creation and spread of IRAs across countries and sectors. What is the weight of national administrative traditions and bureaucratic legacies when politicians choose to delegate? Why are IRAs not always present where I

---

14. In particular, Gilardi's contribution (2002b: 877–8) provides a test of the following hypotheses: [1] the more an economy] is subject to international interdependence, the more delegation there should be; 2) delegation is more likely in sectors that have been recently subject to market opening; 3) there is a significant link between veto-players and delegation'.

would expect them to be? And why do they display a tendency to institutional isomorphism (DiMaggio and Powell 1983) in some policy fields, even in cases where other arrangements would be more suitable? A full account of the answers that neo-institutionalist scholars provide to these questions falls beyond the scope of this book; however, a very useful contribution on how the three major strands of neo-institutionalism (rational, sociological and historical) manage to explain the existence of IRAs as well as organisational change is provided by Gilardi (2002a, 2004). The author points out that these three neo-institutionalist approaches draw attention to different, but equally important, aspects of delegation and concludes that each theoretical strand is better suited to answering some research questions rather than others (Gilardi 2004).[15]

Post-delegation issues and control mechanisms

Delegation of power and competence always comes at a price, particularly in terms of information asymmetries between principals and agents, as often emphasised in the transaction-costs literature. To a certain extent, the delegation of powers to IRAs could be seen as a kind of 'make or buy' decision, in line with Williamson's (1979) theory on contractual relations, where political principals see the delegation of powers as more advantageous than direct exercise of power under certain circumstances. In fact, research questions linked to the post-delegation phase are often tackled within the framework of principal-agent theories that are then tailored to the specificities of IRAs (Bawn 1995).

Bendor *et al.* (2001) provide a very comprehensive analysis of existing formal and informal models of delegation and effectively point out the underlying assumptions, dynamics and practical workings of each model (in particular, authority-delegation models and signalling ones). The authors' contribution sheds light on the logic behind the two delegation approaches described by Majone and extensively addresses the problem of preference-alignment between principals and agents. When delegation happens for efficiency reasons, existing models tend to confirm the intuitive expectation that the principal will choose an agent with similar preferences. However, the authors also demonstrate how, under certain circumstances, a rational principal may actually be better off by choosing an

---

15. In particular, the strengths and weaknesses of each theoretical approach should be borne in mind by scholars when carrying out the case selection for any research on IRAs. For instance, rational-choice institutionalism explains institutional change endogenously, by linking it to issues of credible commitment and political uncertainty. This approach is suitable for cross-national and cross-sectoral comparisons but has a limited ability to take into consideration time factors, as it mainly relies on the longitudinal variations of functional pressures to explain change (Gilardi 2004). In sociological institutionalism, time and historical dimensions are under-specified and this approach does not account for the emergence of IRAs in the first place. On the other hand, sociological institutionalism is very helpful in explaining the spread of regulatory agencies, and its ability to embody a dynamic argument make it well suited for cross-sectoral comparisons. Finally, historical institutionalism is the strongest on the time and historical dimensions and performs better in explaining why change occurs rather than what determines the precise direction of change. As a result, it is somewhat biased towards case-studies applications.

agent with divergent preferences. This is exactly the case of fiduciary delegation in political contexts (Bendor *et al.* 2001: 260), whereby the counterintuitive delegation of powers to an agent with divergent preferences is in fact the most credible way to signal the principal's intention of committing to a certain policy in the future or to tie the hands of its successors (Miller 2005; Gilardi 2007). The strong explanatory power of the mechanisms embedded in the logic of fiduciary delegation also manages to uncover several limitations that traditional principal-agent models have in incorporating some of the contextual factors that are particularly relevant for delegation in political environments (Moe 1990).[16]

A more tailored application of the principal-agent logic to political contexts is often found in scholarly contributions on the control mechanisms that elected politicians devise to monitor the behaviour of their agents. Instead of concentrating mainly on the *ex-post* control of outputs, as is often the case in traditional models, principal-agent theories applied to political institutions allow for the extension of the theory to *ex-ante* monitoring tools. McCubbins *et al.* (1987) extensively discuss the incentive structure created by administrative procedures (for example, deck-stacking, reversal of the burden of proof, decentralised enforcement and the courts, public disclosure requirements) and their link with the standard tools of *ex-post* political control, namely, monitoring the bureaucracy through oversight, 'fire alarms' and sanctions. According to the authors, correctly designed administrative procedures reduce the need to use monitoring and sanctions, and/or manage to reinforce their power, at a limited cost for political principals. This occurs because administrative rules assign different weights to the relevant constituencies responsible for setting up the system; and they ensure that, by operating by these rules, the future actions of an agency will reflect the preferences of those constituencies, even when such preferences change or when there is uncertainty about what the desirable policy outcome is. In other words, administrative procedures limit the range of options available to the agency and in turn do not require constant monitoring and intervention by principals (McCubbins *et al.* 1987: 255; Moffitt 2010).

The tenets of principal-agent theories outlined above coincide with some of the underlying assumptions of this book: in particular, the refined version of this theoretical approach – tailored to political contexts as well as the role of control mechanisms such as administrative procedures, judicial review, and the appointment of agency staff by political principals – will be crucial for the definition and operationalisation of the explanatory variables used in the coming chapters.

---

16. For a thorough discussion of the assumptions of traditional principal-agent models, of the different readings of such models, and of what happens once some of these assumptions are relaxed in a political context, *see* Miller (2005).

Agency independence and expertise

The above overview of delegation theories would be incomplete without devoting special attention to a central variable in the literature, agency independence. What matters more in the context of this book, is that the elements used in the literature to measure the level of agency independence also make the impact of delegation on the use of knowledge in decision-making more explicit.

For instance, in her seminal contribution, Bawn (1995) offers a comprehensive formalisation of the principal-agent and 'deck-stacking'[17] theories described above, and explicitly models the role of expertise in a delegation context. In particular, she shows how the act of delegation puts political principals in front of a trade-off between the need to reduce policy uncertainty (by giving greater formal independence to the agency, and thus more freedom in the use of expertise) and the need to reduce political uncertainty, that is, agency drift (thereby constraining the agency's autonomy in using expertise as it sees fit).[18] These considerations will affect the formal design of the agency, as legislators 'will delegate when the gains from agency expertise outweigh losses from potential agency drift' (Bawn 1995: 62). In other words, the formal degree of agency independence affects the extent to which agencies can use knowledge when making decisions. The preferred choice in the trade-off between political control and expertise will depend on the technical features of each policy field and on the nature of the political environment in question (Bawn 1995: 63; Huber and Shipan 2002: 12, Ringquist *et al.* 2003). This will eventually lead to different equilibria and is reflected in the empirical heterogeneity in the design of existing agencies, as also noted by Gilardi (2002b).

As mentioned, Gilardi (2002b) has developed an index for measuring an agency's formal independence based on five variables: the status of the agency's head; the status of the members of the management board; the general frame of the relationship with the government and the parliament; financial and organisational autonomy; and the scope of regulatory competence (2002b: 880). While this approach is problematic in some respects, particularly as regards the weight of each variable included in the index (Gilardi 2002b; Hanretty and Koop 2012) and the risk

---

17. The expression 'stacking the deck' means to deliberately arrange things (e.g. procedures) so as to obtain a certain outcome (e.g. a result that is favourable to a specific interest group).

18. On this trade-off, *see also* Huber and Shipan (2002) and their concept of 'discretion', intended as the degree of specificity that legislators deliberately include in statutes. Huber and Shipan do not explicitly focus on IRAs and, more importantly, their research question is different from the one I am exploring in this book. Specifically, the authors try to uncover the factors that lead legislators to deliberately choose different levels of precision (ranging from extensive micro-management to extreme vagueness) when legislating on the same policy problem. This entails looking at the broader context in which those legislative efforts occur and doing so in a comparative perspective. As explained elsewhere in this book, while the broader context matters also for questions of knowledge-utilisation, the actual role of expertise in regulatory decision-making can be better observed by looking at specific episodes of policy-making. However, the consequences of the 'deliberate discretion' chosen by political principals in the act of delegation should be borne in mind and will become apparent in the empirical chapters of the book.

of conflating 'breadth of powers with degrees of independence' (Hanretty and Koop 2012: 199),[19] Gilardi's variables remain crucial to structuring empirical research on IRAs.

In fact, several scholars have moved beyond an analysis of the official mandate of an agency to explore the potential discrepancies between formal independence and what happens in practice (Lægreid *et al.* 2008; Maggetti 2007; Yesilkagit and Van Thiel 2008, 2011). This discrepancy and its effects on an agency's behaviour, including its approach to expertise, can be attributed to the relational nature of regulatory policy-making once delegation has occurred. Put differently, delegation is only the first step in the interaction between principals and agents. In this respect, Bawn's analysis brings to the fore the intrinsic uncertainty of procedural controls (that is, formal arrangements), whose effects cannot be entirely foreseen *ex ante*. Hence, rather than reflecting the principal's ideal point, formal delegation arrangements fix the 'distribution from which agency preferences are drawn' (Bawn 1995: 71).

As will be shown in the remainder of this book, the regulatory environment in which the agency operates also draws our attention to crucial questions affecting how an agency can structure its actual independence: what powers does the agency have? Does it share those powers with other entities? Are there many veto-players in the environment in which the agency operates? In addition, looking at the external environment allows us to factor into the analysis the role of other crucial actors, in particular, regulated parties. As argued by Maggetti (2009: 281) 'an agency cannot be a servant of two masters', hence, greater independence from politicians has the potential to increase the avenues for capture by regulatees,[20] although the author shows that this risk can be mitigated by other factors, such as official membership in international networks of agencies. As 'intermediary organisations' (Maggetti 2009: 272) in a continuous interaction with their environment, IRAs have to adjust the exercise of their powers on an ongoing basis.[21] I will come back to this point in the concluding chapter of the book.

In any event, the actual outcome of delegation to a given agency needs to be established empirically. As mentioned above, the post-delegation literature

---

19. In particular, the authors draw an analytical distinction between the breadth of powers formally attributed to an agency and formal independence, which they define as 'the legal ability of an agency to make decisions without political interference' (Hanretty and Koop 2012: 202). The authors argue that an agency can have limited powers but exercise them more independently than an agency with many powers but little independence with which to exercise them. Also, they argue that the absence of certain requirements in the agency's statute (e.g. incompatibility between agency board membership and other offices) is automatically interpreted in the literature as permissibility of that action. While this could indeed be the case, the actual occurrence of that action in real life can only be tested empirically.

20. On this point and on the specific case of the United Kingdom, *see also* Holburn and Vanden Bergh (2006: 36).

21. As noted by Holburn and Vanden Bergh (2006: 8) this is reflected in political strategies of regulated firms 'since regulators generally devise and implement policy on an on-going basis, transactional relations based on one-off specific policy issues become less feasible'.

addresses a set of crucial aspects of the connection between IRAs and political powers by focusing on selected cases. For example, Thatcher (2002b, 2005) analyses the degree of independence IRAs have from elected politicians and regulatees, to investigate the magnitude of external political influence and regulatory capture. In one of his contributions on a sample of agencies in the UK, Germany, France and Italy (2005), he points to a fascinating puzzle in the relationship between European IRAs and their principals. The author observes that the decisions of IRAs are seldom overturned by the political establishment and that formal control mechanisms, such as the dismissal of IRA members or budget restrictions, are rarely used by elected politicians. Thatcher suggests two possible explanations for this phenomenon: either those IRAs are really independent from political factors and actors, or, to the contrary, there are other informal ways for politicians to influence and control IRAs. Other publications focus on the evolution of specific IRAs such as central banks (McNamara 2002), competition authorities (Wilks and Bartle 2002), or systems of judicial review (Shapiro, 2002). In the daily practice of policy-making, control mechanisms often stretch beyond the traditional boundaries of ministerial control (Lægreid et al. 2008; Yesilkagit and van Thiel 2011), leading to the development of more complex forms of accountability (Schillemans 2008; Waterman et al. 1998).

At this point, it is worth recalling that this book only covers a single regulatory agency, Ofcom. Hence, I cannot draw generaliseable conclusions on the impact of independence on the use of expertise by IRAs, as this would require a comparative perspective covering different organisations. In my case, this variable remains fixed (Huber and Shipan 2002: 2).[22] This is the result of a deliberate choice that will become clearer in the next chapter, on research design. My analysis focuses on a fine-grained taxonomy of knowledge usages that are better observed at the level of individual episodes of policy-making, rather than by comparing different organisations. By 'zooming in' on specific regulatory decisions, I can better identify the mechanisms that are at play in knowledge-utilisation, and stand a better chance of isolating the role of expertise from the many variables that affect policy decisions. Nonetheless, the effect of agency independence is captured in the more general explanatory variable of conflict and, particularly, in the potential level of conflict that the formal mandate (intended as the set of powers and duties conferred by statute to the agency) can generate in individual cases of policy-making.

Types of agencies

An additional research question that is worth asking when observing the spread of regulatory agencies (Pollitt et al. 2001; Pollitt et al. 2004) concerns the type of organisation that is created once delegation has occurred, and whether a broad classification of these organisations is possible. Several authors have tackled this issue, from different perspectives. Wilson's classical contribution

22. For further details on the agency covered by this book, see Chapter Four.

on the bureaucracy (1989) classifies organisations on the basis of their tasks and the degree to which their output and outcomes are observable. In general, task-oriented approaches have been used several times in the literature to categorise institutions, mainly for their ability to generate testable hypotheses (e.g. Pollitt *et al.* 2004; Christensen and Lægreid 2007b). In a similar vein, the literature also explores the links between institutional design and the quality of resulting policy outputs and outcomes (Krause and Douglas 2005).

Another way to look at this question is to concentrate on the type of personnel employed by the agency and its links with politicians and regulated firms (McGarity 1991; Thatcher 2005). Finally, agencies can also be classified by looking at their decision-making styles (e.g. Hall *et al.* 2000) and patterns (Brunsson 2007) and by linking them to the organisation's role within a given policy context.

In fact, questions of agency categorisation are only partially related to theories of delegation, given that much of what an agency becomes and does in practice is influenced by what happens in the post-delegation phase (Kerwin 2003). Fitting a given agency type will thus depend on several factors, both internal, such as the structure of the organisation and its human and financial resources, as well as external, such as the characteristics of the environment in which the agency operates, the specificities of its field of competence and the type of stakeholders the agency has to deal with (Coen 2005; Jennings and Hall 2011[23]). In turn, these issues raise another set of research questions that are often better answered in different strands of literature. They will be addressed more extensively in the next two sections.

Organisational theories

The literature offers several theoretical frameworks for understanding the functioning of organisations (e.g. Mintzberg 1979, 1983; March and Olsen 1989; Brunsson 1989, 2007) and the available space would not do justice to such approaches; as a consequence, this section will briefly concentrate on a limited selection of publications that can be helpful in deriving testable hypotheses on the use of knowledge by regulatory agencies.

Drawing on traditional organisational theories, Nils Brunsson (1989) highlights how contemporary organisations are not only expected to deliver products but

---

23. The authors performed the first empirical study on the extent to which US agencies draw 'upon various sources of information to guide their decisions about programmatic operations' (2011: 1). The result of their analysis allowed them to develop a classification of agencies on the basis of the degree of conflict in the policy field and the degree of scientific capacity of the agency (based on the availability, relevance, and credibility of the evidence used by the organisation). The classification is used by the authors to develop hypotheses on the expected use of evidence-based policy-making by an agency. Some of the authors' insights are present in the research design introduced in Chapter Three; however, their classification is applicable to a broader set of organisations than is the case in this book. IRAs tend to fit with only two of the agency types devised by Jennings and Hall, namely, the 'evidence-based agency' and the 'challenged-evidence-based agency' (2011: 17). I will refer to their theory when relevant.

also to cope with complex environments characterised by competing norms and demands. Hence, classical approaches that view organisations as mainly geared towards the generation and co-ordination of collective action for the production of goods or services (Brunsson 1989: 2) only provide a partial account of reality. Against this background, the author identifies two ideal types of structures, the 'action organisation', geared towards efficient production, and the 'political organisation'. The main task of the 'political organisation' is to respond to the complexity generated by the competing demands of the environment in which the organisation operates, by producing ideas/ideologies ('talk', in Brunsson's terms). Real structures rarely fit one of these two ideal types, and are often a combination of political and action components, each meant to achieve different objectives. This state of things will often lead to the emergence of a trade-off between the goal of efficiency attributed to the production perspective and the political goal of gaining legitimacy in the organisation's environment, by successfully handling the challenge generated by inconsistent external demands.

Such conflicting pulls are reflected internally in the division of work between the political leaders/managers of the organisation, whose main role is to produce 'talk', and the 'led' members of the staff, who are concentrating on action. This distinction between action and politics also entails different approaches to rationality: efficient production is normally associated with a sort of unquestioned (which the author terms 'irrational') adherence to a set of norms and values that the organisation has devised to perform its task efficiently (Brunsson 2007). Conversely, political tasks require the adoption of a rational approach towards the conflicting environment surrounding the organisation, in order to guarantee the appropriate selection of norms and demands that the output of the organisation ought to satisfy. Brunsson (1989: 168) identifies four possible interactions between ideas and actions: independence; control of actions by ideas; control of ideas by action; and hypocrisy, when ideas and actions compensate for one another. In turn, each configuration has different implications for decision-making and for the role of knowledge.[24] In this respect, IRAs could be seen as a perfect example of organisations producing both talk and action; as a result, Brunsson's four typologies of interaction between action and politics offer an interesting lens for looking at empirical evidence.

Another strand of literature that is particularly relevant to the focus of this book comprises publications centred on specific aspects of organisations such as size (Egeberg 2003), age, available budget (Pollitt et al. 2004), origin and composition of the work force (Pollitt et al 2004; Thatcher 2005), formal procedural mechanisms and statutes (Christensen 2001) and culture and norms of the organisation (March and Olsen 1989), which can be used as explanatory factors for understanding an agency's functioning and its level of autonomy and accountability (Christensen

---

24. For example, Brunsson (1989: 85) points out that, within the same organisation, there is often a knowledge gap between the leaders and the led, a fact that is not necessarily negative as far as the output of the organisation is concerned.

and Lægreid 2006, 2007b), and so on. This literature frequently contains empirical testing of propositions and is particularly helpful for shedding light on the actual importance of single variables and for isolating those that are most likely to have an impact on the use of knowledge by an IRA. In a way, this approach is linked to the classification of agencies discussed above, although this type of literature is not always linked to issues of delegation and interaction between an agency and its principal(s).

A targeted approach to the type of research questions covered by this book is provided by McGarity (1991) who discusses the clash of rule-making cultures between traditional 'techno-bureaucratic' thinking and 'rational-analysis' approaches in US agencies, following the regulatory reforms launched in the 1970s. The author claims that the best means of discovering the role played by analysis within an agency is to 'focus attention on the role of the regulatory analyst, rather than on the document that the analyst prepares' (McGarity 1991: 179). Hence, McGarity describes several typologies of analysts and their respective roles within US agencies, uncovering five organisational strategies adopted by upper-level decision-makers for incorporating rational analysis in the workings of their organisations. Each strategy/model (hierarchical, outside-advisor, team, adversarial, hybrid) will yield different results in terms of the role and weight of rational analysis; upper-level decision-makers must 'pay attention to agency structure if agency analysts are to function effectively in their assigned role' (1991: 267). McGarity also points out that there is no right or wrong choice between the five strategies, given that the preference for one model over the other should be dictated by a set of conditions such as the degree of discretion of the agency, the complexity of the policy programme at hand, the preferences of top managers and the agency's likelihood of attracting well qualified resources. McGarity's contribution is particularly helpful for deriving testable hypotheses on the effect of human resources and structures on knowledge-utilisation (particularly where instrumental and strategic uses of knowledge are concerned). Conversely, one of the shortcomings of the book is its rather incomplete account of the interaction between the political and technical dimensions operating within the analytical tools themselves (Wood 1993: 252).[25]

Another insightful contribution on regulatory agencies and the inherent conflict between technical and political features is provided by Hall *et al.* (2000) in their analysis of the internal working mechanisms of the British telecommunications regulator Oftel during the 1990s. The authors investigate the impact of culture on Oftel's regulatory efforts and on the telecoms sector in general and describe, through a comprehensive set of case studies, the three different decision-making styles adopted by Oftel to solve policy problems. The authors use the internal structure, culture and management of the organisation, as well as the external pressures generated by actors in the policy arena under examination, as independent variables to explain the decision-making style adopted by Oftel.

---

25. In this respect, Wood's criticism is well founded; on the other hand, this shortcoming in McGarity's approach could be seen as a deliberate choice of the author, given that he explicitly decided to focus on actors and human resources rather than on analytical tools.

Their findings highlight how the link between the internal and external strategies of an organisation have a determining impact on its ability to achieve its goals and to survive and evolve in its surrounding environment, thus bringing back to the table the continuous interaction between action and politics typified by Brunsson. Given that this book treats regulatory agencies as actors in continuous interaction with their policy environment, the insights of organisational theories need to be complemented by a description of the main features of policy-making processes. It is to these questions that we now turn.

Theories of the policy process

The following overview of the main theorisations of the policy process is by no means exhaustive; in fact the purpose of this section is to show how this strand of literature is particularly well suited to setting the scene for discussing the role of knowledge in decision-making by a regulatory agency.

At this stage, it is also worth clarifying that, as there is currently no unifying and encompassing theory of the policy process, and existing approaches normally focus only on a set of aspects or steps of public policy-making,[26] my goal here is to identify the core elements/dimensions that these different approaches have in common, single out their characteristics and role, and link them to research questions on the use of expertise. Hence, I will first describe the general features that are typically discussed in the literature on policy environments and their actors. This will allow me to identify the types of pressures that can be put on an agency and their possible effects on its actions. These general considerations will then be fine-tuned by focusing on the potential differences between policy sectors and the impact of such differences on the strategies of a regulatory agency. After all, each regulator is normally responsible for a specific policy field and, although a shared approach to politics and policy-making within a given country generates similarities across sectors in a national context, the literature (Levi Faur 2006; Thatcher 2005, 2007; Vogel 1996) indicates that sectoral characteristics often have a greater impact on a regulator than the national system in which the organisation is set.

General features of a policy environment

The discussion on the core elements of a policy environment is closely related to the findings of organisational theories outlined above. Drawing again on Brunsson's reading of organisations, the internal mechanisms at work within an agency, be they formal or informal, are a reflection of its strategy for creating an external image and generating appropriate responses to competing external demands. Hence, the need to define the boundaries of the policy environment as a variable, in order to understand an organisation's coping mechanisms.

---

26. For a thorough review of the main theories of the policy process, *see* Sabatier (1999, 2007) and, in particular, Schlager's contribution in Sabatier (2007).

Before I proceed, it should be noted that the organisation–environment relationship is a bidirectional one, whereby contextual features impact on the organisation's behaviour and – at the same time – the organisation itself can play an active role and partially interpret and shape the context in which it operates (Goffmann 1974; Weick 1995). However, for the purpose of this book, it is assumed that the mutual influence between the organisation and the environment is biased in favour of the latter, with the consequence that the organisation tends to react and respond to external influences rather than the other way around.

Given the breadth and scope of the literature on the policy process, a possible option for getting to the core of the issues addressed by this field of enquiry is to focus on the traditional puzzles that this literature tries to solve. Some of the most debated research questions in the field include: what is the nature of policy-making (Lindblom 1959, 1979)? How can policy change be explained and how can policy stability be reconciled with change (Sabatier and Jenkins-Smith 1993; Sabatier 1999, 2007; Thatcher 2007; True et al. 2007; Wilson, C. 2006; Zahariadis 2007)? Why do certain issues achieve prominence on the political agenda while others fade away (Baumgartner and Jones 1993; Kingdon 1995; Peters 2000)? Is there a way to predict the content of policy agendas or specific regulations (Hood et al. 2001; Baldwin 2001)? Who are the key players in the policy-making process and why do they get organised in a certain way (Gormley 1986; Sabatier and Jenkins-Smith 1993, Sabatier 1999, 2007; Weible 2008)? What is the weight of power and resources in the final outcomes of policy processes (March and Olsen 1989)? Are there different types of policies (Kellow 1988; Kjellberg 1977; Lowi 1964, 1972, 1988; Wilson, C. 2006)? Does policy-making vary across sectors (Gormley 1986; Weiss J. 1979)? Can learning occur in policy-making (Bennett and Howlett 1992; Dunlop 2010; May 1992; Sabatier and Jenkins-Smith 1993; Radaelli 2009a; Weible 2008)? These are only a few of the many questions that have been stimulating public-policy researchers in the last decades. While the difficulty of devising a theoretical approach that can satisfactorily answer most of these questions at once is apparent,[27] a pattern emerges amidst such variety: several explanatory variables as well as some dependent ones are quite similar across different publications. In other words, it seems that plausible solutions to these heterogeneous puzzles can be found by looking at certain elements rather than others. For example, policy agendas, the general nature of the policy process, the link between policy stability and policy change, and policy outcomes clearly rank among the preferred dependent variables. However, these are less helpful in this case, as my *explanandum* – knowledge-utilisation – can be seen as a subcomponent of these macro-dimensions of policy-making and thus requires a narrower focus. Instead, what is more relevant for the purpose of this book is

---

27. Some even argue that the very field of public policy contains an embedded contradiction between the need to predict and provide 'usable' advice to policy-making on the one hand and the need to provide a theoretical contribution to the wider discipline of political science on the other hand. This is reflected in the variety and apparent incompatibility of some of the research questions tackled by public-policy scholars. For an insightful discussion of this problem *see* Weimer (2008).

to concentrate on the explanatory variables selected by different scholars and see what guidance they provide for answering research questions on knowledge-utilisation. In this respect, the surveyed literature often draws attention to three broad explanatory variables: the type of actors in the policy process and the relations between them (in terms of institutional structures/arrangements, and distribution of competences, resources, and power); their values and beliefs; and the general features of the political system. Exogenous factors independent from the national political system, such as international events or sudden shifts in the global economic situation are also often pictured as explanatory variables, especially in order to explain policy change (Sabatier 1999, 2007). As regulatory agencies operate at a meso-level in policy-making (Eisner *et al.* 2000) and are normally only indirectly affected by external shocks (with some notable exceptions, such as the influence of international regulation in their field, for example in the case of the European Union and national agencies), this book will account for these exogenous dimensions only when relevant.

To be sure, ideas and beliefs about the nature and composition of these three independent variables depend on the theoretical approach favoured by each author: suffice to compare the different accounts of the role of state institutions in public choice versus neo-institutional theories (Hill 2004; Howlett and Ramesh 2003). But, as stated before, the purpose here is to identify the explanatory variables that matter, without taking a specific theoretical stance.

Going back to the case of regulatory agencies, how do these independent variables operate? What are they drawing our attention to? The remainder of this section will focus on each variable separately.

Agencies do not operate in a vacuum. In particular, actors such as parent ministries, regulated industries, organised interests and consumers have a direct impact on the strategies and position of an agency in the policy environment, and often cause the organisation's behaviour to deviate from the formal arrangements made when the delegation of regulatory powers occurred (Coen 2005). They do so by generating conflicting demands, which in turn trigger reactions within the agency and by its staff, depending on the type of actor who is putting forward each demand and this actor's relationship with the agency (Jennings and Hall 2011; Schillemans 2008; Waterman *et al.* 1998; Yesilkagit and van Thiel 2008, 2011). As shown by several empirical studies on regulatory agencies (e.g. Hall *et al.* 2000; McGarity 1991; Morgenstern 1997), existing equilibria in the distribution of power and resources among actors in a given environment are very powerful in explaining specific policy outcomes.

Formal institutional arrangements are also crucial because they set the rules of the game that the agency and the other actors in the policy field have to respect (Kerwin 2003; Kjellberg 1977; Feldman and March 1981; Pollitt *et al.* 2004; Jordana and Sancho 2004). Here again, the type of arrangements in place will influence both the way the agency is organised internally and the way it responds to external demands when performing its duties. These institutional pressures directly affect the organisation's degree of independence, its ability to carry out its mandated tasks and its freedom in choosing how to do so (Bawn 1995). In some instances, the careful handling of action and political strategies by an organisation outlined by Brunsson may work successfully within a given institutional framework. In other cases, the rules of the game will weaken the agency's position and significantly limit its ability to actively manage external pressures. This type of problem is exemplified by Hall *et al.* (2000) in their study of Oftel. The authors conclude that Oftel's activities in the 1990s were not as independent from the agency's political principal (the Department for Trade and Industry) and the main regulatee (British Telecom) as often pictured in other publications on the agency: in fact, Oftel's position was very much constrained by this triangular interaction in the telecoms policy arena. Ultimately, the image that the organisation had of itself, coupled with path-dependencies in terms of structure and institutional arrangements, had a visible impact on its decision-making potential.

Beliefs and values are also influential in explaining the behaviour of an IRA. In this case, a distinction should be made between core beliefs (Sabatier and Jenkins-Smith 1993) on the ultimate value and purpose of a policy, and beliefs limited to more technical and practical issues, such as the best way to achieve a given policy goal, that is, what Sabatier and Jenkins-Smith (1993) call 'secondary beliefs'. Core beliefs are generally quite difficult to influence and change and are seldom called into question in daily policy-making activities (Hall 1993; Sabatier and Jenkins-Smith 1993; Sabatier 1999, 2007). Conversely, secondary beliefs are often debated in policy-making and can be altered without affecting the core beliefs from which they derive. As regulatory agencies in a democratic setting are normally appointed by political principals embodying the values and core beliefs of the electorate, the mandate of these organisations is generally centred on rather concrete issues, where ultimate goals and values are taken as given. In other words, agencies often operate in relatively technical fields that adopt what Boswell (2009) terms 'technocratic modes of settlement', in which there is 'broad agreement on political objectives [...] but contestation over the best tools for achieving these goals' (Boswell 2009: 80).[28] Only very rarely and in specific policy fields will an agency be required to take decisions affecting core beliefs.

These remarks shed light on the type of problems and pressures that secondary beliefs can generate for an agency, especially when actors exhibit different preferences on the policy options the agency can choose from or is called to implement. In turn, the beliefs held by the agency itself will directly affect the way it reacts to external demands and crafts internal and external strategies. On this point, Carstensen (2011) provides an interesting view on how actors use ideas in

28. The author also specifies that this is the mode of settlement in which expert knowledge is 'considered by the policy community to be a legitimate arbiter of disputes'. Conversely, 'where the dispute is interpreted as revolving primarily around a divergence of values, or interests, or psychological dispositions, then knowledge will not be considered the relevant mode of justification' (Boswell 2009: 79). For those issues, policy-makers will follow a democratic mode of settlement. As mentioned elsewhere, I do not fully follow Boswell's approach, as I wish to move beyond the commonly held expectation that IRAs will essentially make an instrumental use of expertise, thus adhering to technocratic modes of settlement.

decision-making. The author introduces the figure of the 'bricoleur' (in contrast to a decision-maker who adheres to a given paradigm), that is, a (political) actor who adopts a pragmatic and creative approach to policy-making and 'takes stock of his existing set of ideas, policies, and instruments and reinterprets them in the light of concrete circumstances' (Carstensen 2011: 156). This account seems to fit the reality of policy-making by regulatory agencies seeking 'to answer multiple logics simultaneously' (Carstensen 2011: 158), in order to achieve their goals and fulfil their mandate while responding successfully to the demands of actors holding different ideas and interests in relation to policy issues.

A concrete example is provided again by Hall *et al.* (2000), who effectively portray how Oftel's ability to react to the pressures of its policy environment was very much influenced by the type of human resources staffing the agency; by the different belief systems and attitudes of civil servants and professionals; by the high turnover of its personnel and the effects of that on the construction of an organisational memory; and, last but not least, by the personality and beliefs of its head at the time, Don Cruickshank. Each of these components was a crucial ingredient in the organisation's performance and even more in Oftel's ability to exploit its resources, including knowledge (Hall *et al.* 2000: 69) in order to gradually reposition itself as *the* competition authority for telecommunications, in order to survive in an adversarial and ever-changing policy sector. [29]

Finally, the general features of a political system can also impact on the way a regulatory agency goes about performing its mandate. The level of centralisation of competence, the type of parliamentary system, the features of the parties in power, and the number of access points for private actors, organised interests, research communities and so on have a strong influence on how policies are designed and implemented. However, in their daily life, agencies are less influenced by the macro-features of a political system, as these are often filtered by the arrangements linking the agency to its political principal. Hence, this explanatory variable will be taken into account only for the cases where the agency's action crosses the boundaries of its immediate policy environment.

While this short overview of the literature helps us to contextualise the position of IRAs in the policy process, the need to operationalise the link between macro-level independent variables and the actions and strategies of a regulatory agency calls for a narrower focus on the specific components of those variables. This can be best achieved by adopting a sectoral perspective, thus clarifying further the boundaries of the present research.

---

29. For example, the authors point out that the conflict between different subcultures (civil servant versus professionals) within Oftel prevented any one group from obtaining a cognitive monopoly over regulation (Hall *et al.* 2000: 44). Moreover, this clash of cultures proved to be an asset in several circumstances as it strengthened Oftel's reaction abilities and allowed it to develop an interdisciplinary set of skills to tackle policy problems.

Characteristics of a policy sector

In what follows, a sector is intended to mean the set comprising the actors and the policy issues over which the agency has regulatory powers and, in turn, to which the agency has to respond. Note that the relationship is bidirectional, as already pointed out: while the agency's regulatory decisions inevitably shape the sector under its competence, the agency itself is often reacting and responding to external pressures and demands.

The key to distinguishing one policy sector from another is the characteristics of the policy problems typically found in that field. In other words, a clear understanding of the nature of the policy issues facing an agency is necessary to describe, classify and explain the interplay between the different explanatory variables outlined above. Moreover, a sectoral approach brings us back to the delegation theories presented in the first part of this chapter: if the IRA is the agent, who is (are) its principal(s)? What was the logic driving delegation (efficiency *versus* fiduciary) and what consequences does it have in practice? In fact, the link between sectoral features and delegation logics is normally reflected in the formal and informal relations between the agency and external actors. In particular, observing how the mandate of the agency, the institutional arrangements with parent ministries, the degree of formal and informal independence and the procedures for allocating resources to the agency evolve in a given sector is a very effective means for tailoring the main independent variables of the literature on the policy process to the specific case of IRAs.

For example, different policy issues call into question different types of values and beliefs,[30] attract different types of actors depending on the level of complexity of the problem at stake (Gormley 1986; Sabatier 1999, 2007) and are likely to generate different degrees of control from political principals, depending on the saliency and visibility of the policy issue (Gibson and Goodin 2000; Gormley 1986).

A particularly useful framework for operationalising the impact of the features of a policy issue in a regulatory context is provided by Gormley (1986). The author tries to answer an exhaustive set of questions on the type and origin of variations in regulatory politics across issue areas, the possibility of predicting the behaviour of relevant actors, the interplay between the political and technical dimensions of a policy problem and the kind of regulatory pathologies that are likely to emerge in a given context. Gormley uses the public saliency of an issue and its technical complexity at a given point in time to explain which type of actors will participate in regulatory politics and policies, as well as what the relevant fora, timing and modes of participation will be in each case. By focusing on these two variables Gormley (1986: 607) derives an explanatory typology of four types of regulatory-issue networks and their underlying mechanisms. These are: *board-room politics*, in which regulatory choices are mainly driven by business, as complexity is high

---

30. This can be intuitively demonstrated by comparing the type of political debates surrounding distributive policies from those on redistributive ones (Lowi 1964, 1972).

COMPLEXITY

	Low	High
High	Hearing Room Politics	Operating Room Politics
SALIENCE		
Low	Street- Level Politics	Board Room Politics

Figure 2.1: A regulatory politics typology

Source: Gormley (1986: 607)

but low saliency drives policy-making away from the broader public; *hearing-room politics*, in which politicians are in the driving seat, thanks to a combination of low complexity and high saliency, which increases public participation in decision-making; *street-level politics*, for issues of low complexity and low salience, in which lower-level bureaucrats generally have the upper hand; and *operation-room politics*, in which saliency and complexity are both high and where high-level/ professional bureaucrats drive the politics of regulation. Gormley's typology is illustrated in Figure 2.1.

As will be explained in greater detail below, Gormley's framework is particularly helpful for tackling research questions on knowledge-utilisation in a regulatory context.

Back to knowledge-utilisation

This brief overview of the main theoretical contributions on regulatory agencies seems to confirm that research questions on the use of knowledge by IRAs, and more specifically of economic analysis, are often addressed only indirectly in the literature. This is to some extent surprising, given that the question of how knowledge is used by agencies and how analytical tools fit with the political aspects of decision-making is right at the heart of the logic of delegating regulatory powers to appointed institutions. In particular, IRAs should constitute the ideal setting for observing an instrumental/problem-solving use of evidence (Weiss C.H. 1979), due to the 'technical-operational' tasks assigned to them and their relatively detached position from the traditional venues of political debate. However, and as explained above, classical studies on knowledge-utilisation (Weiss 1979, 1999; Radaelli 1995; Boswell 2006, 2009) and learning (Sabatier and Jenkins-Smith 1993; Owens *et al.* 2004; Radaelli 2009a) suggest that expert knowledge is used by policy-makers in several ways, thus raising the questions of whether this happens even in relatively de-politicised settings such as IRAs and, if so, why. Despite some notable exceptions (e.g. McGarity 1991; Morgenstern 1997; Radaelli 2009a), the link between the two streams of literature on IRAs and on knowledge-utilisation is not fully established yet, and what seems to be missing in particular is a set of testable hypotheses on how independent regulatory agencies use knowledge in practice.[31] This section aims to partially fill this gap, by constructing some preliminary hypotheses on the use of knowledge by IRAs on the basis of the three theoretical streams presented above. This attempt will raise a set of additional research questions that will become the main subject of this book.

Delegation and the use of knowledge

Principal-agent frameworks and, more specifically, the logics of efficient versus fiduciary delegation embedded in the statute of an agency are particularly helpful for shedding light on the micro-foundations of the use of knowledge by an IRA. Efficiency-enhancing delegation should be expected to orient the agency towards an instrumental/problem-solving use of knowledge, given that, under this logic, elected politicians normally delegate regulatory powers to a like-minded agency, with the aim of increasing their decision-making abilities and of providing goods and services more efficiently. A symbolic use of knowledge may be present at times, to establish or support the reputation of the agency in the policy arena. Non-use may also occur when available knowledge goes against the (aligned) preferences of the principal and the agency.

Conversely, in the case of fiduciary delegation to an agent with divergent preferences, in order to secure credible commitment, one could expect knowledge-utilisation to assume one of several different forms, depending on who is using the knowledge and for what purpose. From a principal's perspective, knowledge in fiduciary delegation can be used as a means to control the agent, as in the case of monitoring mechanisms such as 'fire alarms' and oversight discussed by McCubbins *et al.* (1987) and by Bawn (1995). From the point of view of the agent instead, the question of knowledge-utilisation is complicated by the diverging preferences of the principal when fiduciary delegation is at stake. Under these circumstances, one could expect the agency to select several uses of knowledge, depending on the behaviour of the principal and the agency's ensuing degree of independence. If the mandate of the agency is clear and control and interference from the principal are limited, the agency will probably prefer an instrumental use of knowledge to carry out its mandate effectively (Bawn 1995; Jennings and Hall 2011). It may, on occasion, also recur to a strategic or to a non-use of knowledge, if expertise goes against the agency's preferences. On the other hand, the greater the risk of interference from the principal, independently of the formal content of the mandate, the more strategic uses of evidence should be expected from the agency. As a matter of fact, the principal's interference may limit the agency's autonomy and its ability to stick to its assigned goals, thus pushing the IRA towards strategic uses to substantiate its policy choices and cope with conflict,

---

31. On the development of a conceptual framework linking the literature on knowledge-utilisation to the one on administrative agencies, *see* Sabatier (1978).

or even towards symbolic uses. Finally, if the agency has no clear mandate or when control from the principal is generally weak, one could observe instances of symbolic uses of knowledge, whereby the agency tries to conform (March and Olsen 1989) to external expectations on the role of expertise, despite the absence of clear directives for action. The agency could also resort to non-use, if available knowledge is in contradiction with its preferences and there is limited risk of control by the principal. These hypotheses are summarised in Table 2.2. As will become apparent in the upcoming discussion, theories of delegation only manage to take into account a small number of the factors that influence an agency's preference in terms of knowledge-utilisation. To a certain degree, one could say that theories of delegation tackle 'ontological questions' directly relating to the creation of the agency and the structure of incentives in terms of knowledge-utilisation which were embedded in the initial set up of the IRA. However, organisations evolve and so does the environment in which they operate: this is why the focus of this work is 'post-ontological' and aims at understanding what goes on inside IRAs after their creation.[32] Hence, the hypotheses described above need to be further specified by including the organisational and contextual variables that come into play in individual episodes of decision-making. As explained above, this book focuses on a single organisation: hence, the potential explanatory power of agency independence cannot be used directly in this analysis but is reflected in one of the explanatory variables of the research design, the level of conflict.

Organisational theories and the use of knowledge

Turning to organisational perspectives instead, Brunsson's model has several implications for knowledge-utilisation, and can be used to elaborate a set of hypotheses on the use of knowledge by an organisation that mixes politics with action, as could be the case of an independent regulatory agency. For example, the technical knowledge required to perform the production tasks (in this case, finding a policy/regulatory solution to a given problem) of the organisation may not always be compatible with the needs of the agency's leaders, whose role is to handle the conflicting demands of the surrounding environment. Under these conditions, it may be wise for leaders not to use the available knowledge and to concentrate instead on talk or other activities unrelated to action, in order to satisfy the demands of the environment, consolidate the position/legitimacy of the agency (Brunsson 1989: 95), and allow the rest of the staff to produce the required output in the meantime.[33]

As a result, one could observe different kinds of knowledge-usages, each located in a different part of the agency and assigned to a different set of actors. In other words, a dichotomy between the technical expertise of some members of the staff and the rather general knowledge of decision-makers interacting with the external

---

32. On this point, *see also* Schrefler (2010).

33. For a discussion of Brunsson's theoretical approach in the context of knowledge-utilisation, *see also* Boswell (2006, 2009).

environment should be expected. According to the classification of knowledge usages used in this book, and in line with the tenets of Brunsson's theory, one should expect agencies to adopt all the types of knowledge usages presented in the beginning of the chapter. However, an instrumental use of knowledge would only be adopted by the action part of the organisation; instead decision-makers interacting with the outside world would adopt either substantiating or symbolic usages, and even refrain from using the knowledge produced internally under certain circumstances.

In order to become operational, this model would need further refinement: first of all, for each IRA, one would have to establish the relationship between ideas and action within the agency, as this link is crucial in determining which type of actor is predominant in the agency and hence which type of knowledge-utilisation is likely to prevail. In agencies where ideas and actions are independent, one should expect the agency to resort to the four types of usages of my taxonomy, although usages will vary depending on whether one considers the leaders of the organisation or the action-oriented staff. If action is controlled by ideas, then strategic uses or non-use are more likely to prevail (that is, leaders mandate the production of the knowledge they need to achieve their goals or ignore available expertise); in the opposite case, the instrumental use of knowledge would probably be dominant instead. Finally, in the case of hypocrisy, where ideas and actions compensate for each other, and which is a rather credible picture of reality for agencies, the four uses covered by this book will have equal importance. As in the case of delegation theories, these hypotheses need to be refined with a set of control variables, such as the capacity of the agency in terms of human and financial resources (Jennings and Hall 2011), the complexity of its mandate, and the main features of the environment in which the organisation operates. The more technical the mandate and the more result-oriented the agency, the more an 'irrational' adherence (obedience to rules without questioning) to and instrumental uses of evidence should be expected (Brunsson 2007). Conversely, when the organisation operates in a hostile environment or shares its competence with other bodies, it is more likely to be biased towards a strategic use of knowledge. Things get even more complicated when the nature of the problems addressed by the agency is added to the picture, so as to reflect the features of the policy sector at stake: this additional dimension highlights the fact that decision-makers sometimes face issues on which they cannot or do not want to act.

Table 2.2 summarises the preliminary hypotheses on the distribution of knowledge usages within an IRA that can be derived from delegation theories and from Brunsson's work. As regards delegation theories, in the case of efficiency-enhancing delegation (third row of Table 2.2) where the principal's and the agency's preferences are aligned, I assume that the clarity of the mandate has a limited impact on knowledge-utilisation. Conversely, this is not the case for fiduciary delegation, as shown in the dedicated rows of the table. In the illustration of the hypotheses derived from Brunsson's model, the table shows how knowledge-usage will depend on the relationship between the action part of the organisation and its political part.

Table 2.2: Hypotheses on the prevailing type of knowledge-use, according to theories of delegation and Brunsson's model

Theories of delegation				
Delegation logics and modalities	**Instrumental use**	**Strategic use**	**Symbolic use**	**Non-use**
Efficiency-enhancing delegation	Prevails		Some (reputation)	Some
Fiduciary delegation with:				
Clear mandate and limited control	Prevails	Some	Some (reputation)	
Clear mandate and control	Some	Prevails		
Unclear mandate and control		Prevails	Some (signal activity)	
Unclear mandate and limited control			Prevails	Some
Brunsson's model				
Type of organisation	**Instrumental use**	**Strategic use**	**Symbolic use**	**Non-use**
Independent actions and ideas	Action-oriented staff	Leaders	Leaders	Leaders
Ideas control action		Leaders		Leaders
Action controls ideas	Action-oriented staff			
Hypocrisy	Action-oriented staff	Leaders	Leaders	Leaders

Knowledge and the policy process

The focus on the external environment and on the nature of the policy problems facing an agency brings us back to Gormley's framework and allows us to add the missing piece of the puzzle of knowledge-utilisation by an IRA. However, and in light of the above review of the literature on the policy process, Gormley's typology is only partially useful for answering the research question under examination. While the technicality and salience of an issue can be good predictors of an agency's attitude to knowledge, they fail to operationalise other aspects embedded in the delegation of regulatory powers to an appointed body, such as the type of mandate an agency has been given or its formal and informal relationship with its political principal(s). These dimensions are very likely to have an equal importance in shaping an agency's strategy towards knowledge, especially taking into account Brunsson's observation on the potential decoupling between action and politics within the same organisation. Hence, Gormley's insight into the explanatory power of the technicality of an issue will be considered in the remainder of this book.

Conversely, in an agency setting, the saliency of an issue is likely to have less impact on questions of knowledge-utilisation, as independent regulators are often dealing with policy problems that do not have great visibility. On the contrary, knowledge-utilisation and – more broadly – knowledge production is primarily related to actors and their preferences and beliefs as regards policy choices. It is by focusing on actors and the possible conflicts arising from their interaction and different preferences that the problematic interplay between expertise and politics is most visible (what Gormley describes as the opposing pressures for accountability and expertise). I will further elaborate on these aspects in Chapter Three.

Concluding remarks

After a brief overview of the literature on knowledge-utilisation, I have introduced the taxonomy of knowledge-usages that I seek to explain in this book. This chapter has then provided a thematic review of the three main streams of literature on independent regulatory agencies, with the aim of identifying elements related to questions of knowledge-utilisation. Most publications on IRAs, be they from a delegation, organisational, or public-policy perspective, do not directly examine the use of knowledge by regulatory agencies; however, they provide valuable insights into concepts and variables that – when adequately linked to the purpose of this book – clarify the role of expertise in IRAs. Hence, the last section of this chapter has reviewed these concepts and adapted them to the classification of knowledge-utilisation introduced above. This exercise clearly shows how, by addressing different types of research questions, these three theoretical streams complement each other in providing a comprehensive set of tools for appraising the use of knowledge by an IRA.

Against this background, the next chapter introduces the research design followed in this book, an explanatory typology built on the two dimensions of conflict and problem tractability. These variables allow us to take stock of the literature on IRAs surveyed thus far and to concentrate on the core dimensions that lie behind the rationale and the dynamics of knowledge-utilisation in policy-making.

chapter three | research design

The use of economic analysis by IRAs: an explanatory typology

In what follows, I will introduce the theoretical background of this book and the set of hypotheses that will be tested in the empirical chapters.[1] The dependent variable of the analysis, namely, the different types of knowledge-usages that can occur within an independent regulatory agency, was presented in Chapter Two and will be briefly recalled below so as to connect each different knowledge-usage and its micro-foundations with the set of indicators used during the fieldwork for this research.

To derive my hypotheses, I use the methodological device of explanatory typologies (Elman 2005), as illustrated in the section below. The typology developed to answer this research question on the scope conditions that lead an IRA towards a given use of knowledge is introduced in the first section. Methodological considerations and case selection are described in sections two and three respectively; while section four offers a brief account of the obstacles faced during the empirical part of this research and the solutions adopted in each case.

Independent regulatory agencies: research questions and findings

Explanatory typologies are based on theories that provide predictions about causality as well as ways to measure a selected dependent variable. As shown by Colin Elman (2005: 296), typologies can be graphically represented by the means of a table (or property space), in which each cell corresponds to the explanation of a possible outcome and thus can be traced back to the theoretical micro-foundations connecting the independent variables with the dependent one (Coleman 1990). The dimensions of the property space (the rows and arrows) reflect the alternative values of the independent variables of the theory under examination and allow me to make predictions based on the various combinations of the different values of the theory's independent variables (Elman 2005: 297).[2] Moreover, through a series of techniques of compression and expansion (albeit with associated costs), the initial property space of a typology can be further reduced or enlarged to clarify the underlying theory and its assumptions, uncover overlooked combinations and make the theory more operational.

---

1. The entire third section of this chapter reproduces and elaborates on Schrefler (2010).
2. For an empirical application of Elman's approach to questions of policy transfer as learning, *see* Dunlop (2009).

Although this research design is not a strict application of Elman's methodological device, the core ideas of his approach are used here to derive, describe and classify a set of causal links drawn from the two separate theoretical streams on IRAs and knowledge-utilisation introduced above. As mentioned in Chapter One, I adopt an eclectic pragmatic approach ('analytic eclecticism', in the words of Sil and Katzenstein 2010) to build a bridge between two complementary, albeit separate, streams of literature. As the authors explain (Sil and Katzenstein 2010: 2) this allows me to make 'intellectually and practically useful connections among clusters of analyses that are substantively related but normally formulated in separate paradigms'. The value added of such an approach

> lies not in by-passing paradigm-bound scholarship or giving licence to explore each and every imaginable factor, but in recognizing, connecting, and utilizing the insights generated by paradigm-bound scholarship concerning the combined significance of various factors when domains of social analysis are no longer artificially segregated. (Sil and Katzenstein 2010: 17)

Hence, before I turn to the research design of the book, it is worth recalling the main tenets of scholarly work on agencies, so as to connect them to the issue of knowledge-usage in policy-making.

As shown in Chapter Two, the majority of publications on independent regulatory agencies can be roughly grouped into three theoretical streams, each focusing on different research questions: the reasons for delegating regulatory powers to unelected bodies; the functioning of IRAs as organisations; and their position in the policy process and vis-à-vis the external environment. Also, the expectation in different theorisations of why IRAs are delegated regulatory powers and have spread so rapidly around the world is that they will make systematic use of knowledge (McGarity 1991; Morgenstern 1997; Vibert 2007). No matter what the normative expectation about legitimacy is (Majone 1996; European Commission 2002; Boswell 2009), it is often assumed that agencies will rely on knowledge to seek legitimacy in output via expertise (Boswell 2009: 78; Everson 2011; House of Lords 2007; Sabatier 1978). In addition, such bodies are often mandated to do so by administrative requirements to 'give reason' or, in other words, to justify their regulatory decisions. A case in point is Section 553 of the US Administrative Procedure Act. In turn, each of these theorisations on regulatory agencies points to different and complementary aspects of knowledge-utilisation.

Theories of delegation mostly focus on the reasons for creating IRAs in the first place as well as on the relationship between the delegated agency and its political principals in the post-delegation phase (e.g. Doehler 2002; Franchino 2002; Gilardi 2002b, 2007; McNamara 2002; Shapiro 2002; Thatcher 2002b, 2005; Thatcher and Stone Sweet 2002; Wilks and Bartle 2002). This strand of literature is crucial for understanding the problems of aligned versus divergent preferences between an agency and its political principal, as pictured in the logics of fiduciary versus efficiency-enhancing delegation (Bendor *et al.* 2001; Majone 2001b; Miller 2005), and offers interesting insights on the functioning of *ex ante* and *ex post* control mechanisms by principals (McCubbins *et al.* 1987). Conversely, these contributions are less helpful in uncovering what really happens inside IRAs once delegation has occurred. In other words, delegation theories mainly focus on ontological questions regarding the existence of regulatory agencies, while the focus of this book is 'post-ontological'. However, theories of delegation remain central in two critical respects: they enable me to formulate the concept of fire-alarm mechanisms (McCubbins *et al.* 1987) and their functioning; and, in relation to knowledge-utilisation, they highlight the direct connection between delegation and the role of knowledge as a tool. That is to say, from the principal's perspective, knowledge can be a tool for controlling the agency but equally, for the agency, knowledge can be a means for responding to oversight and monitoring from the principal by offering proof or justification for its actions and thereby keeping the principal 'at a distance'. In other words, delegation theories bring to the fore the strategic dimension of knowledge-utilisation (Boswell 2009).

Organisational theories applied to IRAs generally highlight specific features of the agencies under examination, ranging from their size to the composition of the workforce, statutory obligations, and culture and norms (March and Olsen 1989). As explained in Chapter Two, all these aspects can be explanatory of an agency's functioning, its level of autonomy and accountability (Christensen and Lægreid 2006, 2007a) and, more generally, of its strategies, including those relating to the production and use of knowledge. In this respect, one of the most interesting lenses for reading empirical evidence on the usage of knowledge is provided in Nils Brunsson's work and, to a certain extent, by Goffman's concept of 'teams' in social interactions (1959).[3] Both authors stress the key role that a logic of appropriateness plays in the daily interaction of an organisation with its environment (in this case, the policy arena), and the opportunities it offers in terms of coupling and decoupling internal resources devoted to politics/ideas from those devoted to action (Brunsson 1989, 2007). These strategies are closely connected to the symbolic dimension of knowledge-utilisation (Boswell 2009).[4] Moreover, the analysis of the formal and informal mechanisms at work within an agency stresses how the internal features of IRAs always reflect the external environment in some way. This, in turn, raises the question of what is meant by external environment and, hence, what type of potentially conflicting demands (Brunsson 1989) are pressuring the organisation. In the case of IRAs, such an environment can be roughly limited to the policy context affected by the agency's regulatory decisions. This will commonly include the regulated industries, the parent ministry(ies), other governmental bodies involved in policy-making (such as local administrations), organised interests, consumer associations, and epistemic communities (academic experts, think tanks and any other actor having

3. Specifically, I find Goffman's theory (1959) of the dramaturgical dimension of presenting oneself to the outside world of particular relevance in the case of an agency that has to demonstrate (for legitimacy purposes and/or because it is appropriate) that it possesses the relevant expertise to perform its duties. For an interesting application of Goffman's theory to international relations, *see* Schimmelfennig (2002).

4. Specifically, Boswell (2009: 61) explains that a symbolic use of knowledge implies that 'knowledge is not being valued for its content, but rather as a way of signaling the authority, validity or legitimacy of certain organisational decisions, structures, or practices.'

expertise or developing standards in a given policy field). Within these boundaries, the most relevant features influencing all actors, including the agency, are – as often pointed out in the literature on the policy process – the conflict dimension (Radaelli and Dente 1996; Sabatier 1999, 2007; Sabatier and Jenkins-Smith 1993) and the characteristics of the policy sector at stake (Kellow 1988; Lowi 1964, 1972, 1988; J. Weiss 1979). In fact, the literature on the policy process is crucial in highlighting how organisational strategies and, in particular, knowledge-utilisation can be seen (and, where necessary, normatively appraised) both as a by-product of the IRA's internal capacity and as a response to the external environment. As a consequence, any empirical research on knowledge-utilisation by IRAs needs to be clearly embedded in the policy context at stake. Ultimately, the rationale behind each type of knowledge-usage reflects the link between the internal and external elements affecting a regulatory agency, namely, its capacity, its mandate, the type and number of political principals and regulatees and so on. In turn, the key question at this point becomes selecting which explanatory factors are most relevant for gaining a better understanding of the mechanisms leading to different types of knowledge-usages. It is to this question that I now turn.

An explanatory typology of policy issues

To illustrate how IRAs can use knowledge – and in this case economic analysis – in the policy process, I have selected two explanatory dimensions that capture both the context and the content of policy: 1) the level of conflict in the policy arena and 2) the degree of tractability of a policy problem. In what follows, I explain what motivated my choice in light of the literature review presented in the previous chapter.

In the former case, the level of conflict is understood as the degree of disagreement over policy values and goals between the actors involved in the policy environment (Radaelli and Dente 1996) and/or between their interests. The higher the number of stakeholders, the greater the degree of conflict, as each player is likely to generate conflicting pressures and demands on the agency (Brunsson 1989; Jennings and Hall 2011; Sabatier 1999, 2007; Sabatier and Jenkins-Smith 1993; Schillemans 2008). When regulatory decisions are concerned, conflict very often develops because of clashing economic/commercial interests of market-players, especially when any possible policy choice is perceived by actors as a zero-sum game with clear (economic) winners and losers (Jennings and Hall 2011).[5] This tendency is exacerbated by the fact that regulatory policies tend to generate concentrated and identifiable costs but diffuse, and thus less observable, benefits.

---

5. The authors clarify that 'agencies that emphasise information from professional/scientific sources are likely those where the central policy questions are in the vein of how to accomplish the established goals rather than what the goals should be; that is, where the questions are instrumental and not political. Even then, we must recognize that the instruments can be questioned, despite the strength of the evidence because their application allocates societal benefits and burdens.' (Jennings and Hall 2011, page number not available at the time of writing as publication was accessible only in HTML format). This description fits with the case of IRAs.

The formal arrangements and power distribution between the agency and its principal(s) are also a crucial indicator of the level of conflict, in particular as far as control mechanisms and sanctions are concerned (Hall *et al.* 2000; McCubbins, Noll and Weingast 1987): stringent oversight mechanisms and the presence of multiple principals are likely to push the agency into adopting strategic behaviour to cope with the external environment. In other words, focusing on the level of conflict allows us to take into account the relevant insights provided by the literature on delegation and by organisational theories.

The second dimension used in this explanatory typology, that is, the level of problem tractability, is intended as a continuum, ranging from policy issues that can be routinely addressed with available knowledge to complex problems for which existing knowledge does not provide any solution or where the medium- and long-term consequences of possible policy approaches are unknown or risky (Boswell 2006; Morgenstern 1997).

In some cases, the concept of problem tractability can overlap with the notion of 'uncertainty': however, I feel the latter is too broad a concept to be used as an explanatory variable in this book, as it can be interpreted in different ways. For instance, it can indicate not knowing what is the most appropriate course of action in a given case (as in problem tractability) but it can also refer to a lack of understanding by actors of the content of an applicable rule or mandate. This second meaning is often evoked by regulatees in policy-debates, when they state that an agency's decision does not provide sufficient regulatory clarity for planning their business strategies; and is also mentioned by regulators themselves, when they feel that their formal mandate/powers are not detailed enough to provide guidance on how to proceed in specific instances. As a result, in this second connection, uncertainty would partially overlap with the level of conflict described above, with the risk of seriously impairing the explanatory power of the two variables of the proposed typology (Brady and Collier 2004, 2010; King *et al.* 1994). Instead, while narrower in scope, the concept of problem tractability eliminates any risk of confusion, as it relates to the content rather than the context of policy, an equally important aspect when addressing questions of knowledge-utilisation (Boswell 2009; Gormley 1986).

Potential indicators of the degree of problem tractability are the existence of epistemic communities (Haas 1992) having accumulated a certain amount of knowledge on the policy issue at stake, the existence of commonly accepted standards and models for tackling a given policy problem (Haas 1992: 11) and the magnitude of uncertainty about the medium- and long-term consequences of potential policy solutions (Morgenstern 1997). As pointed out by Morgenstern regarding the specific case of economic analyses, 'the availability of a modeling framework detailed enough to address new and sometimes subtle policy issues can enhance the likelihood that the analysis will play a significant role in decision-making' (1969: 469).[6] The indicators for the explanatory variables of the typology are summarised in Table 3.1.

---

6. For a discussion of concrete examples at the US Environmental Protection Agency *see* Morgenstern (1997); and for an application of the proposed typology to Morgenstern's examples, *see* Schrefler (2010).

Table 3.1: Indicators of the level of conflict and problem tractability

Level of conflict	Problem tractability
Number of actors	Existence of epistemic communities
Type of actors (their interests/ideas)	Existence of commonly accepted standards in the policy field
Formal arrangements and power distribution with principals	Magnitude of the uncertainty on the consequences of policy solutions

As explained in Chapter Two, an operationalisation of the role of problem tractability in the case of regulatory policies is provided by William T. Gormley (1986)[7] and has also been tested more recently on other types of policies (Eshbaugh-Soha 2006). Although Gormley's framework focuses on different research questions (type and origin of variations in regulatory politics across issue areas; the possibility of predicting the behaviour of relevant actors; regulatory pathologies), the author clearly shows how the tractability of an issue leads to different policy-making patterns and, eventually, to different outcomes. Gormley also uses a second explanatory variable, the salience of the policy being examined, which should be borne in mind in this case, as explained below. As a matter of fact, in an empirical application of the proposed explanatory typology, additional control variables to be included in the analysis are the capacity of the agency and the salience of the problem at stake. In the former case, the availability of adequate human and financial resources within the regulatory agency under examination is likely to influence its general attitude towards knowledge-utilisation, and the ability to properly use available evidence (Bawn 1995; Jennings and Hall 2011). An agency's capacity is connected to the dimension of problem tractability and will mainly affect the agency's decision to use internal or external knowledge/expertise to tackle policy issues. Policy salience is relevant in a different manner: deviations from prevailing uses of knowledge may be expected for cases of increased media attention to or political sensitivity of a problem. Specifically, issue-salience directly impacts on the scope of conflict: salient issues tend to broaden policy conflicts beyond the immediate policy arena of the agency (Gormley 1986; Eshbaugh-Soha 2006). For low-salience issues instead, the configuration of the policy arena and the degree of conflict between the actors involved tends to remain stable, as in the case of Gormley's 'board room' politics.

While the combined effects of issue-salience and problem tractability are already formalised by Gormley (1986), the salience dimension is less relevant for questions of knowledge-utilisation in an IRA setting, as the use of expertise in this case occurs in relation to more technical issues (Boswell 2009: 79) and tends to revolve around the potentially conflicting (economic) interests of the actors involved (Boswell 2009). Moreover, as shown by Christopher M. Weible (2008),

---

7. The author calls it 'technical complexity' (Gormley 1986: 598). For further details, *see* Chapter Two.

issue-salience is endogenous to the conflict strategies pursued by the coalitions involved in policy-making. In addition, and contrary to the degree of conflict, focusing on salience does not allow me to address crucial questions of delegation and the position of the agency in the policy arena and towards principals and regulatees. As a result, the control variables of capacity and salience mainly have the effect of intensifying and/or qualifying the two selected dimensions of conflict and problem tractability, and ensure important features of these explanatory dimensions are not overlooked during empirical research.

Organising empirical research

As mentioned in Chapter Two, four types of knowledge-usage are analysed here: instrumental, symbolic, strategic and non-use. As will become apparent in the empirical part of this book, these usages should be seen as ideal-types (Weber 1949[1904]: 90) for classifying the complexity of reality and guiding this analysis of the use of expertise by an independent regulator. These uses are not mutually exclusive and nor will an IRA adopt the same approach to knowledge-usage all the time. This is why understanding the scope conditions that lead to a certain use of knowledge is likely to be more promising and interesting than trying to identify stable (and possibly non-existent) patterns of behaviour within an agency (Schrefler 2010: 318), as already shown by Boswell (2009) and in Morgenstern's (1997) empirical work on the use of economic analysis at the US Environmental Protection Agency.

One of the most problematic issues in the proposed typology is to find indicators for each type of knowledge-usage, a common problem for scholars working on knowledge-utilisation.[8] Against this background, some preliminary measurements of different knowledge-usages can be derived by looking at selected patterns in the behaviour of a regulatory agency and at the way resources linked to the production and use of knowledge are normally employed.

---

8. As mentioned in Chapter One, the literature on knowledge-utilisation reviewed in Chapter Two seldom contains empirical testing (and thus indicators) of hypotheses on the different types of knowledge-usages. A notable exception can be found in Boswell (2009: 83–6) who develops a system to measure different types of usages based on three indicators: 1) institutional arrangements for knowledge production; 2) research agenda of the organisation; and 3) the level and type of dissemination of research results. While I owe my knowledge-utilisation taxonomy to Boswell (2006, 2009), this book focuses on a specific type of organisation – IRAs – to which Boswell's approach is not fully applicable. Hence, I had to rename some of her knowledge-usages (see Chapter Two), to adapt them to a regulatory context, and I resorted to different indicators to test my hypotheses. This is because, in the case of IRAs, Boswell's indicators tend to remain fixed (e.g. institutional arrangements and research agenda are set by statute and dissemination strategies are often also set in the mandate of the agency). This would prevent me from distinguishing different types of knowledge-usages by an agency. However, I believe that the components of Boswell's indicators are relevant for questions of knowledge-utilisation, and this is why these dimensions (e.g. mandate of the agency, institutional setting) are reflected in the explanatory variables of my typology. In other words, while I tend to follow Boswell's approach, I apply her insights to a narrower object, as I believe that different types of knowledge usages can occur even within technical organisations, in contrast to what is commonly assumed.

In the case of instrumental uses of knowledge, one should expect to observe an optimal use of the resources allocated to the production and use of knowledge across the entire policy cycle. Specific signs of the instrumental approach could be a balanced distribution of financial and human resources between *ex-ante* and *ex-post* policy appraisals, the regular reference to knowledge in policy-related activities. Most importantly, explicit indicators of an instrumental use of knowledge are the existence of guidelines for producing and using knowledge during decision-making, coupled with mechanisms that track how these guidelines are enforced. Such mechanisms can range from the transparent disclosure of how resources were devoted to knowledge-production and use more stringent approaches, such as oversight by a separate body or judicial review.[9] As shown in the literature on evidence-based policy-making (e.g. Dunlop *et al.* 2012; Nilsson *et al.* 2008), the mere presence of guidelines or formal requirements for using knowledge instrumentally is not enough: without monitoring actual implementation, formal guidance can often result in symbolic or strategic usages of expertise.[10]

Conversely, if an agency is using knowledge mainly to cope with external pressures rather than to fulfil its internal needs for information, this should be read as a sign of strategic use. When the strategic approach to knowledge prevails, one could expect knowledge to be produced in conjunction with specific events or phases of the policy process, possibly in response to the production of similar knowledge by other stakeholders or institutions sharing regulatory powers with the agency under examination. Of course, reacting to external pressures can also be a legitimate response to an invitation from stakeholders to explore an issue that the agency has overlooked. In this case, rather, we would be witnessing a case of instrumental usage geared towards learning. Instead, the type of strategic approach I am trying to measure here tends to have a justificatory and, very often, *ex-post* component. A clear indicator of this type of usage is the production of policy-relevant analyses only at a late stage of the decision-making process, or only when expertise is needed to counter arguments that would undermine a predefined solution. Another indication of the occurrence of this type of usage can be obtained by taking a closer look at how the agency frames the policy problem to be addressed in comparison with other relevant analyses on the same topic. If arguments are structured in a way that inevitably channels the policy debate towards a preferred course of action, this can be taken as an indication of strategic use of knowledge.[11]

---

9. An even more stringent mechanism consists of embedding a scientific 'gold' standard in the agency's decision-making framework, as discussed by Mahor (2007) for the pharmaceutical sector. However, this is only feasible (and desirable) in specific policy areas where such a standard exists and can be agreed upon by the policy community.

10. As rightly noted by Bartle and Vass (2007: 899) 'In effect, regulating the regulators requires the same control sequence of setting standards, monitoring and enforcement which the regulators apply to regulated companies – but applied to themselves.'

11. A case in point is when *ex-ante* impact assessments of future policy proposals only analyse a limited set of policy options, with the preferred course of action being the only credible/feasible

Instead, the existence of imbalances or even a complete decoupling between the knowledge that is produced and the objective informational needs of the organisation, as well as a disproportionate attention to only one type of knowledge when a broader array of evidence production would be necessary for decision-making, will be interpreted as indicators of symbolic uses of knowledge. As will be shown in the coming chapters, if the production of a certain type of analysis is part of the statutory duties of an agency, this does not eliminate the possibility of strategic or symbolic uses, as analyses can be crafted at different times and in different ways during decision-making. Finally, the complete absence of produced and used knowledge or the clear identification of alternative means for deciding on policy issues (for example, sticking to the electoral commitments of the principal; unquestioned adherence to in-house habitual decision-making strategies) will be used as an indicator of the non-use of knowledge.

Table 3.2 draws on Peter May's (1992) intuition that different types should be accompanied by information on the type of *prima facie* evidence that would lead one to recognise them. In his work, May was referring to types of policy-learning, while here the emphasis is on types of knowledge-usage. Types of usage are also connected to their micro-foundations, a point on which both Boswell (2006, 2009) and Radaelli (2009a) have insisted in their writing and which has been developed in Chapter Two of this book. This leads us to Table 3.2, which follows the format of Radaelli's table on policy-learning; although the content differs, of course (see Radaelli 2009a). The table summarises the various modes of knowledge-utilisation outlined above; the micro-foundations behind each type; and possible indicators of the occurrence of each type of use.

The four hypotheses

The possible combinations of the two explanatory dimensions described above lead to four hypotheses on knowledge-utilisation, as illustrated in Figure 3.1.

When the level of conflict in the policy arena is low (for example, the stakeholders involved are few and with compatible interests and/or the power and competence of the agency are clear and difficult to challenge), and the degree of tractability of the policy problem with the existing knowledge is high, then one should expect the agency to use knowledge instrumentally to perform its tasks. Given the high tractability of the problem, knowledge-utilisation should be expected to follow a 'routinised' pattern, subject to limited questioning from relevant stakeholders (Jennings and Hall 2011; Weiss, C. H. 1991), with knowledge often applied to the solution of short-term issues, or in other words for 'rational' problem-solving.

solution; another example is stakeholder consultations to gather additional data for the analysis using 'leading questions'.

Table 3.2: Types of knowledge-utilisation by IRAs, micro-foundations, and indicators

Type	Micro-foundations *An agency uses knowledge to:*	Indicators
Instrumental	• Carry out assigned tasks/mandate. • Improve own problem-solving abilities (e.g. problem-solving in Boswell 2006 and partially interactive model by Weiss, C. H. (1979: 427–8). • Increase understanding of an issue (enlightenment model/conceptual use Weiss, C. H. 1979: 430 and 1999: 477) and to learn (Owens *et al.* 2004).	Optimal use of resources allocated to appraisal across the policy cycle and existence of mechanisms to monitor implementation of procedures for knowledge-production and use.
Symbolic	• Gain legitimacy (e.g. prove own rationality and competence, Radaelli 1995: 162). • Emulate similar structures and respond to expectations or external pressures. • Signal political responses to perceived policy problem, in absence of actual measures (Hertin *et al.* 2008).	Imbalance between produced knowledge and the real informational needs of the agency; excessive focus on one type of knowledge.
Strategic (a) *Political*	• Respond to control by principal(s), the judiciary or regulatees (tactical model, Weiss, C. H. 1979: 429). • Expand own power/leverage (Weiss's tactical model; Boswell 2006: 7).	Production and use of knowledge to respond to external needs rather than internal ones, for example in confrontation with stakeholders. Justificatory and/or *ex-post* production and use of expertise in decision-making.
(b) *Substantiating*	• Justifying a preferred/predetermined policy choice. • Use as ammunition in adversarial context (Weiss, C. H. 1979: 429).	
Non-use	• Avoid undermining preferred policy option. • Avoid taking explicit stance on emotional or uncertain policy issues.	Absence of knowledge in decision-making; clearly identifiable use of other means to tackle policy problems.

Source: Elaboration on Schrefler (2010: 320).

H1: a low level of conflict and high problem tractability lead to an instrumental use of knowledge.

When the level of tractability of the problem at stake is high but so is the level of conflict in the policy arena, one should expect a strategic use of knowledge to occur. Under these conditions, knowledge can be particularly effective as ammunition against other stakeholders or institutions questioning the power of the IRA, or as a tool to support the agency's choices in the presence of oversight mechanisms and judicial review (strategic political use). Knowledge can also be used to advocate a preferred policy solution in the face of alternative options proposed by other stakeholders (strategic substantiating use).

H2: a high level of conflict and high problem tractability lead to a strategic use of knowledge.

When the level of conflict is high and the tractability of the policy problem at hand is low (that is, there is no available or broadly accepted knowledge on the issue or no technical model for addressing the long-term consequences of available policy solutions), one should expect either a non-use of knowledge or a symbolic use. In the former case, the agency is stuck with no possibility of moving in any direction, because of the sustained levels of conflict in the policy arena and the lack of real answers to the policy problem under examination. However, if the level of conflict results in pressure on the IRA and an expectation that it will unblock the situation, in the absence of adequate knowledge, the agency could be expected to use knowledge symbolically, to respond to external demands partially without pursuing any concrete action to address the problem at hand. For instance, if the production and use of knowledge is formally requested from the agency, one could observe the classical 'box-ticking exercise', in which knowledge-utilisation conforms to the rulebook but has little connection with the real decision-making needs of the IRA.

H3: a high level of conflict and low problem tractability lead to a symbolic use of knowledge or to non-use.

When the level of problem tractability is low and so is the conflict in the policy arena, one could expect the agency to use knowledge instrumentally, to increase its problem-solving ability in the long term. One could object that low pressure level on the agency in this case could also lead to the non-use of knowledge. However, it is commonly assumed that the very credibility of an agency depends on its ability to tackle policy problems: low levels of conflict provide ideal conditions for using knowledge instrumentally, for learning and strengthening the agency's future coping skills. Hence, I assume that, under these circumstances, instrumental use will be dominant.

H4: a low level of conflict and low problem tractability lead to an instrumental use (in the learning sense) of knowledge.

These four hypotheses are illustrated in Figure 3.1.

While these hypotheses point to the prevailing types of knowledge-utilisation, the two control variables on the agency's capacity and the salience of the policy issue should always be taken into account during empirical testing, to check whether they could justify deviations from the proposed hypotheses. As noted above, the salience of an issue is likely to broaden the scope of conflict beyond

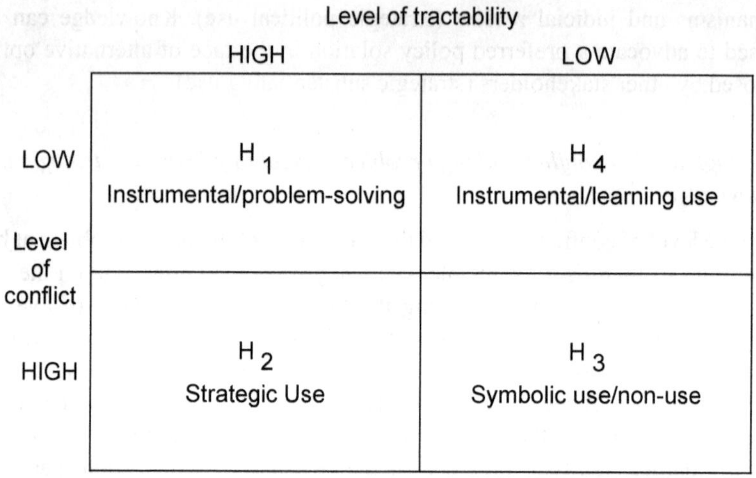

Level of tractability

	HIGH	LOW
LOW	H_1 Instrumental/problem-solving	H_4 Instrumental/learning use
HIGH	H_2 Strategic Use	H_3 Symbolic use/non-use

Level of conflict

Figure 3.1: Hypotheses on knowledge-utilisation by IRAs

Source: Elaboration of Schrefler (2010: 321)

the traditional regulatory arena at stake, thus possibly strengthening strategic behaviour. The capacity of an agency instead affects the agency's choice of whether to rely on internal or external expertise. For example, an agency with limited human and/or financial capacity may be more prone to symbolic uses of knowledge in the face of more intractable problems, while it will probably rely on external knowledge for highly tractable issues. These questions, however, pertain more to the production of knowledge than to its final use (Sjörgen 2006), as will be shown in the empirical chapters of this book.

Before turning to questions of methodology and case selection, it is worth giving a few additional words to the justification and the possible limitations of this approach to the research question on the use of knowledge by independent regulatory agencies. Although less parsimonious than more statistical approaches, explanatory typologies reduce the risk of omitting relevant variables and interaction terms (Bennett and Elman 2006: 263). By allowing for the refinement of concepts, they also offer valuable guidance in the selection of cases that can be productively compared (Dunlop 2009: 299; Munck 2004: 111). Thinking of limitations, besides the inherent limits embedded in any simplification of reality, the proposed typology does not assign any relative weight to the independent variables. This is because the relative importance of each variable probably varies on the specific circumstances of each case, even though I believe that both the level of conflict and the degree of tractability of a policy problem influence the agency's approach to knowledge and should thus be accounted for in each case. Additional insights into the relative importance of each dimension will emerge in the empirical chapters of this book.

Another limitation of this research design stems from the fact that expectations in terms of knowledge-utilisation are not always unambiguous: in one case (H3), the same combination of independent variables leads to two different possible outcomes. Empirical testing and a better understanding of the mechanisms at work in each case will shed further light on this point.

Methodology

One of the first considerations that springs to mind when thinking about the right methodological approach to test these four hypotheses empirically is that the mechanisms leading to each outcome are not made explicit in the proposed typology. In fact, this is not surprising, as these mechanisms are indeed what I try uncover in this book and this constitutes the core of the research question. The purpose of this work is not to establish 'the truth', or to draw generalisable conclusions about how regulatory agencies will use knowledge in decision-making under certain circumstances but rather to better understand if and how certain scope conditions generate the mechanisms that will ultimately lead to different knowledge usages. This will allow us to add one of the missing pieces from research puzzles on the link between knowledge and policy and also to gain more insight into a crucial ingredient in the 'internal cuisine' of regulatory agencies, and deepen our understanding of what happens in the post-delegation phase.

Against this background, qualitative methods such as process tracing (Bennett 2010; Brady 2010; Freedman 2010) and case studies (Gerring 2004, 2007) seem to offer the highest chances of observing causality *in vivo* and therefore generate insights on sequences and causal mechanisms (Abraham and Sheppard 1999; Checkel 2007; George and Bennett 2005; Munck 2004). Given the type of hypotheses to be tested, the case-study method can follow several approaches, in particular as regards the treatment of the sources (that is, written documents and oral testimonies) that are needed to appraise the hypotheses. Before I turn to the methodological approach to those sources, the next section clarifies the nature of the documents used for the case-study analysis.

Type of economic analyses used in this book

So far, I have referred to economics in very general terms. The concept of economics is often used imprecisely, to indicate different things ranging from sub-disciplines such macro and micro economics to specific tools such as cost-benefit analysis, or even specific models and methods of calculation. In this work, the terms economic expertise/knowledge, economic analysis or even economics is used interchangeably to indicate a body of knowledge systematically produced in line with the two criteria outlined in Chapter One to differentiate expert knowledge from other types of information. Hence, the focus is on the outputs of the discipline (normally in the form of documents) and not on specific theories or models. The analyses that will be taken into consideration in this book include both the product of internal research as well as external studies commissioned by a regulatory agency.

Economic analysis is also a broad category in itself and each organisation uses several types of analyses, often bearing different labels, such as evaluation, background note, literature review, study, internal research, and so on. In order to draw up a classification that can be used for operational purposes and clarify what I will be looking at in Chapters Five to Seven, it is best to focus on the rationale behind each type of analysis as well as its position in relation to decision-making. As a result, four types of documents will be used in this book: literature reviews, *ex-ante* impact assessments, *ex-post* evaluations and foresight studies. In what follows, the features of each category are briefly described and will be used as a template for the empirical part of the research.

Literature reviews are documents used for general informative purposes. Sometimes called background notes or studies, they contain an overview of the state of the art on a topic and may present existing theories and models dealing with a specific issue. They often compare different approaches to a problem or describe practices adopted by other organisations in other countries or sectors. Literature reviews may take a critical stance on the existing body of knowledge or instead simply limit themselves to covering available expertise on a topic. What distinguishes them from other types of analysis is the fact that they serve as a general tool to keep the policy-maker up to date and are not specifically linked to a given decision or course of action.

Ex-ante impact assessments, instead, are one of the core elements in the decision-making phase of the policy process, when different possibilities to solve a policy problem are considered and evaluated. The National Audit Office explains that:

> impact assessments assess the need for, and likely impact of, proposed policy interventions of a regulatory nature. They seek to identify appropriate and cost-effective options for policy development and ensure that decisions are well informed. They form an important part of a wider agenda of regulatory reform which is seeking to improve the design of regulation whilst maintaining the protections it affords society. (NAO 2010a: 9)

In reality, impact assessments vary in their degree of depth and comprehensiveness. Partial analyses of specific aspects, such as the consequences of a given policy on small and medium enterprises (SMEs), are often also labelled as impact assessments. As a result, the broad umbrella of impact assessment covers different types of analyses, ranging from the measurement of administrative burdens for firms to competitiveness tests, partial-risk analyses, cost-effectiveness analyses and fully fledged cost-benefit analyses. Impact assessments contain both quantitative and qualitative information and use different methodologies (for example, the standard-cost model; specific types of environmental tests; different methods to evaluate saved lives and so on), depending on the type of issues addressed by the analysis. While I acknowledge the difference between each of the above types and the perils of presenting them as an homogeneous analytical tool carrying the same weight in policy-making (Radaelli 2005a), for the purpose of this work I will use the general label of impact assessment to indicate all types of economic assessments that are undertaken and used before a policy decision is adopted.[12] When relevant for the question of the use of economics in decision-making, the distinction between different types of analyses will be made explicit.

Ex-post evaluations fulfil the same function as impact assessments but *after* a policy has been enacted. They normally contain qualitative and quantitative information on the general and specific goals of a policy and compare this with the results achieved in practice, normally with the help of specific indicators. In a comprehensive evaluation, both outputs (short-term effects of the policy) and outcomes (long-term and general effects of the policy) are assessed. The purpose of this type of analysis is to take stock of what has been already achieved with a specific initiative and pave the way for future decisions. As a result, *ex-post* evaluations normally contain a section with recommendations about the preferable course of action for the policy under examination, such as continuing with the current approach, fine-tuning the policy, taking a completely new direction, or terminating the policy. Here again, there are several methods and templates for performing the analysis, depending on the sector and the context of application.

Finally, foresight studies are analyses devoted to exploring possible future developments in a given sector or the potential consequences of policy intervention in cases with a strong degree of risk or uncertainty. They are normally undertaken when immediate action is not foreseen, to increase the knowledge and problem-solving abilities of an agency or more generally to identify possible future challenges and opportunities. While foresight studies often take stock of existing knowledge and policies, as literature reviews and evaluations do, they also tend to contain a set of predictions and scenarios for pushing the frontier of available knowledge towards less well explored ground. The difference between this type of analysis and impact assessments and evaluations, which also contain alternative policy options, is its disconnection from any immediate policy action: foresight studies are seldom directly linked to a specific decision. But they nonetheless remain quite relevant either to anticipating potential problems or to signalling the possibility of future regulatory intervention in a given sector. In the last case, this often triggers reaction from other actors in the policy arena, who may, in turn, produce studies on the topic. A case in point could be when a regulatory agency investigates how to tackle a new situation but lacks sufficient information on the risks and consequences of potential regulatory/policy approaches, to which different stakeholders react by providing additional (and often conflicting) data and information on the issue. This often clarifies possible risks and can also reduce the degree of uncertainty surrounding the problem; as a result, foresight studies are the type of analysis that relates most closely to learning in organisations.

While the above is undoubtedly a simplification of reality, it is also true that, in the face of the great variety of analyses that can be used by regulatory agencies, these four categories are commonly found in the majority of organisations and

---

12.   This is why they are known as '*ex-ante* impact assessments'.

more importantly, despite their idiosyncrasies, most analyses performed by IRAs normally conform to one of the four types described here (Biegelbauer 2007; PTS 2008[13]).[14]

Coding

In the episodes covered by Chapters Five to Seven of this book, the relevant sources are the four types of economic analyses described above, regulatory statements and decisions, public consultation documents, consultation responses and any other type of evidence provided by stakeholders in each case, minutes of board meetings, minutes of public hearings, articles in the press, online blogs and commentaries, other relevant content posted on the website of the agency (such as press releases and communication campaigns) and, of course, direct testimonies in the form of transcripts of interviews with various actors involved in the cases under examination.

The first methodological question that comes to mind is how to meaningfully organise these sources and, more importantly, how to select the right approach to analyse content systematically and locate the instances that allow the testing of the hypotheses.[15] In this respect, two different coding approaches were considered.

---

13. Interview at PTS, the Swedish Regulator for Postal Services and Telecommunications, September 2008.

14. It is worth mentioning here that the official documents pertaining to the case studies covered in this book are almost always labelled as impact assessments, because of Ofcom's statutory duty to perform an impact assessment before major policy decisions. However, depending on the circumstances, the content of these documents can indeed correspond to an impact assessment or instead be closer to a foresight study or an evaluation, as they are described here. As I look at the actual content of each document, regardless of the label, whenever necessary I will specify to which of the four categories a given economic analysis belongs to.

15. I use here Krippendorff's definition of content analysis, (2004: 18), namely, 'a research technique for making replicable and valid inferences from text (or other meaningful matter) to the context of their use'. This definition is built by considering six characteristics of texts, that I believe capture key elements that are relevant for the rigour of both quantitative and qualitative approaches to the analysis of content: 1) texts have no objective, that is no reader-independent qualities, as the meaning of a text 'is always brought to it by someone'; 2) texts do not have single meanings; 3) the meanings invoked by texts need not be shared, which is not a problem for content analysis unless the analysts fail to spell out the criteria for validating their results; 4) meanings (contents) speak to something other than the given texts, and this requires the analyst to look at the broader picture and not just the text – an inherent limitation and problem in automated/computer content analysis; 5) texts have meanings relative to particular contexts, discourses or purposes, which help reduce the difference in interpretations as soon as a text is put into context; 6) the nature of text demands that content analysts draw specific inferences from a body of texts to their chosen context, bearing in mind that context is always constructed by someone, in this case the analyst (2004: 18–25). This definition allows the author to build a conceptual framework for content analysis based on the following conceptual elements: text; a research question to be answered by analysing the body of text; a context chosen by the analysis to make sense of the body of text; an analytical construct to operationalise what the analyst knows about the context; inferences intended to answer the research question; validating evidence to validate the analysis in principle (2004: 39), i.e. the researcher must have in mind how his claims can be validated by others

To minimise subjectivity and the risk of human error, quantitative text analysis[16] (Krippendorff 2004; Laver and Garry 2000; Laver *et al.* 2003; Neuendorf 2002) was initially envisaged as a suitable solution. However, it quickly proved to be inapt to research questions on knowledge-utilisation, as indications of different types of usages, as well as other portions of text linked to the explanatory variables, would probably materialise only once or twice in documents; and most often the same word or 'evidence-based' claim would be used for different types of usages.[17] For example, a hypothetical sentence such as 'the economic evidence on the substitution between product X and Y leads us to restrict our market definition to [...]' could indicate that we are witnessing a classical case of the instrumental use of knowledge, in which economic analysis is used in a problem-solving manner to conclude that product X is not part of a given market subject to regulation; or alternatively, the same sentence could hide a strategic use of assumptions in the analysis or a disputable interpretation of evidence, both indicating that a strategic substantiating use of knowledge is taking place. Even with the most sophisticated software and with a fine-grained coding system, quantitative text analysis would not allow me to capture those differences, let alone reflect the richness of the details behind a case and in the stories gathered through interviews (Bazeley 2007). This led me to revert to qualitative text analysis,[18] with its well known trade-offs between the advantages of in-depth analysis and the potential risks of subjectivity and human coding errors.

To systematise the work and keep track of the different stages of analysis, test potential relationships between variables, identify patterns, uncover mechanisms and their direction in the case studies under examination, I chose the NVivo software, which provides a complete and user-friendly system for qualitative text analysis.[19] This led to a second methodological step, namely, the development of a coding system to analyse the sources collected for each case study systematically. As the literature explains (Bazeley 2007; Miles and Huberman 1994: 61), coding is an iterative process that evolves along with the research: it often starts as a theory-driven exercise which gradually becomes enriched as the fieldwork progresses. Thus, I first developed a limited set of codes[20] to cover the explanatory variables, their indicators (for example, the mandate of the agency, the conflicting preferences of regulated companies), different intensities of each variable, and also dedicated codes for the four usages of knowledge. In order to distinguish between

and not simply by redoing the content analysis itself (as redoing the content analysis is about reliability, not validity).

16. Also known as automated/computer content analysis.
17. I am grateful to Kenneth Benoit and Will Lowe for their feedback and suggestions on this point.
18. For a discussion of the core features of qualitative text analysis, see Miles and Huberman (1994).
19. I am particularly indebted to Marie-Hélène Paré for having taken the time to discuss and structure my research with NVivo and to Tony Onwuegbuzie for his additional suggestions on methodology.
20. In line with Miles and Huberman (1994: 56), I define codes as 'tags or labels for assigning units of meaning to the descriptive or inferential information compiled during a study'.

knowledge-utilisation claims made by the agency, those made by regulatees on the agency and the perception of the researcher, three separate 'knowledge-utilisation' coding systems covering the same concepts were developed. In other words, the coding was built so as to distinguish these three different narratives (Goffman 1979) of the same event.

As the field work progressed, it became apparent that some additional concepts were regularly surfacing and/or that interviewees gave different interpretations of the same notion. Relationships between individual codes, such as the association between learning and judicial review (see Chapter Four), progressively emerged; some codes grew in importance while others turned out not to be very useful. In this respect, a few more words have to be given to the frequency of a given code's occurrence across sources. The fact that a code has a prominent presence in the different sources associated with a case study may be confidently taken as an indication of its relevance; conversely, the same weight should not be attributed to the *absence* of certain codes in a given set of text sources. This is because absence does not automatically imply irrelevance: it can also indicate that the very nature of the concept at hand cannot easily emerge from the available portions of text, especially when the examined source is an official document. Hence, the need to complement my coding exercise with within-case analysis and as accurate a reconstruction of events as possible, so as to get the broader picture and gain additional insight into the relevance and/or presence/absence of a given code in the sources.

The list of codes was progressively enlarged and finally stabilised when the successive coding and recoding of documents did not bring any new 'label' to the fore (Miles and Huberman 1994: 62). As the above description of the coding process indicates,[21] this book is the result of constant feedback between a deductive and an inductive approach. This will become even more apparent in the empirical chapters and is the result of a deliberate choice. On the one hand, I wanted to start the fieldwork with a simplified map (the typology) that would allow me to 'zoom in' on the role of knowledge without losing track of the insights provided by the different theories described in Chapter Two. I also wanted to avoid the situation so colourfully described by Becker (1998: 122) of not knowing 'what constitutes [...] "data" '. A purely inductive approach would have introduced too much distance between the fieldwork and the two strands of literature on IRAs and knowledge-utilisation that I try to connect in this analysis. Hence, the explanatory typology allowed me to describe and classify what I wanted to observe, very much in line with the tenet that concept-formation comes before measurement (on this, see Maggetti *et al.* 2012, forthcoming).[22] On the other hand, conscious of the inevitable simplification that a purely deductive approach would bring to the analysis, I wished to ensure that the richness of the empirical findings would

---

21. For further details, *see also* the methodological appendix at the end of the book.

22. For a detailed description of the different types of concepts and the trade-offs and costs embedded in concept formation, *see* Maggetti *et al.* (2012, forthcoming) and Becker (1998, Chapter Four).

not be straitjacketed by the typology and its hypotheses. In particular, I tried to minimise the risk that a purely deductive approach would cause aspects that were not included in the initial categorisation to be overlooked (Becker 1998). For instance, fieldwork showed that judicial review, one of the components of the conflict variable, has a much more prominent role than initially expected. This cross-fertilisation between the deductive and the inductive directly stems from the 'relational quality' (Becker 1998: 133) of concepts in the social sciences: concepts only acquire a meaning when they are contextualised in the 'full set of relations they imply' (Becker, 1998: 138). To be sure, this interaction may appear rather 'messy' to readers. However, I found it to be a valuable approach[23] for providing a plausible account of facts and, more importantly, for highlighting the mechanisms and turning points of the three regulatory episodes that are analysed in this book. I will come back to this discussion in Chapter Eight.

In line with the functionalities of NVivo and of the logic of coding itself, I have used both of what are called 'free nodes' (Bazeley 2007: 32) – codes that are not specifically linked to other concepts and that cannot be grouped into macro categories of items that are logically connected – and 'tree-nodes' (Bazeley 2007: 100), whenever a set of codes are linked to each other in such a way as to form a logical and often hierarchical set. Broadly speaking, the codes used in this book can be grouped into the following categories: first, descriptive codes, which relate to background information on a given case and set the scene or refer to objective facts such as the number of stakeholders consulted and the data used in a research. Then, I have research-design-driven codes (the 'deductive' codes), which are derived from the explanatory typology presented above and the set of hypotheses to be tested. A third category is related to the features of the policy process and includes a mix of descriptive and more interpretational (Miles and Huberman 1994) codes that cover the specificities of the policy-making process in the telecoms sector, which is the object of analysis. Finally, I have also devised a category of subjective codes containing judgements – presented in official texts and by interviewees – on the regulator, the decision-making process under examination in a given case and, of course, knowledge-utilisation. This is where the inductive part of the research comes into play. For the sake of clarity, these judgements were grouped according to the actor that originated them: stakeholders, the regulator or the researcher. As with the codes on knowledge-utilisation, this structure allowed me to distinguish between the different narratives that unfolded in each case (Goffman 1959; Jones and McBeth 2010).

Within these four categories, all codes related to knowledge/expertise have been flagged separately, so as to be easily retrievable and groupable when needed. Table 3.3 provides an example of the different types of codes subsumed under each of the four categories described above.

---

23. For a discussion of alternative and more inductive approaches to questions of knowledge-utilisation, *see* Chapter Eight.

Table 3.3: Classification of codes

Sample list of codes	Code description
Descriptive codes	
Mandate	Statutory duties of the regulator
Type of knowledge	Nature (economic/legal/technical) of the knowledge used in a case
Commercial problem	Commercial issues faced by market players in a given case
Research-design-driven codes	
Relationship regulatees	Relationship between the agency and market players
Salience	Visibility of a given policy issue
Size of policy arena	Number of actors involved in a policy case
Policy process codes	
Consultation	Text or interviewee refers to the consultation process
Policy options	Different courses of action considered in a given case
Reporting obligation	Duty to report on a given aspect in the telecoms market
Subjective codes (i.e. reflecting narratives)	
Industry learning	Perceived learning process by market players
Influence on the regulator	Reference to instances where the regulator was/could have been influenced by external sources/actors on an issue
Evidence-based claim	Text/interviewee claims decision is grounded in evidence/facts

Last but not least, I turn to the question of what to do with the results of this coding exercise, as outputs significantly differ depending on the type of document being coded. For instance, it soon emerged that, in official documents, references to the explanatory variables as well as to knowledge-uses were quite scarce and, generally, the ratio between the coded parts of the text and the overall length of documents (on average a few hundred pages) confirmed my suspicion that these sources, being the final product of the decision-making process, have been re-worked and polished several times, thus neutralising any 'narrative' component that could help to test the research question. Undoubtedly, one can find several claims of evidence-based decision-making and references to the robustness of supporting facts and evidence but, as will be explained in the second case study (Chapter Six), this is rather the sign of a special type of strategic behaviour, related to the make-up of the text in presentational/rhetorical terms (McCloskey 1998), which has a limited link with the knowledge usage that occurred behind the scenes and before the publication of the final official document. Among these official sources, however, consultation responses from stakeholders and the way they are dealt with by the regulator in the official statements still offer interesting insights and help to locate and verify the different positions of stakeholders in the debate, identify the type of economic model used and understand the chronological

Table 3.4: Number of codes used per type of source in narrowband retail services case study

Source	Number of codes used
Interview 1	63
Interview 2	58
Interview 3	57
Interview 4	49
Interview 5	38
Official documents	
BT response	17
Regulatory statement	**16**
COLT response	14
Consultation document	**13**
Kcom response	11
bSkyb response	11
TalkTalk Group response	7
UKCTA response	5
Cable&Wireless response	3
T-mobile response	3
FCS response	2
SSE response	2

unfolding of events and arguments. Finally, as expected, interviews offered thick accounts of the case studies under examination and proved to be very informative coding material.

As an illustration of what I have just described, Table 3.4 shows the number of codes (denominated nodes in the NVivo software) that were used for the different types of sources in the case study on fixed, narrowband retail services markets described in Chapter Five. As the table shows, the number of codes used for interview transcripts (which are on average ten single-spaced pages long) and in stakeholder consultation responses (normally ranging from three to ten pages) is significantly higher than the number of codes used in the official consultation document and the regulatory statement (in bold in Table 3.4), which are respectively 160 and 103 pages long.

Another indication of the heterogeneous informative value[24] of the various types of sources used to test the hypotheses can be derived by observing the difference in coding density (the proportion of text that is actually coded) between

---

24. The expression 'informative value' refers to the number of clues to knowledge-utilisation the document contains and is by no means a judgement on the quality of the document itself.

official texts and interview transcripts for the same episode. In the case of official documents (the consultation and the regulatory statement), each of the most-used codes covers between 1 and 2 per cent of the total text. Conversely, the density of individual codes for interview transcript N.1 (see Table 3.4) never falls below 5 per cent of the text. This difference cannot only be attributed to the varying length of documents.

Finally, as regards the categories of codes (according to the classification provided in Table 3.3) emerging from the qualitative text analysis, there are no fixed patterns per type of document, although an official regulatory statement will rarely include any 'subjective codes', while still offering portions of text corresponding to research-design driven codes and, naturally, descriptive codes. In contrast, interviews are the richest in terms of interpretative codes that reveal what was happening behind the scenes of the official narrative, albeit with anecdotal accounts. As a result, the output of this coding exercise cannot be used to draw generalisable conclusions about any of the aspects covered by this book; on the other hand, coding has proven particularly valuable for identifying patterns and associations present in certain types of documents or that are typical of certain categories of interviewees. Hence, coding helped to easily retrieve, monitor and contrast the key pieces of the different narratives, in order to uncover the mechanisms behind the usage of economic analysis in each of the case studies and also to compare cases, without getting 'carried away' (Miles and Huberman 1994) by first impressions.

Interviews

As mentioned, besides official documents, the other main source of information for this book is constituted by thirty-four interviews (face-to-face and via telephone) with a selection of relevant actors. This approach can be inscribed in the tradition of elite interviewing (Dexter 2006; Richards 1996),[25] which I find particularly suited to research questions on knowledge-utilisation and for collecting the type of information needed to complement the analysis of official/public documents.[26] Specifically, these interviews served the purposes of clarifying contexts, corroborating my reconstruction of events and, where relevant, gathering insights on the respective positions and beliefs of the different actors in each episode. I discarded the alternative approach of performing a survey with a standardised questionnaire, as this method would not have elicited the type of answers (for example, on the process that led to the adoption of a certain decision, the choice of

---

25. Dexter (2006:18) defines elite interviewing as 'an interview with *any* interviewee…who in terms of the current purpose of the interviewer is given special, non-standardized treatment. By special nonstandard treatment I mean: 1) stressing the interviewee's definition of the situation; 2) encouraging the interviewee to structure the account of the situation; 3) letting the interviewee introduce to a considerable extent (an extent which will vary of course from project to project and interviewer to interviewer) his notions of what he regards as relevant, instead of relying upon the investigator's notions of relevance'.

26. On the different goals of elite interviewing, *see* Goldstein (2002: 669).

a given economic model rather than another, the role of judicial review) needed. Moreover, elite interviews are among the best means for getting actors to give their own account of the story and thus drawing attention to specific mechanisms and aspects that my questions and reasoning had not anticipated (Berry 2002; Gerring 2007: 48). In other words, this approach addresses the risk of 'straitjacketing' findings that comes with testing pre-defined hypotheses, as is the case in this book, and overcomes some of the limits of a purely deductive approach.

Of course, elite interviews raise a set of specific challenges (Aberbach and Rockman 2008; Berry 2002; Richards 1996) that need to be taken into account before embarking on the interview process itself.

The first problematic area concerns the representativeness of the sample of interviewees, which can be significantly affected if only one type of respondent agrees to be interviewed. However, as pointed out by Goldstein (2002: 670), the advantage of elite interviewing when compared to surveys is that the researcher knows much more about the non-respondents and can thus estimate the impact of the 'missing interview' on the overall validity of the findings. For each case study, I first proceeded with a mapping of all relevant contacts: in most cases, these corresponded to the respondents to the public stakeholder consultation, because, in order to take part in the debate, each organisation had to respond to the consultation, otherwise the regulator has no grounds for taking its position into account. For the regulator, the Communications Office of the agency directed me to the right person in each case (as no full organigramme is publicly available); additionally, I relied on my network of contacts inside the agency to verify whether I had spoken to the right person and, if needed, to access some additional interviewees.[27]

Another classical problem of this method concerns the ethical implications of interviewing elites. Often, the number of interviewees for a case-study is rather limited and each person can be easily identified by any reader who is familiar with the episode under examination. Hence, researchers have a duty to ensure that their work does not damage interviewees. In this case, there were potentially two risks: 1) interviewees, especially on the industry side, sometimes had to comment on commercially sensitive information that was relevant for their position and career; 2) the regulation of telecommunications is a 'repeated game', hence actors are particularly careful when it comes to their reputation and to sharing views on other players in the policy arena, if their comments can be attributed. As a result, and in agreement with each interviewee, the material included in this book is treated entirely on a 'not for attribution' basis (Goldstein 2002: 671): while I quote interviewees *verbatim*, I never specify their organisation (except in the case of Ofcom), their name or position. In addition, I deliberately do not provide a list of interviewees, as the limited number of actors actively working on each case, especially from the industry side, makes them easily traceable for anyone who knows the UK telecoms policy arena. On the other hand, this choice allowed me to record the interviews and thus gain greater accuracy in reporting the subtleties of my conversation with each actor.

---

27. For further details, *see* Appendix.

A third challenge of elite interviewing is linked to conducting the actual interview, which requires a certain amount of flexibility (Richards 1996), gaining rapport with the interviewee (Berg 2001; Leech 2002), and avoiding leading questions that would artificially steer the conversation and undermine the very purpose of hearing the story 'from the horse's mouth'. To sharpen interviewing skills and correct potential problems with the questions, a set of background interviews among experts (academic and not) were conducted and a pilot test of the questionnaires with regulatees and in another comparable agency was run, before I embarked on the real fieldwork for this book.

Finally, elite interviews entail specific issues when it comes to analysing the collected data. A first concern is reliability, which can be affected both by the number of interviewers and by the intended use of the interview data. As explained in this chapter, I do not use responses and coded portions of text to make quantifications or estimates, as this would indeed lead me to make claims that I cannot corroborate with my findings (Berry 2002). In addition, all interviews were performed by the same person, thus eliminating problems of inter-reliability among interviewers.

This method also requires balance from the researcher, as the quality of interviews differs and some accounts seem more persuasive than others, which does not necessarily imply that they are closer to 'the truth' (Berry 2002: 280). Besides triangulating findings with different sources and interviewing actors from different groups, following Berry (2002), I also inserted a set of 'probes' in the interview sheet, and asked each interviewee 'to critique its own case' (Berry 2002: 680) or to describe an opposing view on some crucial points of each episode (for example, the definition of the policy problem or the quality of a previous regulatory decision). In this respect, the fact that I had pre-coded all the relevant official documents before the interviews, and that I waited for the final (that is, approved by the interviewee) version of all interviews before coding them (Berry 2002) and then constructed tables comparing all the quotes on a given aspect/question,[28] helped to identify biased and/or exaggerated views.

Questionnaires were adapted to each case and type of interviewee; however their structure was somewhat standardised to allow for greater comparability of collected data and narratives within and between cases. Specifically, all questionnaires included a general part with questions on the agency and its position in the policy arena; on the origin of regulation in the field (are policy/regulatory initiatives taken essentially by parent ministries, the agency, or by other sources?); on the role of judicial review, and general impressions on the type of evidence used by the regulator; on the importance of economics; and a request to describe a case where the interviewee felt that economics had a visible impact on a final decision, versus a case where the decision seemed decoupled from economics. Then followed a section of questions on the specific episode under examination, covering: its origin; the two explanatory variables; the role of evidence; the weight

---

28. Here again, I chose not to insert these comparative tables in the book, as it this would have facilitated the identification of the interviewee, as soon as his/her comments were compared to those of all the actors involved in a given episode.

of economics; the type and origin of the studies/analyses used in the process; their perceived impact on decision-making; the impact of the interviewee's input (and of its organisation) on the final decision (with sub-questions on economics when relevant); and, finally, an open question in which the interviewee could add additional comments on the specific case or on another topic that had emerged as particularly relevant during the interview, most often the role of evidence in policy-making and/or the influence of judicial review.

Before each interview, ethics consent forms were submitted and signed by the interviewee and the researcher; often, interviewees required a copy of the transcripts and suggested some limited revisions or asked not to be quoted on some points.

All interviews were taped, with the previous consent of the interviewee. Half were carried out face-to-face and others by telephone, often because of the availability constraints of the interviewee. As the research progressed, it also became apparent that interviewees tended to be more open over the phone than in face-to-face contacts. This seems to be somewhat counterintuitive, as face-to-face interviews are expected to facilitate rapport and allow the observation of body language and other non-verbal clues (Berg 2001: 82). However, the topic under examination is rather technical and questions rarely touch on emotional aspects or the core beliefs of the interviewee, two elements that would have made visual contact of paramount importance. Moreover, for some, the constant presence of a tape recorder could have hampered the flow of the discussion when commercially sensitive information would naturally come into the conversation. Perhaps the latter is the main reason why interviewees were more open over the telephone, almost as if they were somehow speaking to themselves. This also seems to corroborate Goffman's (1959) insights on the different attitudes that actors have when they are 'on stage' (in my case, during a face-to-face interview, often in the interviewee's office or meeting room) and have to play their part, versus 'backstage' behaviour, where interaction is less controlled. In some cases the same person had to be contacted for two case studies, as, besides the regulator and a limited number of big market-players, other organisations are rather constrained in terms of human resources.

Case selection

The empirical part of this book was carried out by analysing a set of regulatory cases in the sector of telecommunications in Europe. As explained in Chapter One, the use of knowledge by regulatory agencies is under-tested and especially so in the case of European IRAs, due to their relatively short existence. However, in telecommunications, IRAs were created more than a decade ago, their functioning has been observed (e.g. Thatcher 2002b, 2005), and some of these organisations have clearly invested in the development of in-house economic expertise, openly embraced evidence-based policy-making and produced a body of economic knowledge that is documented and traceable. Moreover, and in contrast to other policy fields, the regulation of telecommunications is particularly well suited to the use of economic analysis, due to the type of issues (for example, existence of monopolies, auctioning of licenses, industrial policy decisions) facing the regulator.

The hypotheses to be tested generated constraints on case selection: individual episodes (our cases) had to belong to the past so that I could credibly claim to observe which type of knowledge-utilisation was at work; however these episodes also needed to be recent enough to ensure that interviewees would be able and willing to respond and would have fairly accurate recollection of events, and that the relevant documentation and economic analysis would still be available. I also needed regulators with longitudinal experience with the tools of better regulation and evidence-based policy-making, especially cost-benefit analysis and impact assessment, to test whether usage(s) or lack of usage were manifestations of the types described in Chapter Two, rather than being explained by sheer lack of capacity or adoption of the tools not followed by implementation.[29]

This led to the choice of cases from within the UK Regulator, Ofcom: it was the first telecommunications IRA to be established in Europe (as Oftel, in 1984) and has seen several waves of reform and consolidation as well as an explicit move to evidence-based policy-making in recent years, as is the case for other Government departments and agencies in the UK. Also, Ofcom is widely seen in telecommunications policy circles as the EU telecoms regulator with the strongest economic-analysis capacity. This was confirmed by most interviewees and also by other experts in Brussels and elsewhere abroad. Hence, Ofcom seemed to be a paradigmatic case of the type of organisation I wished to study in this book.

Finally, the rationale for focusing on economic knowledge was outlined in Chapter One. The particular relevance of this type of expertise in policy areas that have been subject to liberalisation and deregulation has already been noted by others (De Streel 2008a; Gilardi 2002b; Larouche 2008), and is corroborated by Gilardi's finding that delegation is more likely to occur for economic than for social regulation (2002b: 887). Ofcom itself is defined as an 'economic regulator' in British political circles (e.g. House of Lords 2007) and, as we will see in the next chapter, acts as the competition authority for electronic communications in the UK. While this confirms the relevance of choosing economics to tackle the research question, in some instances other types of knowledge (for example, engineering) are more appropriate than economics for solving a policy problem in telecommunications regulation. In those cases, observing a non-use of economics would have had little to do with the hypotheses of the explanatory typology. Hence, to counter the risk of erroneously interpreting these episodes as examples of non-use of economics, the interviews included a set of questions on the type of expertise used in and outside the agency in each case. When types of expertise other than economics were mentioned, I have covered them in the analysis.

---

29. Radaelli (2009c), argues that regulatory impact analysis has been adopted by most European countries, yet most of them have used it rather seldom, at least at the time his research was carried out.

chapter four | setting the scene for the empirical research

We shall create a new unified regulator (OFCOM) responsible for the communications sector. The regulator will be independent, will act at arm's length from the Government but will work closely with the DTI, DCMS and other relevant departments, including on European and other international negotiations. (White Paper on Communications, 2000)

The Office of Communications (Ofcom)

In this second part of the book I will test the four hypotheses presented in Chapter Three, with the help of three case studies on regulatory policy decisions taken by Ofcom between 2005 and 2010. All cases are in the field of telecommunications and were selected on the basis of my explanatory variables (the level of conflict and problem tractability). As mentioned, to allow for a reliable testing of the hypotheses, the case selection was subjected to two main constraints: I chose only closed episodes, so as to be able to cover each story and the use of economic analysis for the whole duration of the decision-making process under examination. I also decided to focus on recent cases, to maximise the chances of locating the relevant interviewees and count on a relatively accurate recollection of facts. Prior to turning to the individual case studies, this chapter introduces Ofcom as an organisation. The remainder of this section covers the agency's history, structure and mode of functioning; the following section locates Ofcom in its institutional context both nationally and internationally and sets the scene for the upcoming empirical chapters. I conclude with some additional remarks on the telecommunications policy area and the markets for which Ofcom is responsible.

While the content of this chapter is essentially based on official/institutional publications, when relevant, I have also drawn on interview transcripts; some of these contain rich accounts on Ofcom as an organisation and are a good complement to the materials used in the individual case studies.

The creation of Ofcom

Ofcom as we know it today was created by merging five separate regulators in 2003. Specifically, as shown in Figure 4.1, under the Office of Communications Act of 2002, Ofcom took over the duties of the Broadcasting Standards Commission, the Independent Television Commission, the Office of Telecommunications, the Radio Communications Agency, and the Radio Authority. The decision to create Ofcom was taken in December 2000 and the organisation started operating three years later, on 29 December 2003. Following the merger of its five predecessors,

The creation of Ofcom

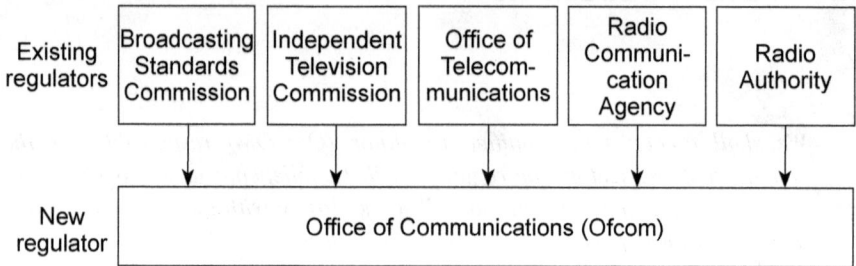

Existing regulators	Broadcasting Standards Commission	Independent Television Commission	Office of Telecommunications	Radio Communication Agency	Radio Authority

New regulator	Office of Communications (Ofcom)

Figure 4.1: The creation of Ofcom

Source: NAO (2006: 4)

Ofcom became the independent regulator and competition authority for the UK communications industries, with responsibilities for television, radio, telecommunications and wireless communications services.

As regards telecommunications, Ofcom's direct predecessor was the Office of Telecommunications (Oftel). The latter was set up with the Telecommunications Act of 1984, right after the privatisation of British Telecommunications (BT). As other regulators established around that time for water, electricity, gas, and so on, Oftel was a non-ministerial government department responsible for regulation and competition in its area of competence. Oftel had a staff of 234 civil servants at the time of Ofcom's creation (NAO 2006: 8), many of whom remained in the new organisation.

The rationale and the logic for the merger were outlined in the White Paper *A New Future for Communications*,[1] and the publication of the White Paper was accompanied by extensive public consultation and a regulatory impact assessment for the upcoming Communications Bill. The main drivers behind the creation of Ofcom were the technological convergence taking place in the electronic communications market (for example, phoning over the internet, TV on mobile phones) and the resulting need for a co-ordinated regulatory approach between previously separated policy areas. In addition, the UK had to transpose into national legislation by mid-2003 five EU directives often referred to as the 'second telecoms-package'. The importance of putting in place a regulatory framework suitable for the future evolution of the sector was at the centre of debates at that time:

---

1.   CM 5010, White Paper of December 12, 2000. Initially, the regulation of telecoms was supposed to fall under the Utilities Bill of 2000, together with gas and electricity. However, the marked diversity of the telecoms sector, the speed of technological change, and its forecasted impact on economic growth led the legislator to regulate telecoms separately.

We are living at a time of revolution in the ways in which we communicate. The worlds of telephony, broadcasting, mobile communications and the internet are changing and converging with astonishing speed. Meanwhile, our current regulatory framework was designed for a different age. We need to update the framework of regulation, and put in place a system that recognises the current fast-changing picture and can cope with the inevitability of change in years to come. The White Paper prepares us for that future, and will set up modern regulation for a modern world. (Chris Smith, Secretary of Culture, December 2000)

Two government departments – Trade and Industry (DTI) and Culture, Media and Sport (DCMS) – shared responsibility for the creation of the new independent agency. Transition from the previous structure was carefully planned and, on top of the steps and analysis included in the Communications Bill's impact assessment, two studies on how to manage the merger were commissioned from external consultants.[2] In its *ex-post* evaluation of the merger, the National Audit Office (NAO) estimates that the total cost of Ofcom's creation exceeded initial expectations and amounted to at least £80 million (NAO 2006). The milestones of Ofcom's creation are summarised in Table 4.1.

Table 4.1: Milestones in creating Ofcom

Date	Milestone
December 2000	White Paper *A New Future for Communications* published.
September 2001	Ofcom Scoping Report presented to Ministers.
March 2002	Ofcom Act receives Royal Assent.
May 2002	Draft Communications Bill published.
July 2002	David Currie appointed Ofcom chairman.
September 2002	Main board non-executives appointed.
January 2003	Stephen Carter appointed chief executive.
July 2003	Communications Act receives Royal Assent.
December 2003	Ofcom vesting day: December 29.
March 2004	Designed staff performance review process.
September 2004	First set of financial accounts laid before Parliament.
February 2005	Colleague Survey work of all Ofcom staff undertaken.
September 2005	Work begins on Project Progress, looking at organisational effectiveness.

Source: author's elaboration on NAO (2006: 7)

---

2. Both consultancy projects were led by Towers Perrin. The second project was carried out by a consortium that also included Ernst&Young and Differentis.

Ofcom was viewed as a new organisation from the very beginning and the narrative surrounding its creation depicts it as a start-up rather than the successor of the entities it replaced (Ofcom 2006d: 65). Besides major decisions on financial and practical aspects, the transition to Ofcom required a significant change of culture for the legacy staff; there were extensive internal and external communication campaigns to 'set the tone' of the new independent regulator. The tension and difficulties accompanying this transformation are carefully described by Ofcom (2006d) and by the National Audit Office (2006). In short, the newly created agency was meant to be 'something different' for a challenging and ever-changing policy field.

The new structure is a synthesis of public and private organisations and, around 2003, strong emphasis was put on reinforcing Ofcom's private-sector dimension through targeted recruitment policies and a new approach to human-resources management. Ofcom's governing Board was set up to mirror the boards of the (private) companies it regulates and, in comparison with other, similar agencies, Ofcom offers very competitive salary packages (House of Lords 2007, House of Commons 2009).

In legal terms, Ofcom is a statutory corporation established by the Office of Communications Act 2002, while its primary duties are specified in the Communications Act of 2003. As mentioned, the latter is the transposition into UK legislation of the second EU 'telecoms package' of 2002.[3]

According to the Communications Act (Article 3.1), Ofcom's principal duty is to further the interests of citizens in relation to communications matters and of consumers in relevant markets, by promoting competition if appropriate. The Act clearly differentiates between citizens and consumers and Ofcom is the only regulator that is required by statute to make this distinction when carrying out its duties. Specifically, duties towards consumers are those that are traditionally expected by (economic) regulators and are broadly related to the concept of consumer-protection matters in connection to products and services available on the market. Instead, Ofcom's duty towards citizens entails a broader perspective and 'involves ensuring that people have access to the services, content, and skills needed to participate in society, and that they are protected appropriately' (NAO 2010b: 9). Official sources (House of Lords 2007; NAO 2010b) report that Ofcom is clearly aware of this difference when performing its mandate, although it might occasionally have to reconcile tensions between these two objectives. By way of example, there could be a trade-off between mandating access to a given service that would benefit society as a whole if this also implies an increase in prices for current consumers.

---

3.   After several years of negotiations in Brussels, the 2002 EU regulatory framework for electronic communications was revised in 2009 and was under transposition in EU member states at the time of writing. In the UK, the transposition of this third telecoms package was an occasion to update existing legislation and align it with new policy priorities. The framework had to be transposed in the UK by May 25, 2011.

The Communications Act also sets out the following specific duties:

1. Ensuring the optimal use of the electro-magnetic spectrum;
2. Ensuring that a wide range of electronic communications services – including high speed data services – is available throughout the UK;
3. Ensuring a wide range of TV and radio services of high quality and wide appeal;
4. Maintaining plurality in the provision of broadcasting;
5. Applying adequate protection for audiences against offensive or harmful material; and
6. Applying adequate protection for audiences against unfairness or the infringement of privacy.

Ofcom is required by statute to respect better regulation principles (that is, regulatory activities should be consistent, transparent, proportionate, accountable and targeted); Article 7 establishes the duty to carry out impact assessments and to justify policy decisions explicitly. The article also specifies under which conditions an impact assessment should be carried out and in which instances this duty does not apply (that is, for urgent matters). Article 7 is particularly relevant for this research, as it embeds evidence-based policy-making in the mandate of the agency.

Moreover, in the exercise of its functions, Ofcom is also bound by the following regulatory principles:[4]

- Ofcom will regulate with a clearly articulated and publicly reviewed annual plan, with stated policy objectives.
- Ofcom will intervene where there is a specific statutory duty to work towards a public-policy goal that markets alone cannot achieve.
- Ofcom will operate with a bias against intervention but with a willingness to intervene firmly, promptly and effectively where required.
- Ofcom will strive to ensure its interventions will be evidence-based, proportionate, consistent, accountable and transparent in both deliberation and outcome.
- Ofcom will always seek the least intrusive regulatory mechanisms to achieve its policy objectives.
- Ofcom will research markets constantly and will aim to remain at the forefront of technological understanding.
- Ofcom will consult widely with all relevant stakeholders and assess the impact of regulatory action before imposing regulation upon a market.

Ofcom's duties are disciplined by an additional set of UK and European Acts. As regards the UK, Ofcom's work is affected by the Broadcasting Acts, the

---

4. Online. Available: http://www.ofcom.org.uk/about/ofcom-reorganisation/ (accessed 25 March 2013).

Table 4.2: Legislative Acts affecting Ofcom's activities

Broadcasting Act 1990
Broadcasting Act 1996
Competition Act 1998
Communications Act 2003
Enterprise Act 2002
The Electronic Communications Code (Conditions and Restrictions) Regulations 2003, SI 2003/2553
The Regulation of Investigatory Powers Act 2000
The Wireless Telegraphy (Spectrum Trading) Regulations 2004, SI 2004/3154
Universal Service Directive
Unfair Terms in Consumer Contracts Regulations, SI 1999/2083
Wireless Telegraphy Act 1949
Digital Economy Act 2010
Postal Services Act 2011

Competition Act, and the Enterprise Act. Recently, the Digital Economy Act of 2010 gave Ofcom new responsibilities in areas such as copyright infringement, infrastructure, internet domain names, public service content, radio and spectrum. Since 2011, Ofcom is also responsible for the regulation of postal services, following the adoption by Parliament of the Postal Services Act 2011, and will also take over the duties of the previous regulator, Postcomm. The UK legislation spelling out Ofcom's duties and responsibilities is listed in Table 3.2. The Acts that are of particular relevance for the case studies covered in this book are indicated in bold. I have not included the EU Directives and other obligations that affect Ofcom's work, as these are normally transposed into UK legislation and thus indirectly covered in the table.[5]

Current structure and functioning

From its creation, Ofcom adopted a matrix organisational structure (Ofcom 2006d: 55) in which work is organised on a project basis. Ofcom's main decision-making body is the Board, which comprises both executive and non-executive members and is in charge of setting the overall strategic direction for the agency. The Board has a non-executive chairman (Ms Colette Bowe at the time of writing), Executive Directors including the Chief Executive Officer (Mr Ed Richards at the time of writing) and non-executive directors. The Board is also responsible for overseeing

---

5. For further details on the latest EU-driven changes to Ofcom's mandate, *see* the consultation document on Ofcom's draft annual programme for 2011–12. Online. Available: http://stakeholders.ofcom.org.uk/binaries/consultations/draftap1112/summary/ap201112.pdf (accessed 15 March 2013).

Ofcom's overall funding and expenditure, and meets once per month (except in August). The agenda and minutes of Board meetings are publicly available on the agency's website; however, minutes are very terse and could not be used for the coding exercise performed for this book.[6]

Ofcom's senior executive team is known as the Executive Committee and runs the organisation. The Executive Committee answers to the Board. Ofcom has also a Policy Executive that is charge of the agency's regulatory agenda. It acts as a forum for discussion and has the power to take certain decisions itself. As explained by one of Ofcom's interviewees, the Policy Executive can, for example, finalise regulatory statements once these have been broadly approved by the Board. While official sources do not extensively describe how decision-making occurs within Ofcom, the following interview excerpts shed some additional light on this aspect:[7]

> The Board sets the strategy, to be honest we are very executive-driven in that the Executive will spend their time working through what our duties are and structuring what it is we should be doing and then it will bring it to the Board for the Board to take a view about whether we are going in the right direction or to ask some quite challenging questions and then it goes back to the Executive. It's not the Board that decides at the outset what we are going to do; it's much more...the Board reacts to what the Executive suggests. That's not to say the Board doesn't occasionally make suggestions but if I look at where we are at the moment, the Board's principal concern is around our annual planning process, our strategic, what it is that we want to do over the next 3, 4, 5 years, what the implications are going to be of a change of government, a coalition government, the impact on the public sector, what impact there is going to be on us.... And the Policy Executive, the one that meets weekly, that's chaired by the CEO, and he has all the senior, the policy-makers at that meeting, so the general counsel, the chief economist, and the various people who head our spectrum and content standard, competition, all turn up at Policy Executive, so you have actually sitting in this very room, about a dozen people around the table, and between that dozen people you have access to every aspect of Ofcom, so when a paper comes up the CEO has everyone he needs to talk to, and they can either give him a view or go and get the view. (Board Member, June 2010, Ofcom)

The role of the Board has evolved with time and increasingly mirrors the function of a private company's board. This was not the case in the beginning, as the Board was set up during the transition from the legacy regulators and had to take on several executive tasks to ensure that Ofcom would be able to perform its

---

6. For further details on this point, *see* Chapter Three.

7. During the fieldwork for this book, I had the opportunity to examine internal guidelines that specify how responsibilities are allocated within the organisation, and which type of decisions can be taken at each organisational level so as to ensure smooth and timely functioning of the agency. These guidelines also specify which tasks are reserved to the Board and include a sliding scale for the approval of funding to external projects.

duties appropriately by the end of 2003. In fact, official documents (Ofcom 2006d; NAO 2006) and some of the interviews show how the Board was instrumental in ensuring both continuity and change during this transition period and how it fostered the development of a new organisational culture at Ofcom:

> The Board's role was also to converge the heritage regulators, the five regulators into one, so the role of the Board was also to set the tone, and by choosing the building, choosing the chief executive, choosing the style and design, just little things, like saying 'yes we will have free coffee machines on every floor' that you know, it sounds tiny, but it indicates what your culture is going to be. And culture was very important. So I think it was important in setting both policy and culture, and making some fundamental decisions, like saying that we would not go with public sector pay scales, that we would aim to have fewer people, who were better and better paid, that was a Board, along with the Chief Executive, but it was a Board decision. (Former Board Member, May 2010, Ofcom)

Ofcom has also a set of additional boards and committees in charge of overseeing specific policy areas. These include: the Spectrum Clearance and Awards Programme Management Board (responsible for the 800 MHz and 2.6 GHz spectrum frequency bands); the Operations Board, which supports, guides and challenges Ofcom's operational performance and reports directly to the Executive Committee; and the Content Board (a sub-committee of the main Board), responsible for setting and enforcing standards for television and radio. The Content Board was set up to counter initial fears that, because of the economic weight of telecoms, broadcasting and content would receive less attention from the merged regulator (Ofcom 2006d). The Communications Act also foresees additional committees and advisory bodies to assist Ofcom in its work: the Communications Consumer Panel, the England, Northern Ireland, Scotland and Wales Advisory Committees, the Ofcom Spectrum Advisory Board and the Older Persons and Disabled Persons Advisory Committee.

Ofcom's total expenditure is agreed on an annual basis with the Treasury and the regulator has to perform its duties within this limit. As foreseen in the Communications Act, Ofcom raises its funds from the sectors it regulates, specifically from: television broadcast licence fees; radio broadcast licence fees; administrative charges for electronic networks and services and the provision of broadcasting and associated facilities; funds in the form of grant-in-aid from the Department for Business, Innovation and Skills[8] to cover Ofcom's operating costs for spectrum management; and grant-in-aid funding to cover statutory functions and duties which Ofcom must discharge but for which there is no matching revenue stream. In 2011–12, the agency's operating budget was £108.7 million, the lowest annual running costs for the regulator (Ofcom 2012a: 70).[9]

---

8. Formerly known as the Department for Trade and Industry.

9. Online. Available: http://www.ofcom.org.uk/files/2012/07/OfcomAnnualReport11–12.pdf (accessed 1 April 2013).

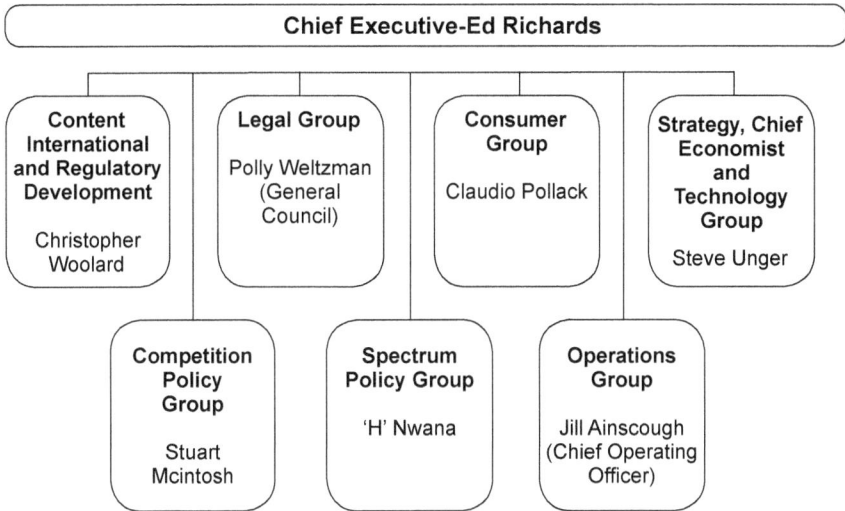

Figure 4.2: Ofcom's organigramme

Source: Ofcom's website (2011)

Ofcom has about 800 staff, composed of a mixture of people with public- and private-sector backgrounds so as to reflect the structure and working methods of the companies it regulates. Under the Cameron-led coalition government, and following the 2010 public-sector spending review, the agency will see a 28.2 per cent budget reduction (about £30 million) over four years and 170 job cuts.[10] As a result, Ofcom completed a review of its internal spending on 1st February 2011 and established how the budget cuts will be distributed. The review also led to a restructuring of the organisation according to the following groups (that is, departments): Competition Group; Content, International & Regulatory Development; Consumer Group; Legal; Operations; Spectrum Policy Group; Strategy, Chief Economist and Technology.[11] Figure 4.2 shows Ofcom's organigramme in 2011.

Ofcom's in-house expertise

In terms of expertise, Ofcom has a strong pool of economists, lawyers, engineers, statisticians and finance experts. Reportedly, economists and lawyers constitute the two biggest groups. Economists are essentially divided in two teams: the biggest one, known as the Competition Group, follows on a day-to-day basis all

---

10. *The Guardian* (2010), 'Ofcom to cut 170 jobs and reduce budget by 28.2% over four years', published on 21 October. Online. Available: http://www.guardian.co.uk/media/2010/oct/21/ofcom-job-losses-spending-review (accessed 15 March 2013).

11. Online. Available: http://www.ofcom.org.uk/about/ofcom-reorganisation-2011/ (accessed 15 March 2013).

the regulatory dossiers for which Ofcom is responsible. These range from appeals and dispute-resolution (that is, *ex-post* regulation) to market-analysis and *ex-ante* regulatory policy decisions. A second and much smaller team of economists, under the direction of Ofcom's Chief Economist, carries out additional research to support the Competition Group, to build additional expertise and develop a more long-term view of the communications market. As mentioned, Ofcom's mode of working is essentially project-based. Ofcom interviewees explained that, for each dossier, a dedicated team with mixed competences is normally set up. The composition depends on the topic under examination but economists are always involved in the organisation's decisions, as are the so-called 'policy-people'. The latter often have a strong background in a particular area of expertise (such as economics or engineering) but carry out a 'generalist' function in the organisation. As explained by a senior member of staff, there are fewer senior positions available in Ofcom's individual areas of expertise; hence, the move to the category of policy-people is often dictated by opportunities for career advancement.

While not all interviewees explicitly referred to Ofcom as an 'economic regulator',[12] all confirmed that economics plays a central, if not the main, role within the agency. Insiders and outsiders also pointed out that the weight of economics is clearly signalled by the economics background of those who hold key positions (for example, either the Chairman or the Chief Executive is always an economist). Of course, the relevance of different types of knowledge for a given policy dossier may create tensions between different experts; for instance, when economists in a team privilege 'efficiency' while engineers advocate the primacy of 'technical quality'. While the nature and extent of such tensions would have to be appraised on a case-by-case basis, from official documents and interviews it generally emerged that there is a deliberate attempt by Ofcom not to sideline non-economic domains of expertise, given that the agency is also responsible for broadcasting regulation.

In some instances, Ofcom relies on external expertise, most often for market-research purposes. Normally, an externally contracted firm selected through classical tendering procedures carries out data collection for the regulator; this information is then processed and analysed internally. Ofcom has also a panel of external economic consultants, which includes some prominent academics and is meant to complement in-house economic skills. These consultants are selected on the basis of their area of specialisation so as to cover the different types of problems that Ofcom may have to address; they are regularly contacted for targeted advice and feedback on specific economic questions. The regulator also organises *ad hoc* workshops, with other regulators in the EU and beyond and with experts from academia and the policy world.

Ofcom regularly stresses the importance of evidence and research in its decision-making processes. The agency saw the light under a Labour Government that put considerable emphasis on evidence-based policy-making and this is

---

12. The House of Lords Review of Economic Regulators in 2007 places Ofcom in this group.

reflected in Ofcom's statutory duty to perform regulatory impact assessments for most of its decisions and in all official publications.[13] In a way, Ofcom corroborates the normative expectation that the use of expertise is a founding element for (independent) regulatory agencies. In turn, the importance attributed to expertise is closely linked to one of the control variables in the explanatory typology presented in Chapter Three: the capacity (in terms of human resources) of the agency.

As we will see in the following chapters, Ofcom is consistently perceived by interviewees and in consultation responses as an organisation with high level of capacity and expertise. In fact, the two concepts are used as synonyms by many interviewees and also in official publications on the agency (for example, written and oral submissions to the House of Lords 2007). To be sure, Ofcom signals quite clearly that it possesses the relevant expertise for carrying out its mandate and is open about the fact that this is the result of a deliberate choice. In public speeches and when probed during hearings in Westminster about the rationale of paying its employees (particularly the senior staff) more than any comparable organisation, Ofcom representatives stress that this is a Board's strategy to give the organisation the means to regulate the communications market successfully and attract and retain the best talents among its staff.[14] Quite interestingly, this approach is supported by regulatees, although this has clear repercussions on the fees levied on them to finance Ofcom's work. As Orange, one of the biggest mobile operators in the UK market, famously put it: 'good regulation is not cheap regulation' (House of Lords 2007: 588). In fact, regulatees are Ofcom's shareholders and thus have high expectations in terms of performance; Ofcom has established a strong reputation among them. This is corroborated by comparisons with Oftel, for instance; there is now a healthy flow of expertise between Ofcom and the private sector, while previously a job at Oftel was mostly viewed 'as a meal ticket to a job in the private industry' (House of Lords 2007: 303).[15] Also, during the fieldwork for this book, industry representatives did not hesitate to praise Ofcom's in-house

---

13. Ofcom developed its own impact assessment guidelines in 2005 and includes in its Annual Reports an overview of all policy decisions for which an impact assessment was performed as well as those for which there was no impact assessment. Ofcom impact assessment guidelines: Online. Available: http://stakeholders.ofcom.org.uk/binaries/consultations/better-policy-making/Better_Policy_Making.pdf (accessed 15 March 2013).

14. On this point during a hearing in front of the House of Lords Select Committee on Regulators, Ofcom's Chair of the time, Lord Curry of Marylebone explained: 'We were set up as a public corporation and we are not a non-departmental public body. That distinction gives us freedom in our salary and remuneration policy. I have to say that freedom has been absolutely essential to what we have achieved because I think what we quite consciously did very early on with Stephen Carter and his successor was to create an organisation with a lot of capability at the top but slimmer in other parts of the organisation, so overall smaller, overall cheaper, but with a lot more capacity at the top. That has enabled us to do the job of joining up what is a complicated scene and a fast-moving scene [...]' (House of Lords, 2007: 20).

15. It is also interesting to note that, in their submissions to the House of Lords in 2007, regulatees and other contributors did not always have the same opinion of other sectoral regulators and Ofcom always came out favourably in comparison exercises.

teams of sectoral experts and, as regards economists, interviewees stressed that the regulator scores well both in terms of quantity ('they have an army of economists'; 'I have been working with Ofcom's economists for very long, and I still bump into some that I have never met before') and quality of available expertise ('they are a well qualified bunch [...] one benefit of Ofcom is their expertise, and their professionalism').

In a way, these insider/outsider perspectives are broadly in line with the assumption and expectation that expertise is a necessary ingredient for a regulator's legitimacy, so much that it justifies above-average salaries. I will come back to a more detailed discussion of these normative aspects in the concluding chapter of this book. For the moment, we can safely anticipate that Ofcom's capacity remains high in all the case studies covered here. Whether and how this ability to produce relevant economic knowledge has an impact on knowledge-utilisation is one of the research questions I plan to answer with the case studies. Before I turn to the individual episodes that I have selected to test the explanatory typology, let me present the policy environment in which Ofcom operates and, in particular, the other institutions with which the agency interacts when performing its duties.

The institutional environment in which Ofcom operates

As can be expected for a merged regulator with such a wide range of competence, Ofcom has several (political) principals. At the ministerial level, Ofcom has essentially two parent ministries:[16] the Department for Business, Innovation and Skills (BIS) and the Department for Culture, Media and Sport (DCMS). In addition, the Treasury determines Ofcom's annual spending. While Ofcom must ultimately account to these bodies for its activity, and particularly to the first two as far as its policy choices are concerned, the regulator is by statute independent. Hence, the degree of ministerial and political interference in its daily activity is formally limited.

This is in line with the argument put forward by Bawn (1995) in the concluding section of her article, in which different political systems are compared. In particular, Bawn (1995: 70) explains that the British parliamentary system tends to reduce intrinsic procedural uncertainty;[17] hence independence (and the weight of expertise in agency decision-making) should be less restricted than in other political systems once delegation has occurred. If one refers to the variables included in Gilardi's index (2002b), Ofcom also scores better than its European counterparts in terms of formal independence.[18] This is confirmed by a similar index

---

16. At the time of the Communications White Paper, there was a plan to create a unique Communications Department to which Ofcom would report. This was to avoid possible delays and clashes between two departments that could potentially have conflicting preferences. Following a general election, this plan was abandoned. For further details, *see* House of Commons (2002).

17. For further details on Bawn's model, *see* Chapter Two.

18. Note that the data used in the empirical part of Gilardi's contribution refer to Ofcom's predecessor, Oftel.

developed by the OECD (2006b) for telecommunications independent regulators, which looks at autonomy both from political principals and regulatees. Yet, as explained in Chapter Two, formal and *de facto* independence may not always coincide; the latter must be observed empirically in the post-delegation phase.[19] In this respect, Ofcom's independence is not questioned in public debates and publications (House of Lords 2007). One of Ofcom's former Chief Executives explained:

> I think people under-estimate the extent to which the idea of independent regulation has become almost quasi-constitutional. In my experience, it is accepted by all the political parties and no-one at a senior level in a political party in my experience has ever seriously questioned it. (Ed Richards, House of Lords, 23 January 2007)

Most of the interviewees explicitly stated that Ofcom is independent from its parent ministries. However, a couple of stakeholders pointed out that there seems to be more politicisation than in the past on some highly salient dossiers (see Chapter Seven). Quite naturally, Ofcom is aware of a ministry's preferences on certain topics; still, the agency's autonomy was not questioned in any of the interviews and Ofcom officially reported that the

> Secretary of State may give general or specific directions for the limited purposes of national security, foreign relations, international obligations, public safety/health and prompt standards in a specific area. To date, the Secretary of State has never exercised these powers. (non-confidential answer, Annex UK, ECTA 2010)

Perhaps, the relationship with the parent Ministry is best described by the words of one of Ofcom's senior staff members:

> I cannot immediately think of any decisions where the Ministry had a big role; I mean there are cases where we need to understand where they are, but that doesn't mean that we will give them what they want. (Interviewee 1, Ofcom)

In parliament, Ofcom's work falls under the responsibility of two different committees in the House of Commons – the Culture, Media and Sport Committee and the Trade and Industry Committee – and the regulator's annual plans are traditionally discussed in a joint session. The minutes of the debates are publicly available on the Parliament's website. Additional sessions of the joint Committee are organised when necessary, for example, in view of the appointment of Ms Colette Bowe as Chairman in 2009. Ofcom's work is also scrutinised by the Public Accounts Committee and by the House of Lords Select Committee on Regulators. The latter published a comprehensive review of economic regulators in the UK,

---

19. As explained in Chapter Two, this book does not use independence as a separate explanatory variable in the analysis; however, the empirical chapters discuss Ofcom's independence where relevant.

including Ofcom, in 2007, and asked the National Audit Office to report on the use of impact assessments by these bodies on the same occasion (NAO 2007).[20]

One of the expectations embedded in Ofcom's creation was that its lean structure would prevent the duplication of effort of its five predecessors and deliver better value for money[21] to British taxpayers (House of Commons 2002; House of Lords 2007; NAO 2006). As a result, the National Audit Office regularly reviews Ofcom's activities and value for money is one of the performance indicators on which the agency is searchingly examined in the House of Commons. While the National Audit Office (2010b) recently concluded that Ofcom has indeed achieved some cost savings and works more efficiently than its predecessors, it also stressed that the goals and targets of the organisation are not fully transparent yet: hence, it remains difficult to fully assess whether the agency meets its intended objectives effectively and efficiently. However, the NAO and the stakeholders it interviewed for its periodic assessment concluded that Ofcom's performance is positive in most areas and is reflected in the competitive state of many of the markets that the agency regulates.[22]

Ofcom is also the competition authority for the communications sector and thus has concurrent powers with the Office of Fair Trading (OFT), the UK's competition authority. The two organisations have a Memorandum of Understanding to co-ordinate their activities. Under the Communications Act, sections 192–7, Ofcom is subject to extensive judicial review on the merits.[23] This obligation was included in British legislation to meet the requirements of the EU telecoms package of 2002. This means that, when appealed, the regulator's decisions can be reviewed not only on procedural grounds (how the decision was made) but also on content and on the analysis supporting it. The main body to which regulatees appeal Ofcom's decisions is the Competition Appeals Tribunal (CAT),[24] except for pricing matters, which are referred to the Competition Commission. Once the latter has come to a

20. In the NAO Report (2007), Ofcom comes out as a top performer among UK economic regulators as far as impact assessments are concerned, although the assessment is based on the examination of two impact assessments per regulator and all showed room for improvement.

21. Value for money is defined by the National Audit Office as 'the optimal use of resources to achieve the intended outcomes'. The NAO has a dedicated value-for-money programme, whereby it undertakes around 60 studies per year covering different UK departments and agencies to assist the Parliament and government in providing better public services. Online. Available: http://www.nao.org.uk/about-us/role-2/what-we-do/value-for-money-programme/ (accessed 25 March 2013).

22. For further details on the indicator developed by the National Audit Office to assess Ofcom's performance, see NAO (2010b: 33–4).

23. All decisions by an economic regulator can also be appealed by regulated companies on procedural grounds to the High Court. This approach is applied to all the other economic regulators (e.g. Ofgem, Ofwat); conversely, appeal on the merits only applies to Ofcom and stems from EU obligations.

24. The CAT can appeal certain decisions made by the UK Competition Authority and sectoral regulators made under the Competition Act 1998, the Enterprise Act 2002, and the Communications Act 2003.

£ millions

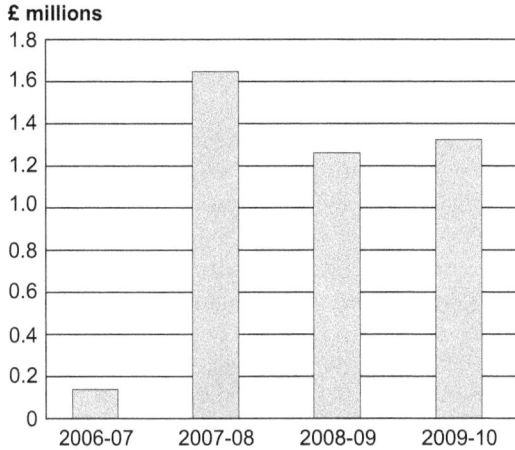

Figure 4.3: Ofcom's appeal costs

Source: NAO (2010b: 32), elaboration on Ofcom data

conclusion on a pricing matter, it normally communicates its findings to the CAT, which will then go on with the other elements of the dispute. If the CAT upholds an appeal, Ofcom's decision is overturned.

The importance of judicial review on the merits cannot be overstated and it has had visible impacts on the policy fields falling under Ofcom's remit. Since its creation, Ofcom has been appealed thirty-five times (NAO 2010b) and other appeal procedures were ongoing at the time of writing.[25] According to the NAO (2010b: 32), these thirty-five appeals led to twenty-five proceedings, as some cases could be treated together. Eight of these cases were still ongoing, and five were withdrawn. Of the twelve remaining cases, Ofcom lost four, won six, and achieved a split decision in two. Most of the interviewees in and outside Ofcom commented extensively on judicial review and on its pros and cons. One of the most critical issues is undoubtedly the cost of proceedings, which, according to recent estimates have cost Ofcom over £1 million per year since 2007–8. The number of appeals has seemed to be on an upward trend and there is no sign of it decreasing in the near future. As a result, the Department for Business, Innovation and Skills launched a consultation in 2010, to explore the possibility of reviewing the appeals system and to address some of the shortcomings that have emerged in terms of the cost and duration of proceedings.[26]

---

25. On more recent appeals, *see also* Larouche and Taton (2011).

26. The consultation was launched on the occasion of the transposition of the third telecoms package adopted at the EU level in 2009. For further details, *see also* Chapter Eight. Online. Available: http://www.bis.gov.uk/Consultations/revised-eu-electronic-communications-framework?cat=clo sedawaitingresponse (accessed 22 September 2012).

The average cost of appeals is illustrated in Figure 4.3. One has to take into account that these are only the costs borne by Ofcom. The costs for the plaintiffs and the defendants as well as for other parties involved should be added to these total amounts.

Regardless of the impact that judicial review or the threat of being appealed may have had on knowledge-utilisation in the different episodes covered in this book, it is worth adding some general remarks here, given the prominent place held by the appeals process in electronic communications policy. Views on judicial review differ somewhat different between Ofcom staff and external actors; however, all interviewees raised some common points. On the positive side, judicial review is seen as a means by which to discover and clarify the boundaries of Ofcom's competence, as these are not always clear in statutes. On the negative side, besides its costs for all parties involved, judicial review can also be used by market-players as a weapon, often to delay regulation inappropriately. In turn, this has both positive and negative effects on Ofcom's decision-making and can affect the agency's approach to knowledge. The importance of judicial review in some individual cases will be examined in greater detail in the next three chapters; in the meantime, the following quotes illustrate the advantages and disadvantages of the current system quite clearly:

> Judicial review is very influential in the way Ofcom works. In some ways, in a helpful way, in some ways in an unhelpful way. The helpful way is that it works as it should do against sort of arbitrary decision-making. We are always aware of the fact that we've got to be able to justify decisions, we've got to have evidence, we've got to reason things properly, and that's a good discipline. The bad side of it is, I think, that we feel that we have to be more thorough than is really necessary, so that and I think that it's not so much about the fact that you are reviewable but about the way the review is taking place, where the level of detail of the review has been such that you kind of feel that there are 100 questions and you have to get a 100 out of a 100 [...] if you get 99 out a 100 it's not good. (Interviewee 2, June 2009, Ofcom)

> Overall Ofcom tend to lose, they have a poor appeal track record to start with; I think they are learning from their losses in their understating of where the CAT's judgement is going to get them; to be fair the Communications Act 2003 doesn't always [...] it was not always 100 per cent clear so some of the CAT's judgements have given them clarity about what they need to do as a regulator, so that's all part of the process [...] some of them are bad decisions, but some of them are about Ofcom not understanding or not having the clarity about what its duties are and how to interpret them. It can look back at the Communications Act but the Communications Act only goes so far and it needs to understand some of those issues and the CAT has helped them to do that. (Industry 1, July 2010)

> We are seeing [...] in the UK now, loads more litigation and this again reflects the fact [...] Ofcom make a decision and if we are happy with it, someone else normally isn't happy and appeals. And if we're not happy, we've told them,

that we are going to use lawyers as a way of freezing the system, we've got to protect our interests and we will appeal. (Industry 2, November 2009)

I think the CAT, from our perspective, has been hugely beneficial. I remember the first half of this decade, the frustration that industry had with Oftel's ability to resolve disputes, the lack of scrutiny over some of the rather bizarre decisions, and the CAT has improved things greatly. So if you think there are pros and cons: the pros are that clearly there is a place to go if you are not happy or feel that Ofcom's decisions are fundamentally flawed, and we think that the track record of CAT's judgements makes it clear that they have made serious flaws over the last five years. On the downside there is that it's a further legal opportunity and legal hoop for prevarication or for parties to try and delay the implementation of policies that they are not comfortable with. (Industry 3, November 2010)

Overall, both Ofcom and the regulatees agree that judicial review instils greater rigour in decision-making and fosters learning by the regulator. In a way, their views also converge on the view that the system can generate strategic incentives among all parties concerned, although the mechanisms at play are obviously described from two opposing perspectives.

As regards scrutiny by civil society, Ofcom receives feedback through open public consultation processes and is considered a good performer in this area (House of Lords 2007; NAO 2010b). Besides individual regulatory proposals, Ofcom's annual plan is also subject to public consultation. In addition, the regulator's work is often monitored by the media, consumer organisations and other initiatives such as OfcomWatch, a dedicated internet blog that aims at providing 'an independent, informal, non-partisan, well written, easily readable, occasionally humorous online resource'.[27] Other more specialised websites/blogs follow specific parts of Ofcom's activities and serve as additional fora for debate, although the technicality of their content tends to attract mostly contributors with a specialised background.

Ofcom is also part of a network of institutional relations at the international level and particularly within the European Union. Since the adoption of the EU telecoms package in 2002, which mandated the creation of an independent national regulatory authority (NRA) for electronic communications in each member state and a set out a series of obligations for these organisations, Ofcom's work and that of its EU peers has been affected by decision-making in Brussels and by the European Commission in particular. One of the core obligations imposed by the EU telecoms package on NRAs is to regularly assess the state of competition in a variety of electronic communications markets (for example, fixed telephony, mobile telephony) and perform a specific test to decide if and what type of regulatory intervention is appropriate at the national level in each case. National

---

27. Online. Available: www.ofcomwatch.co.uk. I am grateful to Russ Taylor of OfcomWatch for his time and valuable input to this research.

regulators are required to inform the European Commission of the result of this analysis and receive non-binding feedback on it.[28]

The European Commission also set up a network of NRAs to co-ordinate the application of EU legislation and facilitate cross-national learning and the exchange of best practice. The network, known as the European Regulators Group (ERG), also gives opinions on the functioning of the EU telecoms market. During the recent debates that led to the adoption of the third EU telecoms package (2009), one of the proposals initially put on the table was the creation of a pan-European regulator for electronic communications. The rationale behind this idea was to accelerate the development of an EU internal market in this policy field and remedy the current lack of a single market offering more competition and greater consumer choice to European consumers (De Streel 2008b; Pelkmans and Renda 2011; Renda 2009). Eventually, the proposed agency did not see the light of day but the ERG was replaced by a more formal structure known as the Body of European Regulators in Electronic Communications (BEREC).[29] In 2006, Ofcom chaired the ERG and has always played an active role in the network, with the aim of influencing policy decision-making in Brussels (House of Lords 2007). More generally, Ofcom tends to be viewed by stakeholders as being at the forefront of many of its European peers. This view is echoed by the European Competitive Telecommunications Association (ECTA), which publishes annual comparative Regulatory Scorecards for the European Union and places the UK (that is, Ofcom) in the top position(s) among EU independent telecoms regulators, together with France, the Netherlands, Denmark, and Ireland. While the UK occupied the top position in previous reports, it was overtaken by the Netherlands in 2009 (on the basis of unweighted results). With equally weighted results, the UK would still hold the top position by one point (ECTA 2010: 32).[30]

ECTA also provides another interesting set of indicators (ECTA 2010: 8) on aspects covered in this chapter. In particular, ECTA's analysis combines the results obtained by each EU regulator on two indicators, institutional performance and regulatory performance respectively. Institutional performance scores cover aspects that regulators cannot influence but that affect the environment in which they operate, namely: the level of transposition of the EU framework; the enforcement powers of the regulator; the scope and scale of its resources;

---

28. This process is known as Art. 7 procedure under the telecoms package of 2002. While giving a comprehensive explanation of the market-review principles falls outside the scope of this chapter, further details will be provided in the individual case studies when relevant.

29. BEREC was established by EC Regulation 1211/2009, and is made up of a board composed of the heads of the 27 NRAs. Their work is assisted by an Office, which is a Community Body located in Riga (Latvia) with a Management Committee in which all NRAs and the Commission are represented. Online. Available: http://berec.europa.eu/ (accessed 25 March 2013). On the creation of BEREC and more broadly on the lack of EU-level agencies engaged in 'economic regulation', see Thatcher (2011: 801 and 803).

30. Online. Available: http://www.ectaportal.com/en/REPORTS/Regulatory-Scorecards/Regulatory-Scorecard-2009/(accessed 25 March 2013).

independence; the dispute-settlement body; and the effectiveness of the appeals procedure. Regulatory performance indicators cover aspects that are generally influenced by a regulator's activity: the implementation of the EU regulatory framework; the transparency of the regulator's processes; its enforcement record; and the efficiency of the dispute-settlement body. Again, the UK is among the top scorers.

Telecommunications in the UK

In the coming chapters I will describe three case studies on different aspects of the telecommunications market, namely, the regulation of fixed narrowband retail services; an episode on mobile telephony (mobile termination rates) and a complex case on the deployment of next-generation networks. Each chapter will include an introduction with more detailed elements to explain the technical, economic and legal implications of the case under examination. In this section, I provide a few concluding data and remarks on the market for electronic communications (and more specifically on telecommunications) in the UK, so as to set the empirical analysis in a broader context.

Since the privatisation of British Telecommunications (BT) in 1984[31] telecommunications have evolved considerably in the UK, and so has the role of the regulator. Initially, regulation of the sector mainly consisted in breaking the monopoly held by BT after privatisation to gradually open the market to competitors. Since then, and as previously explained, technological convergence has completely changed the shape of the market so as to make the exclusive use of the term telecommunications somewhat misleading. In a nutshell, telecoms are now only a portion of the broader market for electronic communications. According to the latest data provided by Ofcom (2012b: 23), the communications industry's revenue in 2011 amounted to £53.2 billion. The market for telecommunications and networks, which is the focus of this book, includes fixed and mobile telephony and telecoms-based internet connections and infrastructure; it still accounts for the biggest portion of the communications industry as a whole, as shown in Figure 4.4.

As Figure 4.4 shows, 2009 is the first year exhibiting a fall in revenues for the sector since Ofcom began monitoring the market. One of the most likely causes of this decrease is the recent economic and financial crisis. Demand patterns have also changed, with UK consumers using communications services more than ever; however, households tend to spend less than before on mobile and fixed telephony. The average monthly expenditure by British households is shown in Figure 4.5.

When compared to the situation facing the legacy regulator Oftel, the policy arena that Ofcom has to deal with is more complex in many respects. In the first decades after privatisation, telecoms regulation offered a relatively predictable scenario to the regulator. In terms of the explanatory typology, while there were undoubtedly some intractable problems, these usually fell within clearly

---

31. For further details, *see* Chapter Five.

£ billions   **Total**

							5 yr
						1 year	**CAGR**

Figure 4.4 bar chart:

£ billions

- 2006: 52.4 total (Telecoms 40.7, TV 10.6, Radio 1.1)
- 2007: 54.2 total (Telecoms 42.0, TV 11.0, Radio 1.2)
- 2008: 54.8 total (Telecoms 42.5, TV 11.2, Radio 1.1)
- 2009: 53.4 total (Telecoms 41.2, TV 11.1, Radio 1.1)
- 2010: 53.4 total (Telecoms 40.5, TV 11.7, Radio 1.1)
- 2011: 53.2 total (Telecoms 39.7, TV 12.3, Radio 1.2)

Total: 1 year / 5 yr CAGR
- −0.3% / 0.3%
- 3.5% / 0.6%
- 4.9% / 3.0%
- −1.9% / −0.5%

Legend: Radio, TV, Telecoms

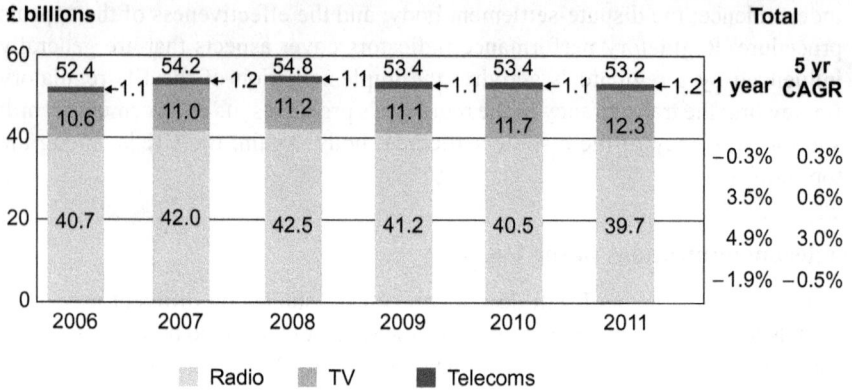

Figure 4.4: Communications industry revenue
Source: Ofcom (2012b: 23)

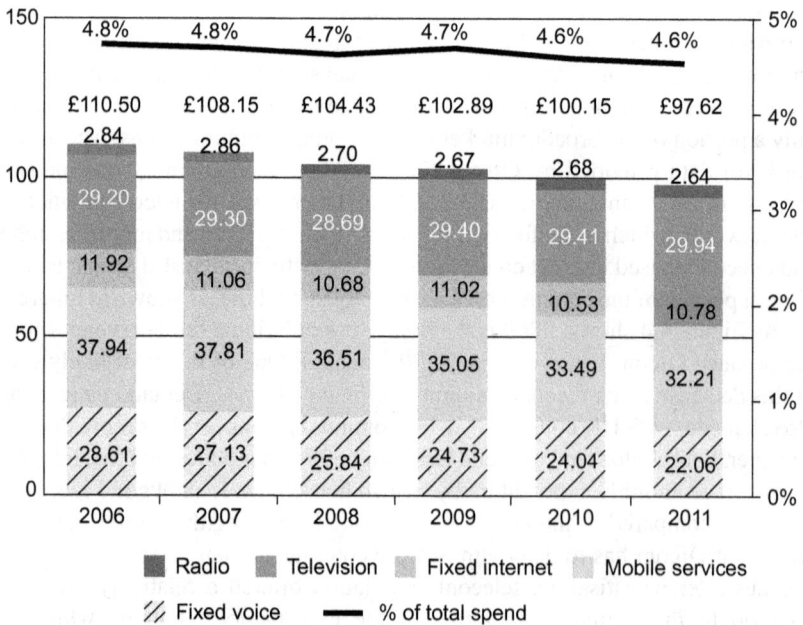

Figure 4.5 bar chart:

% of total spend line: 2006 4.8%, 2007 4.8%, 2008 4.7%, 2009 4.7%, 2010 4.6%, 2011 4.6%

Monthly household spend totals: 2006 £110.50, 2007 £108.15, 2008 £104.43, 2009 £102.89, 2010 £100.15, 2011 £97.62

	2006	2007	2008	2009	2010	2011
Radio	2.84	2.86	2.70	2.67	2.68	2.64
Television	29.20	29.30	28.69	29.40	29.41	29.94
Fixed internet	11.92	11.06	10.68	11.02	10.53	10.78
Mobile services	37.94	37.81	36.51	35.05	33.49	32.21
Fixed voice	28.61	27.13	25.84	24.73	24.04	22.06

Legend: Radio, Television, Fixed internet, Mobile services, Fixed voice, % of total spend

Figure 4.5: Average monthly household spend on communications services
Source: Ofcom (2012b: 32)

identifiable economic and technological areas. The sectoral convergence that has taken place in recent years has greatly increased the complexity and the speed of the evolution of policy problems. The level of conflict, the second explanatory variable of the typology, varied on a case-by-case basis, as it does today but there were generally fewer opposing interests on any given issue. Often, conflict took place between the former monopolist BT and the regulator, or between BT and another competitor. Nowadays, there are many more sides to each issue, as pointed out by several interviewees, and this makes Ofcom's work more challenging. The stakes vary from market to market, of course, but, overall, regulation in the telecoms sector tends to be a zero-sum-game, in which any decision is likely to generate winners and losers among regulatees. Before we turn to a more detailed analysis of how the selected explanatory variables played out in the individual case studies, it is worth concluding with a few words on the companies operating in the UK, so as to identify the key actors in the episodes I am about to describe.

The fixed telecoms market, which had a total revenue of £8.9 billion in 2011 (Ofcom 2012b: 280) still sees BT as the major player, with a 47.1 per cent share of total fixed voice revenue (Ofcom 2012, quarterly data Q1 2012[32]), albeit with decreasing voice-call volumes (36 per cent of the total). The second biggest player in fixed telecoms is Virgin Media. According to the latest data available (Ofcom 2012, quarterly data Q1 2012), the UK has 20.9 million non-corporate fixed broadband connections, showing an increasing trend. BT is again the main player, with a market share of 29.3 per cent.

The mobile market had retail revenues of £15.1 billion in 2011 (Ofcom 2012b: 281). The biggest players in this market are Everything Everywhere (born in 2010 from a joint venture between Deutsche Telekom and France Télécom and resulting in the merger of former T-Mobile UK, Virgin Mobile and Orange UK), Vodafone, and O2. 3UK is another active mobile player but with less weight on the market.

Because of technological convergence and the fact that, in some cases, mobile subscriptions are being substituted for fixed-line ones, it is more appropriate to take a cumulative view of the market, to show the respective weight of all players, mobile and fixed. Figure 4.5 shows that the market-players with the biggest number of connections are O2 (mobile, increasing share), Vodafone (mobile, increasing share), and BT (fixed, decreasing share). Since the 2010 merger, however, Everything Everywhere (mobile) has the highest number of connections on the market, with £5.2 billion mobile retail revenues in 2010.

---

32. Online. Available: http://stakeholders.ofcom.org.uk/market-data-research/market-data/communi-cations-market-reports/tables/q1_2012/. The general page where data are being regularly updated is: http://stakeholders.ofcom.org.uk/market-data-research/market-data/communications-market-reports/tables/.

Proportion of connections (%)

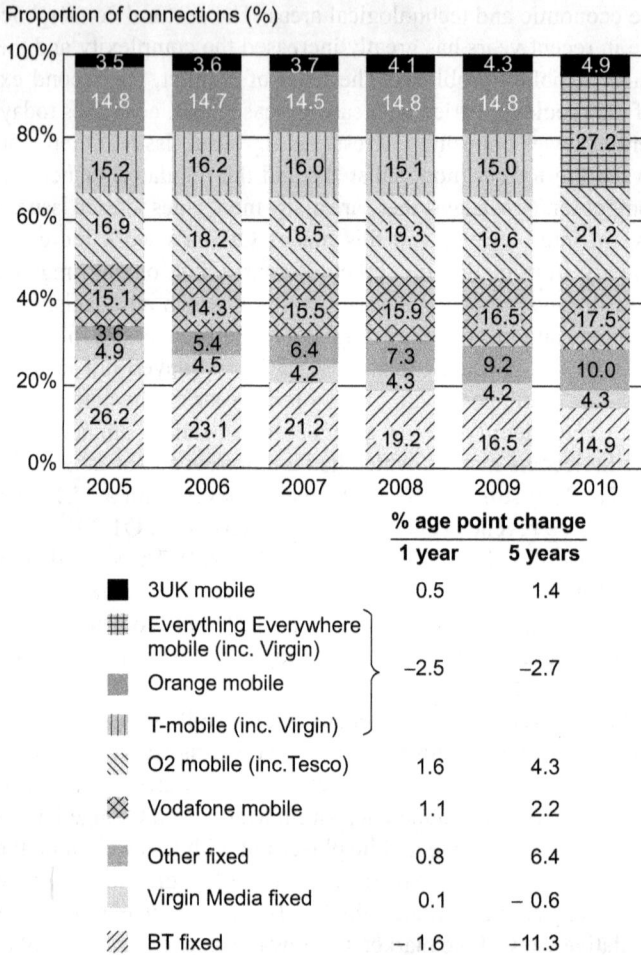

	% age point change	
	1 year	5 years
■ 3UK mobile	0.5	1.4
▦ Everything Everywhere mobile (inc. Virgin)		
▨ Orange mobile	−2.5	−2.7
⦀ T-mobile (inc. Virgin)		
⦦ O2 mobile (inc.Tesco)	1.6	4.3
⦼ Vodafone mobile	1.1	2.2
▨ Other fixed	0.8	6.4
░ Virgin Media fixed	0.1	− 0.6
▨ BT fixed	− 1.6	−11.3

Figure 4.6: Share of total UK fixed and mobile telecoms connections
Source: Ofcom (2011: 280)

Concluding remarks

As this chapter has shown, Ofcom appears as the paradigm of an independent regulatory agency that makes extensive use of expertise and derives its legitimacy from an evidence-based approach to policy-making (that is, through an instrumental use of knowledge). This is, in fact, the normative assumption that prompted this research in the first place, particularly when it is contrasted with the findings of the knowledge-utilisation literature, as explained in Chapter One. This expectation is often reflected in the statutes of independent agencies and supported by the official image that these organisations intentionally project to the outside world (Boswell

2009).[33] As mentioned, this point is also closely related to one of the control variables in the explanatory typology: the capacity of the agency. In this respect, the information provided in this chapter shows it is safe to assume that Ofcom's capacity level was consistently high in all the episodes covered by the book.

Finally, this chapter has brought to the fore two other important elements for the case studies: the importance of judicial review in the UK electronic communications sector; and the fact that the policy questions tackled by Ofcom easily lead to regulatory solutions that are zero-sum-games for regulatees.

With these points in mind, let us now move to the empirical analysis and explore how Ofcom used economic analysis in three specific episodes.

---

33. On this point *see*, among others, Ofcom's written and oral evidence submitted to the House of Lords (2007) and, more recently, Ofcom CEO's speech at the Oxford Media Convention on January 24, 2011. Online. Available: http://media.ofcom.org.uk/2011/01/24/oxford-media-convention-speech-by-ed-richards/ (accessed 15 March 2013).

chapter five | a classical tale of problem-solving: the instrumental use of economic analysis

Introduction

Our first empirical chapter presents a case where (relatively) low conflict[1] in the policy arena is combined with high problem tractability, that is, when the analytical approach and economic modelling is generally accepted by actors in the policy community for tackling the policy issues under examination. According to the proposed typology, this combination of the selected explanatory variables should lead to an instrumental use of knowledge (H1), in which economic analysis plays a problem-solving role and helps identify the most appropriate regulatory solution for the case at hand. To test our hypothesis, I have selected a recent episode, the 2009 regulatory statement on the fixed narrowband retail services markets in the UK and Kingston-upon-Hull area (hereafter, Hull).[2] While this decision received less public attention than others, it constitutes, in fact, a first in the history of UK telecoms: it is the first case of full de-regulation in the fixed telephony sector and the end of a 'regulatory saga' of over twenty years' duration.

As regards methodology, for this episode, a qualitative coding (see Chapter Three) of the following sources was performed: Ofcom's consultation document and the regulatory statement; the ten consultation responses submitted by stakeholders; and the transcripts of five interviews with Ofcom and industry representatives performed during the summer and autumn of 2010.[3] Before putting our case in context, let me briefly discuss why it constitutes a good testing of the H1 hypothesis.

---

1. This judgement should be read in a comparative perspective and bearing in mind other regulatory cases in the market for electronic communications. As explained in Chapter Four, the regulation of electronic communications is very often a zero-sum-game in which any advantage for a market-player is mirrored by a loss for another, hence the virtual absence of zero-conflict situations.

2. This chapter will focus on the general UK market, excluding the Hull case, which is an exception in the UK and warrants a separate analysis. Specifically, Hull is a unitary authority located in the East Riding of Yorkshire and is the only city in the UK to have a municipality-owned telephone system (Kingston Communications, founded 1902, nowadays KCOM Group, listed on the London Stock Exchange) that was not absorbed by BT. As Hull has a small territory and population, competitors have limited interest in entering the market and KCOM still holds a monopoly. This situation is unique in the UK and is treated separately by Ofcom as well. Excluding the Hull case does not alter our findings in this chapter. For further details on Kingston Communications and the market in Hull, *see* Turner (2002).

3. The regulatory statement. Online. Available: http://stakeholders.ofcom.org.uk/binaries/consultations/retail_markets/statement/statement.pdf (accessed 18 March 2013). The text of the consultation can be found at /stakeholders.ofcom.org.uk/binaries/consultations/retail_markets/summary/

The regulation of narrowband retail services

Narrowband retail services still represent a key share of the telecoms market and include fixed analogue and digital (ISDN) telephone lines, which allow both residential and business consumers to make telephone calls, access the internet (via narrowband) and use other related services such as payment terminals in shops. Given the monopolistic position of BT in the market for fixed telephony when telecommunication services were liberalised in the 1980s (Waverman 1998: 23), narrowband retail services have been subject to regulation for over two decades. Since then, the sector has considerably evolved: new services have become available, including narrowband internet connections. Most importantly, several new players have entered the market, increasing both competition between providers and choice for consumers. What may have seemed impossible for British consumers when telecommunication services were first liberalised is now a reality: different products can be purchased from different providers or bought as a bundle (for example, internet + telephone; or internet + telephone + TV) from the same operator. [4] Moreover, Ofcom's market research and the data provided by individual operators in the fixed narrowband retail services markets show that consumer awareness of the availability of several providers on the market is growing.[5] Also, while market shares remain unevenly distributed between operators, and BT still retains a considerable portion of customers (when compared to other players on an individual basis), both public and confidential figures indicate that even consumers who do not switch provider increasingly choose positively not to do so rather than not switching because of a lack of information on existing alternatives.

Past regulatory decisions have played a considerable part in this evolution of the market. In particular, the creation of Openreach in 2005 and the removal of retail-charge controls on BT in 2006 represent milestones in the transformation of the UK market for fixed narrowband retail services, as will be explained in greater detail below. Technologically, this market is now fairly stable and less prone to innovation than others, thus limiting the regulatory questions to be tackled by Ofcom to a series of well known critical points. *Prima facie*, this seems to have limited the degree of conflict surrounding the 2009 regulatory statement: while diverging positions and commercial interests remain, these tend to be established, easily identifiable and – in a way – more manageable for the regulator and for market-players.

In terms of problem tractability, regulatory choices on this specific policy issue are based on classical economic tests, such as the definition of market power for the different players; assessments follow standard and widespread economic

---

fnrsm_condoc.pdf. The consultation responses. Online. Available: http://stakeholders.ofcom.org.uk/consultations/retail_markets/?showResponses=true (accessed 22 September 2012).

4. Thanks to technological convergence (*see also* Chapter Seven), these services can be provided through different (and competing) infrastructures, for example via telecom networks or via cable.

5. For further details, *see* Ofcom's additional reports *Consumer Preferences in Narrowband Communications – Research Report* (19 March 2009a); and *SME Preferences in Narrowband Communications – Research Report* (19 March 2009b).

methodologies and additional guidance for European regulators on this type of market analyses is provided at the EU level by the European Commission's services. Hence, while the interpretation of results may be subject to debate in some cases, the underlying methodology is widely accepted, making this a clear case of high problem tractability.

The regulatory dilemma facing Ofcom in 2008–9 was whether there was room for withdrawing regulation in the market, given the state and degree of competition at the time, and whether available evidence and economic analysis provided an answer to this question.

Chronology of events and policy questions

Historical background of the regulation of fixed narrowband markets

The regulatory statement under examination represents the latest development in a long history of measures beginning when telecommunications were liberalised in 1984. Without attempting to cover the full evolution of regulatory remedies in this field, it is worth recalling the turning points in the regulation of fixed narrowband services (both at the retail and wholesale levels), as these have had a considerable impact on the current state of the market and on the two explanatory variables of our typology. By the same token, this brief excursus puts the case studies covered in this book in their historical context and broadens our understanding of the mechanisms at play in each episode, and of the origin of the different narratives provided by actors.

The regulation of fixed narrowband services affects two levels of service provision: retail services (that is, those being sold to final users, residential and industrial consumers) and wholesale services, namely the access products (exchange lines) provided by the former incumbent, BT, to other operators wishing to offer telecommunication retail services to consumers. The demand for wholesale services is what can be called a 'derived demand' as the wholesale inputs are logically determined by the demands of the retail level.

The need to regulate at the wholesale level stems from the very nature of the existing infrastructure for providing narrowband services and is, more generally, a classical feature of network industries (Shy 2001):[6] due to economy-of-scale considerations, it is most often not economically viable for potential new entrants in the market to replicate an existing network fully. Hence, competition at the retail level and greater choice for consumers can be achieved through regulation by mandating and setting specific conditions for allowing alternative service providers

---

6. Shy (2001: 1) lists the four characteristics that distinguish network industries from traditional markets: complementarity, compatibility and standards; consumption externalities; switching costs and lock in; significant economies of scale and production. The last two aspects are often at the core of telecom markets debates. Other classical network industries include, among others, software and hardware production, airlines, electricity and gas.

to offer their services via access to the existing network.[7] This is exactly what Oftel, and then Ofcom, have been doing with BT's infrastructure, so that new entrants could develop and offer a range of alternative services to consumers.[8] Another key regulatory instrument for fostering competition in fixed narrowband markets is the application of a price-control scheme to prevent the incumbent operator (BT in this case) from abusing its dominant position in the wholesale and/or retail market. In the case of the UK, the price-control formula was developed in 1982 by Stephen Littlechild, during the privatisation of telecommunication services (Burton 1997; Cave and Williamson 1996).[9] While subject to several revisions to establish the appropriate level of charge control in each case, this formula has remained the cornerstone of regulation in the fixed narrowband market. In the case of retail services, it was applied to a basket of selected products to ensure that consumers (both business and residential) would not be penalised by BT's former monopoly on the provision of fixed telecom services. As the market evolved, Oftel and, since 2003, Ofcom regularly undertook market reviews to update the charge-control scheme and the other obligations imposed on the former incumbent (Burton 1997; Dassler *et al.* 2006).[10]

As a result of these regulatory interventions, the initial monopoly position held by BT in the wholesale and retail markets was gradually eroded (NAO 2002), first during the BT-Mercury duopoly (1983–91),[11] and then by growing competition from other players offering fixed telephony services and, since the 1990s, internet as well. A major review of the fixed narrowband services market was carried out in 2003 and Ofcom concluded that BT still had Significant Market Power (SMP)[12] both at the retail and wholesale levels, despite the growing number

---

7. This practice, also known as access pricing, is adopted in all liberalised network industries to preserve the efficient large scale use of existing infrastructure, while offering to consumers increased welfare thanks to competition between providers (Shy, 2001: 8).

8. A clear example is the use of carrier pre-selection (CPS) to allow fixed telephony customers to place calls with their BT phone using an alternative provider.

9. The formula takes into account the rate of inflation (RPI = retail price index) minus a factor (X) that is established on an *ad hoc* basis to reflect expected efficiency savings achieved by the regulated company.

10. The authors provide a detailed and critical assessment of how the RPI-X formula was managed and updated by Oftel/Ofcom until the removal of charge controls in 2006, in particular as regards the use of Shleifer's (1985) benchmarking approach, which is commonly adopted in utilities regulation to set price caps. On this point, *see also* Cave and Williamson (1996) and NAO (2002).

11. For additional details on the duopoly period, Mercury, and Oftel's regulatory approach, see Waverman (1998) and Hall *et al.* (2000).

12. The SMP concept is analogous to the one of dominant position in competition law and economics. The definition applied by Ofcom follows the one established at the EU level in the 2002 Framework Directive on Electronic Communications, whereby 'an undertaking shall be deemed to have significant market power if, either individually or jointly with others, it enjoys a position equivalent to dominance, that is to say a position of economic strength affording it the power to behave to an appreciable extent independently of competitors, customers and ultimately consumers'. The presence or absence of SMP in a given market is established by looking at: market shares; barriers to entry and expansion; the intensity of competition in the markets and the costs imposed on consumers wishing to switch provider; prices and profitability; countervailing buyer power; other competitive constraints; and international comparisons.

---

of retail competitors present on the market. However, the scenario at the retail level changed drastically in 2005, when, having completed its periodic Strategic Review of Telecommunications,[13] Ofcom was about to refer BT to the Competition Commission under the Enterprise Act 2002[14] for a series of anticompetitive practices revealed by the market analysis. In lieu of referral to the Competition Commission, BT offered what are commonly called 'the Undertakings' and created Openreach, a separate division within the company in charge of the fixed infrastructure only, and whose main purpose is to guarantee equality of access to BT's own local network to all rival operators. In other words, the provision of retail services by BT is now separate from the management of and access to the underlying infrastructure, an arrangement that is also known as functional separation.[15] This way, BT's retail services are treated on an equal footing with those provided by its competitors and BT cannot discriminate between different retail-service providers, including itself, when granting access to its network.[16] This change was crucial for the retail level and soon resulted in the end of price regulation on BT's retail services in 2006, after almost two decades, while leaving some other less intrusive regulatory obligations in place for the incumbent.[17]

Our case study starts from the subsequent review of the fixed narrowband services markets and the ensuing regulatory statement of 2009, which concluded that BT does not hold SMP in the retail market. This led to the first full de-regulation of a series of telecom services since the liberalisation of the 1980s. Table 5.1 summarises the key events between the privatisation of BT in 1982 and the 2009 statement.[18] The third column includes some comments detailing the impact of each event on the retail market.

---

13. For a discussion of the tensions between BT and other players in the market before the Undertakings and the content and process of the 2003 strategic review, *see* Whalley and Curwen (2008).

14. For further details, *see* Chapter Four.

15. The Undertakings were officially accepted by Ofcom on September 22, 2005 in accordance with the Enterprise Act of 2002, thus making the functional separation of BT's infrastructure legally binding on the entire UK territory, with the exception of Hull, where BT does not operate (KCOM Group is the local incumbent). The official text of the Undertakings: Online. Available: http://stakeholders.ofcom.org.uk/binaries/telecoms/policy/bt/btundertakings.pdf. For further details on the rationale behind functional separation, *see* OECD (2006a) and Cave, Correa and Crocioni (2006).

16. This principle is known as 'equivalence of inputs' (EOI) and, as Ofcom explains, entails that 'BT provides, in respect of a particular product or service, the same product or service to all Communication Providers (CPs) (including BT) on the same timescales, terms and conditions (including price and service levels) by means of the same systems and processes, and includes the provision to all CPs (including BT) of the same commercial information about such products, services, systems and processes.' Online. Available: http://stakeholders.ofcom.org.uk/telecoms/policy/bt-undertakings/glossary (accessed 22 September 2012). For a theoretical assessment of the equality of access principle, *see* Whalley and Curwen (2008).

17. For further details, see for example, *Financial Times* (2006) 'Ofcom may ditch pricing controls imposed on BT' March 22.

18. For an assessment of the initial milestones of UK telecoms privatisation and liberalisation in light of the theoretical expectations embedded in Littlechild's approach, *see* Burton (1997).

Table 5.1: Key events in the UK telecoms markets and impact on narrowband retail services (1982–2009) [19]

Date	Event	Impact on the retail markets
1982	Privatisation of BT	
1983	Government accepts recommendations of the Littlechild Report	Setting of the charge-control model limiting BT's price increase with the formula RPI-X, with X=3% for the first 5 years of privatisation (until July 1989). Mercury is allowed to compete on the market with BT and the BT-Mercury duopoly era begins.
1984	Telecommunications Bill	BT becomes a public limited company with 51% of shares sold to the public by November. Creation of Oftel.
1988	Consultation on price formula	New agreement on formula RPI-4.5% to run out in July 1993.
1991	Publication of the Duopoly Review	End of the duopoly (BT and Mercury). Sale of BT's share, government ownership reduces to 25.8%.
1993–7	Revisions of the RPI-X formula	Formula set at RPI-7.5% for a basket of key BT retail services until July 1997. Launch of big debate on what to do afterwards.
1997–2001	Several consultations and market reviews to monitor considerable evolution of communications market and convergence of services. Growing competition powers to Oftel.	Development of methodology for assessing if company has SMP, following imminent adoption of two EU Directives.
2002–3	Debate and adoption of Communications Act.	Ofcom established 29 September 2003 and inherits – among others – Oftel's duties.
2003	Market review for fixed narrowband retail services[20]	BT found to have SMP in several retail markets; new price controls set until July 2006.

(Cont'd.)

19. Online. Available: http://www.ofcom.org.uk/static/archive/oftel/about/history.htm (accessed 22 September 2012).

20. Online. Available: http://www.ofcom.org.uk/static/archive/oftel/publications/eu_directives/2003/fix_narrow_retail0803.pdf (accessed 24 September 2012).

Table 5.1: (Cont'd.)

Date	Event	Impact on the retail markets
2004–5	Strategic review of the telecoms market	Ofcom about to refer BT to the Competition Commission under the Enterprise Act 2002.
Sept. 2005	Undertakings	BT Undertakings, accepted by Ofcom in lieu of referral to the Competition Commission after public consultation, result in legally binding functional separation for BT. Creation of Openreach.
2006	Lifting of retail price controls	Retail price controls no longer imposed on BT; other remedies still in place.
March 2009	Consultation	Public consultation in the framework of the market review of fixed narrowband (retail and wholesale) services.
Sept. 2009	Regulatory statement on fixed narrowband retail services markets	BT found to have no SMP in retail market. All regulation in retail market removed.

The situation at the wholesale level remains more complex, due to the presence of enduring bottlenecks that that cannot be removed by increased competition at the retail level alone. In this respect, some of the changes initially hoped for by the regulator did not fully materialise: for instance, it was assumed that new entrants in the retail markets would gradually start building alternative infrastructures to compete with BT at the wholesale level as well.[21] This would have reduced their dependence on BT's wholesale inputs and, as a consequence, the need for regulation by Ofcom. Ofcom's periodic market reviews indicate that existing wholesale investments are not of sufficient magnitude to warrant de-regulation for the time being and even the presence of Openreach and of the principle of the Equivalence of Inputs (EOI) leaves some issues unresolved. Thus, the level of conflict remains higher and the debate less stable in the wholesale part of the market. This means that, while I will refer to the wholesale level when necessary in the analysis, the appropriate level to test the hypothesis H1 remains the retail one.

The 2009 market review: decision-making steps and content of the analysis

It is still relatively early to draw definite conclusions on the impact of Openreach and the Undertakings on the UK market for fixed narrowband services (Cave, Correa and Crocioni 2006). However, one thing is certain: the new arrangement leads all market players, including BT, to expect further (de)regulatory changes at the end of the charge-control period (for wholesale markets) and the scheduled review of the fixed narrowband markets. In fact, at the time of the Undertakings, Ofcom committed to de-regulate certain markets in the future (Whalley and Curwen 2008: 284). As we will see below, each market-player prepared its strategy accordingly.

On the side of Ofcom, work for the 2009 statement on fixed narrowband retail services started towards the end of 2008 (reportedly, in September) in view of the consultation to take place in March 2009. As in most cases, during the pre-consultation period an in-house team of economists, lawyers, technical (that is, engineers) and policy experts was put together. The team's brief was to deal with the review, gather the necessary data from market-players and organise a series of multilateral and bilateral meetings with stakeholders; at these meetings they were to discuss possible policy orientations, outline data needs for the consultation and

---

21. A similar set of expectations was embedded in the EU regulatory framework for electronic communications adopted in 2002. The underlying theoretical model, known as the 'ladder of investment' was proposed by British economist Martin Cave and assumes that, if new entrants are successively provided with different level of access to an existing infrastructure, with access charges gradually increasing over time or with some access obligations on the incumbent being removed after a certain date, new entrants will have an incentive to slowly 'climb the rungs of the ladder' by investing in building alternative infrastructure rather than competing only at the level of services provision. In the long run, increased competition should allow the removal of *ex-ante* regulation from a given market, a clear indicator that the chosen policy approach was successful. For further details, *see* Cave *et al.* (2001) and Cave (2006).

hear any comments that stakeholders had at that point. Although the wholesale and retail reviews were carried out in parallel, two separate teams were set up at Ofcom. As reported by most interviewees in and outside the agency, this pre-consultation phase is crucial to influence Ofcom's 'direction of travel', as this is when key data and analytical assumptions that could alter the course of the debate can be submitted and potentially incorporated in the regulator's economic assessment. While no interviewee raised any issue as regards the transparency of this procedure, whose outputs are indeed reflected in official documents, views differed as regards the open-mindedness of Ofcom on the possible outcome of the debate in this specific case. After a couple of months' work on the data received, and following the elaboration by Ofcom's market research unit of two reports, on consumers' and on SMEs preferences respectively, the official consultation document for the retail markets was published in March. Consulted parties were allowed to submit responses until June of the same year. Ten stakeholders submitted their comments, which were addressed by Ofcom during the summer. The final statement for the retail markets was adopted on 19 September 2009 without further consultation rounds.[22]

The consultation included a preliminary assessment of the market for access and retail services, and was structured around the classical steps of a market-review exercise: 1) market definition, to establish the relevant markets for the statement at hand; 2) market analysis, to assess competition in each market and establish whether some players held significant market power (SMP); and finally 3) the analysis and selection of appropriate regulatory remedies where there has been a finding of SMP. The eighteen consultation questions followed the structure of the analysis and required feedback and comments on the three phases of market definition, market analysis, and suggested remedies, as well as leaving space for further general comments. This confirms that Ofcom indeed does consult on every aspect for which a decision could be taken. In fact, this statutory duty is further reinforced by the existence of judicial review on the merits, as explained in Chapter Four: this combination creates a set of post-delegation control mechanisms (Majone 2010; McCubbins et al. 1987) that cannot be ignored by the regulator.

Both the consultation and the statement include extensive references to Ofcom's market research on consumers' preferences to illustrate the evolution of the sector and thus flesh out the traditional approach to market definition and the assessment of SMP. Market-research data cover all recent relevant trends, such as the decrease in retail prices for fixed telephony,[23] the increasing portion of

---

22. The consultation and the statement cover two different markets, the UK market with the exception of Hull, and Hull as a separate geographic market. As mentioned, I will focus on the UK part only.

23. For instance, the consultation explains: 'Our analysis shows that in nominal terms BT prices for the bottom eight deciles has fallen if the additional charge for non-direct debit is excluded and risen by 2.2% if the non-direct debit charge is included. This is in a period of inflation of around 4% – thus a reduction in real terms. Further analysis shows that consumers in the bottom three deciles have experienced greater price reductions with a net reduction of 3.5% (nominal) if the non-direct debit charge is excluded and an increase of only 0.2% if the charge is included. This is

calls placed via mobile rather than fixed telephones and, most importantly, the growing demand for bundled products by British consumers. As shown in Figure 5.1, bundling was a key issue in the debate as, under the rules existing at the time, BT was not allowed to provide products in a bundled form because of the risk of unfair competition.[24] While this was understandable from a competition policy viewpoint, in practice it also implied that BT's fixed telephony customers could not add internet and/or TV to their BT contract and had to look for a second provider to purchase those services.

The analysis supporting the market definition in the consultation and the statement is influenced by Ofcom's EU obligations and follows the common approach used by EU regulators in the electronic communications sector. This is commonly known as the 'hypothetical monopolist test', whereby a product is considered to constitute a separate economic market

> if it would be profitable for a hypothetical monopoly supplier of the product to impose a 'small but significant non-transitory increase in price' (SSNIP) above the competitive level. If a hypothetical price rise would not be profitable then the market definition should be expanded to include substitute (either demand or supply-side) products. (Ofcom 2009c:15)

Also, while newly available retail products make the distinction between services directed to businesses and those intended for residential customers less evident than in the past, especially when SMEs are concerned (SMEs can choose between purchasing a residential or business tariff), Ofcom's assessment concluded that these still constitute separate markets with different competitive dynamics.[25] Access and calls, too, should be considered as separate markets, given that a certain portion of consumers both in the residential and business markets treat them separately in their purchasing choices. Conversely, there are no separate markets for different types of residential calls (local, international, etc.) as consumers normally purchase them from the same provider. Finally, Ofcom's analysis established that, with the exception of Hull, the UK should be considered

---

approximately a reduction of around 7% in real terms excluding the non-direct debit charges and around 3.8% if it was included' (Ofcom 2009c: 14).

24. Specifically, as BT's fixed narrowband retail services such as telephone lines were still subject to regulation, in contrast to the case of other market-players, the possibility of offering bundles of services would have implied that a bundle would include SMP products subject to regulation (fixed telephony) and non-SMP products (e.g. TV, a market in which BT does not have a dominant position). In turn, this could potentially have allowed BT to unfairly leverage the advantages provided by its dominant position in the SMP market on the non-SMP one.

25. Specifically, the consultation document explains that: 'in the residential market BT faces competition from a number of large retailers such as Sky, CPW and the Post Office, while in the business market, BT faces competition from a large number of smaller retailers[...]The nature of competition is different in the two markets. In the residential sector, the predominant strategy is to bundle access and calls to other products such as pay-TV and broadband. In the business market, bundling is much less prevalent, and prices are often bespoke' (Ofcom 2009c: 19).

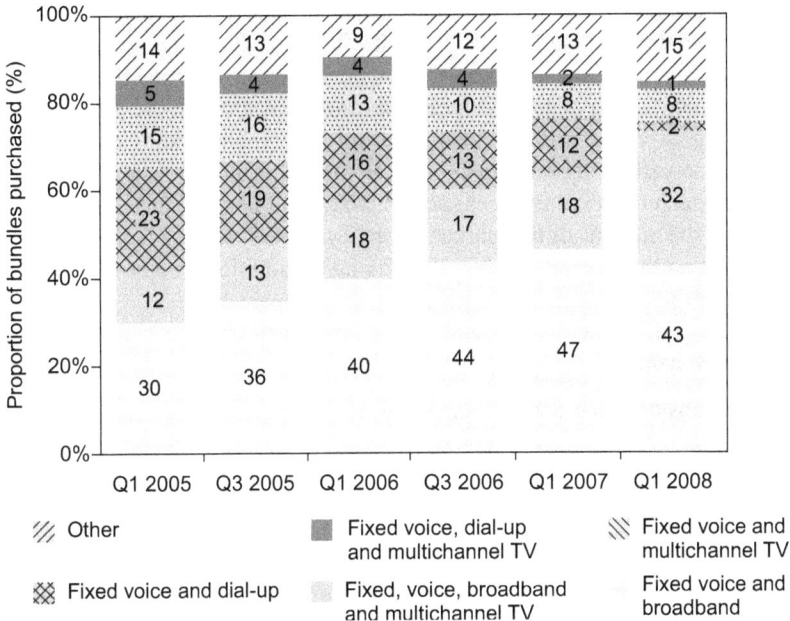

Figure 5.1: Bundled services purchased by consumer by type

Source: Ofcom/operators in consultation (Ofcom 2009c:12)

as a single market with no further geographical distinctions. As a result, the following fixed markets are included in the statement for the UK: residential fixed narrowband analogue access; business fixed narrowband analogue access; residential fixed narrowband calls; business fixed narrowband calls; ISDN2 Access; and the ISDN30 Access.

As regards the assessment of SMP, Ofcom followed the guidelines and methodology adopted at EU level. Ofcom's economic analysis was informed by the results of its market research, as described in the consultation document, by market-share information on the different providers compiled by Ofcom itself and by additional figures provided by operators in response to a formal Ofcom request and, finally, by the regulatory returns of BT. As explained in detail in the consultation document, the analysis of this evidence and the recent and prospective evolution of market shares (that is, the expectation that BT's share would continue decreasing in the future) lead Ofcom to conclude that no operator holds SMP in the UK (excluding Hull) for the analogue access markets for business and residential customers, while BT was still found to hold SMP in the ISDN2 and ISDN30 markets. For calls markets in the UK instead, Ofcom's analysis concluded that no company holds SMP for residential and business markets.

The market analysis is followed by a section on impact assessment, to establish the preferred regulatory options for the case at hand. Applicable rules require Ofcom to withdraw regulation from all markets where BT is found to hold no

SMP. The expectation in Ofcom's analysis is that such a de-regulatory move will benefit consumers and market-players, as it will allow BT to offer bundled products like those from other communication providers, furthering competition, lowering prices and generating additional incentives for innovation. In the long run, these benefits are expected to reach also the most vulnerable strands of society and bridge the so-called 'digital divide' between those that already take full advantage of existing technological services such as broadband internet and consumers who are still on the margins of the market. In any event, BT remains bound by General Conditions and Universal Service Conditions, in addition to non-sector specific consumer-protection legislation, which covers all operators.

For the ISDN markets instead, Ofcom put forward two regulatory policy alternatives, namely:

- imposing price controls on BT to reduce prices closer to a competitive level; or
- removing existing retail remedies, relying on wholesale remedies to control the cost of market entry.

The first option was considered less advantageous, because price controls would undermine incentives for other communication providers to innovate in an already mature market. Hence, the second option is presented as the preferred one, to be dealt with in the companion review of the wholesale markets. In the final statement, the second option was selected for ISDN2 markets, while no decision was taken for the ISDN30 case, as Ofcom needed additional evidence from the wholesale market analysis to decide.

Low conflict and high problem tractability: paving the way for an instrumental use of knowledge?

As mentioned, the composition of the policy arena and the evolution of the debate, as well as its content, indicate a situation of intermediate–low conflict and high problem tractability. According to our explanatory typology, this combination should foster an instrumental/problem-solving use of economic knowledge (H1). Before I turn to the appraisal of our hypothesis, let me better qualify our explanatory variables in this specific episode by looking at the features of the debate that developed in 2008–9.

The debate

In addition to the discussions that took place during informal stakeholders' meetings before March 2009, in response to the formal consultation ten contributions were sent by the following operators: BT, KCOM (mostly commenting on the Hull case where the company is the incumbent), COLT, Scottish Southern Energy (SSE), the UK Association of Competitive Providers (UKCTA), Cable&Wireless, the Federation of Communication Services (FCS), Sky, TalkTalk Group, and T-Mobile. In contrast to other policy cases, consumer associations, academia, and individual consumers did not submit any contributions, which indicates that the salience of the debate was low, with discussions remaining among the 'usual suspects'. As a result, the size of the policy arena remained quite small, with a limited number of conflict sources. This was explicitly confirmed by Ofcom's representatives and by another interviewee, who described the set of actors involved in the 2009 narrowband review as a policy community in which

> there may be only a hundred people or so who work in the companies and Ofcom on certain policy things, so usually relationships are already formed, people know each other and it's just about kicking off the project and pulling it through. (Industry 1, July 2010)

Several responses to the consultation covered both the wholesale and retail markets and corroborate our intuition that the level of conflict was higher in the former. Interviewees confirmed this point as well. For the retail market, despite a lower level of conflict, positions were entrenched, with BT on one side advocating full de-regulation as a logical next step after the Undertakings and the removal of price controls and, on the other side, most other communications providers expressing concern that a removal of the SMP finding at a time when BT had a decreasing but still large market share would allow the incumbent to engage in anticompetitive practices, for example, by locking in consumers through its freshly introduced twelve-month rolling contract. BT's counter argument on that point was that, in fact, competitors had everything to gain from keeping the SMP finding on BT for as long as possible, thus preventing BT from entering the very lucrative market of bundled retail services. Somewhat predictably, various tenets of BT's position were supported by KCOM (the incumbent in Hull), which could face similar issues in the future. These stakeholders' arguments show how the clash between these two sides of the debate mostly revolved around commercial interests, even when economic arguments and more general assumptions on the role and duties of the regulator were used to support positions. As in most regulatory decisions, Ofcom had to be the referee of this zero-sum-game.

This low–intermediate level of conflict still fits with our H1 hypothesis: the number and type of pressures that characterised the debate, as well as the arguments supporting different positions, were easily predictable beforehand. After all, one must not forget that this was the conclusion of a regulatory adventure of over twenty years!

This leads to our second explanatory variable, problem tractability. As mentioned, tractability was high, given the wide acceptance of the hypothetical monopolist test. Hence, the debate revolved around the interpretation of the test's results by the regulator, certainly not on the formula to establish market shares or on the potentially thorny question of market definition (for example, the issue of fixed–mobile substitution). This is confirmed both in our coding of official documents and of interviews.

Finally, it is worth adding a few words on the type of knowledge used by Ofcom, given that the accounts of the different interviewees are somewhat discrepant on this point, particularly as regards the weight of economics in the final decision. All interviewees as well as official sources indicated that used knowledge included economic analysis, market research (data on consumer preferences and trends in the market, with no economic modelling involved) and the input of Ofcom's legal team (market reviews are a statutory duty that must follow a certain procedure). Three out of five interviewees, including Ofcom's representative, claim that economics had an important/central role, with market research being a crucial complement to shed light on consumer behaviour and interpret the findings of the economic analysis. However, the remaining two interviewees were more critical, stating that – in spite of the very economics-centred appearance of the argumentation – economic reasoning was in fact secondary to market research and legal input. Among the critical voices, a senior regulatory economist from the industry side even described the analysis as all 'legalese and the work of commercial people',[26] with 'no hard and fast fact [...] to get one's teeth into'.

Undoubtedly, market research had an important place in the discussion but I could not establish whether its impact was excessive or pinpoint all the reasons for giving to market research data the space they received. These could include the fact that market research was indeed essential for the economic evidence-base needed by Ofcom to make a decision. The laws of supply and demand also influence the production and use of knowledge for policy-making purposes. Thus, the emphasis on market research could be motivated by renewed attention to Ofcom's consumer-protection mandate. Or it could also have been driven by a growing interest in behavioural economics inside and outside the agency. Whether this may signal an evolution in Ofcom's way of dealing with economic analysis would warrant separate research. In the analysis I note that the two types of input are closely linked to each other but also that the general line of argumentation is typically economic and so is the reasoning put forward by stakeholders in their consultation responses. Hence, while we cannot conclude that 'pure' economics was the only basis for the decision, economic analysis was certainly very important. As to the question of how and if it was used, this is the topic of the next section.

Clashing narratives

Several clues to the role of economics in this particular episode can be found in the judgements on Ofcom's analysis provided by the sources coded[27] for this case study. Predictably, the tone and content of the feedback differ according to the position of each actor vis-à-vis the SMP/no-SMP finding question at stake. For example, in the regulatory statement, Ofcom explains that it selected a cautious approach to market definition to support a 'robust determination of market power' and the finding of no-SMP. Among consultation responses, BT judges Ofcom's assessment as thorough and its approach appropriate but too cautious on ISDN.

---

26. Namely, Ofcom's market research department.

27. For further details on our approach to the qualitative coding of sources for the case studies, *see* Chapter Three.

Positive judgements are echoed by T-Mobile and by KCOM for what concerns the UK market. Unsurprisingly, the opposing camp has some severe critiques on the interpretation of the market analysis' results: COLT and Sky find it unconvincing and superficial in some points, while Cable&Wireless and FCS require more justification for ignoring BT's large market share in concluding that the incumbent has no SMP. When these judgements are put into context with other portions of text on the policy process itself, two different stories gradually take shape and draw our attention to the possible mechanisms that influenced the use of economic analysis.

On the one hand, some stakeholders describe Ofcom's decision to de-regulate as a predictable and logical step in the de-regulatory path that followed the Undertakings of 2005. Their tone is relatively neutral. When present, negative comments concern the open-endedness of the debate and the real potential for 'knocking Ofcom off their course' but do not automatically imply that Ofcom's final policy choice was wrong. Others, such as UKCTA, bluntly portray the decision as pre-ordained. In this perspective, judgements on the depth and soundness of Ofcom's analysis turn, in the consultation responses, into open references to a strategic use of knowledge to substantiate the decision to de-regulate. For example COLT's consultation response states that:

> The analysis of market power is superficial and apparently designed to tell the story[28] Ofcom wants telling rather than presenting the thorough and objective analysis of markets we have come to expect from Ofcom.

This was also the view of TalkTalk Group:

> Although Ofcom's analysis is thorough, we are concerned that it is also heavily coloured by a strong and unjustifiable ambition to deregulate BT in these markets whatever the evidence and/or other circumstances.

This view was also shared by Sky, which termed Ofcom's conclusion that BT had no SMP in the retail market 'perverse'.

Along these lines, two interviewees hinting at a strategic use of knowledge by the agency point out that, following the Undertakings, Ofcom had a strong incentive to de-regulate, as this would make it 'look good in the eyes of the Government' and eventually prove that the regulatory approach adopted since the liberalisation of the telecoms sector delivered the expected results, with competition allowing the regulator to withdraw from markets, as foreseen in the 'ladder of investment' theory (Cave *et al.* 2001; Cave 2006). Among these, the interviewee who described Ofcom's analysis as 'legalese and the work of commercial people' added that the final outcome of the decision-making process had a lot to do with the interpretation of available evidence, as

> You could imagine that if Ofcom had decided that they would want to maintain regulation on BT Retail, then they could have used exactly the same evidence to argue the other way [laughs]. (Industry 2, September 2010)

---

28. It is interesting to note this explicit reference to a 'narrative' in an official document. This tends to be an exception, as explained in Chapter Three.

On the other side, Ofcom naturally presents the analysis and its use as instrumental, explaining in the statement that market share cannot be the only factor in reaching a conclusion on whether BT holds SMP and that the final decision was made by looking at all the available evidence. As explained by one of Ofcom's senior economists, the agency kept an open mind in the process as

> There was no specific reason to conclude one way or the other. It is one of those cases were you really want to do the right thing [...]. and the evidence was in favour of the no-SMP. (Ofcom 1, September 2010)

This open-minded attitude and a reference to an instrumental use of economic analysis is also mentioned in the account of one of BT's major competitors,[29] who described the debate in those terms:

> One side with BT obviously pushing for deregulation, a deregulatory agenda, and on the other side you had Ofcom who appeared keen to try and deliver some degree of deregulation but weren't sure where to stop, and the market information was key for them to understand where it was appropriate to retain regulation. (Industry 1, July 2010)

Another interviewee explains that Ofcom used (instrumentally):

> Market analysis, the data analysis: it's about 'evidence in the broader sense'. It was hard to argue against the evidence this time. (Industry 3, June 2010)

It would be inappropriate to draw from these sources definite conclusions on whether Ofcom used economics instrumentally or strategically, as our analysis is certainly not a voting context and the account of each actor tends to be broadly in line with the interests of its organisation. In fact, these different versions of the story could be seen in dramaturgical terms (Goffman 1959; Schimmelfennig 2002), whereby each narrative corresponds to what an actor is 'supposed to say' on a given topic in a particular context. Also, as noted again by Goffman (1974: 8–9) the question:

> what is it that's going on here is – in a way – suspicious, and it is plain that retrospective characterization of the 'same' event or social occasion may differ very widely, that an individual's role in an undertaking can provide him with a distinctive evaluative assessment of what sort of an instance of the type the particular undertaking was. In that sense it has been argued, for example, that opposing rooters at a football game do not experience the 'same' game [...]

Moreover, as explained in Chapter Three, it is not our intention to establish 'the truth' and take an explicit stance on which story is more credible; after all, even our description and interpretation of facts is another, albeit external, narrative of

---

29. For reasons of confidentiality I cannot be more specific on the affiliation of interviewees; however, it is important to point out that BT's representatives were not the only ones who openly supported Ofcom's conclusions and version of the story.

the same set of events.[30] Conversely, these different formal and informal accounts were quite enlightening on the mechanisms at work during this decision-making process and their influence on knowledge-utilisation. Specifically, three elements appear to have had an impact on Ofcom's decision-making and use of economic analysis for the 2009 statement: historical developments in the regulation of retail markets as reflected in the level of conflict; the theoretical and policy expectations embedded in the chosen regulatory approach; and the presence of judicial review. The latter links both with conflict and problem tractability.

To be sure, the historical evolution in the regulation of the narrowband retail sector had an impact on the composition and size of the policy arena, as well as on the nature of the policy problems faced by Ofcom during this market review.[31] Without the imposition of charge controls for over two decades, the economic assumptions embedded in the RPI-X formula and the granting of licenses to different operators, the UK market would have looked very different in 2008–9. In recent years and since the adoption of EU legislation on electronic communications, the evolution of policy choices in the UK retail market should also be observed with the tenets of the 'ladder of investment' theory in mind. As explained, this theoretical model is at the core of EU telecoms legislation and of the approach taken by other European regulators. The underlying assumption that *ex-ante* regulation will deliver increased competition in the long run and, ultimately, lead to de-regulation under certain conditions, clearly creates a set of expectations among political and economic actors. In the case of the UK, these expectations and the ensuing set of incentives on the regulator may have been reinforced by the fact that the country was the first EU member state to liberalise telecoms and embrace these theoretical views on the evolution of the market. In addition, the functional separation of 2005 may have strengthened the weight of these expectations. Specifically, one could argue that this succession of events generated two sets of incentives for Ofcom: first, towards its political principals, to show that good use was being made of delegated powers; and second, towards market-players, to signal that regulation would indeed be removed when appropriate. In both cases, de-regulation delivers positive reputational gains to Ofcom in the UK and abroad. This does not mean that the de-regulatory outcome of the 2009 review of the retail markets was driven by these pressures rather than by strong evidence that the desired level of competition had finally been achieved; however, these expectations and incentives mechanisms were also at work to a certain extent. At the very least, when Ofcom took the major step of accepting BT's Undertakings in 2005, it positioned itself as a first mover among EU regulators and ensured that a lot of attention would be given to what would happen next: this could not have been overlooked by the

---

30. This is why, when coding sources, I distinguished between Ofcom's narrative, stakeholders' narratives and our narrative, as explained in Chapter Three.

31. As pointed out by Larouche (2007: 23) regulatory decisions, such as those on SMP, are never 'taken in a complete vacuum. There is historical experience with the various markets, the players on these markets and their behaviour'.

agency. It is too early to assess the real effects of functional separation but there is indeed a chance that it had a significant effect on competition, making retail regulation for fixed narrowband markets truly unnecessary, even given BT's large market share. This would indicate that the conclusions of the 2009 statement are the fruit of an instrumental use of economic analysis and its findings. On the other hand, the Undertakings were a major step for BT and, despite the advantage they generated for competitors on the market, some industry interviewees (from both sides of the debate) claim that, at the time of the Undertakings, many were under the impression that a lot of deal-making was taking place and that further de-regulation would have happened at some point. In this light, the 2009 statement was (neutrally) perceived by some as a logical step after such a major decision; others saw it as a 'done deal' (hence, implying a strategic use of knowledge). A representative of BT mentioned that the company was hoping to get something in exchange for the Undertakings, otherwise there would have been no point in going for functional separation in the first place, at a time when the company was already under severe competitive pressure in the fixed retail services. Was the 2009 statement the *quid-pro-quo*? Perhaps not, as the same interviewee added that de-regulation in the 2009 statement came as a surprise and that, although the decision to keep regulation on ISDN was disappointing and could have been appealed by BT:

> if you are being given more than you expect, you are not going to stay up in arms, but still it would now be nice to have a clean break in terms of de-regulation across all of the services as opposed to doing ninety per cent.[32] (Interview, June 2010)

This brings us to the third mechanism at work in this case, namely the threat of judicial review on the merits. This element is linked to knowledge-utilisation in two different ways. First, judicial review on the merits affects the level and depth of the analysis produced by Ofcom and the regulatees to support their position. This point was introduced in Chapter Four and will be discussed again for the next episodes included in this book. Undoubtedly, the fact that the Competition Appeals Tribunal and the Competition Commission take different stances on the analytical approach followed by Ofcom or on the interpretation of findings generates additional constraints on the assumptions and reasoning underpinning the regulator's economic analysis. For instance, it becomes very difficult to ignore conflicting analyses and each line of argument has to be thoroughly supported and justified, as any weakness would offer an easy opportunity for appeal for stakeholders who were either legitimately unhappy with a decision or simply wished to delay the regulatory process (NAO 2010b). This logically strengthens an instrumental use of knowledge.

Secondly, in terms of conflict, the possibility of judicial review puts further pressure on a regulator (Alemanno 2009; Majone 2010) and makes the opposing

---

32. Namely, still keeping ISDN regulated.

stances of stakeholders in the policy arena clearly visible and often more entrenched. Under those circumstances, it is probable that the regulator will also consider who is most likely to appeal; this is reflected in Ofcom's cautious approach to market-definition in this case and also in the way statements were written (in presentational terms), as explained by several Ofcom representatives. Could this also imply that the content of the decision itself is in some way influenced by the likelihood of appeal from a given party, thus suggesting an additional element of strategic thinking in the production and use of economic analysis? As noted by Yandle *et al.* (2011: 243) in their work on litigation (although from an opposing perspective, that is, when litigation is instigated by the regulator to achieve a certain regulatory outcome) 'making a regulatory decision is far more complex than simply going after every activity that seems to impose costs on society and the economy'. Rules are made by humans serving as decision-makers, and 'constraints and incentives matter' (Yandle *et al.* 2011: 244). In the case at hand, one could, for example, imagine that BT was the most probable candidate to appeal because of the Undertakings, hence the decision to de-regulate in the retail market and the general feeling of having been faced with a 'done deal' reported in some interviews.

However, as pointed out by Coglianese (2011: 256), when one cannot draw conclusions from a single or a limited number of cases (without falling into the trap of over-determination), one should at least explain why alternative explanations are not convincing and what one 'finds lacking in the alternative hypotheses suggested by [...] respondents' (Coglianese 2011: 256). In this respect, suspecting a strategic use of knowledge in this particular case fails to take into account the structure of the UK appeal systems and the fact that its costs, when compared to the gains in case of victory, are relatively limited for any of the major market-players. As mentioned by almost every interviewee, this has spurred a surge of litigation in recent years (*see also* NAO 2010b). Hence, an indicator that supports the thesis of an instrumental use of knowledge is the fact that the statement was not appealed, and this is one of the rare cases in the past few years, as pointed out during interviews. Had there been clear economic weaknesses in the analysis or a strategic use of assumptions, appeal would have certainly been a good option for some of BT's major competitors, especially given the significant commercial interests at stake. BT could also have appealed, and reportedly threatened to do so during the process, claiming that they would have commissioned an alternative economic analysis. As I was told by one of Ofcom's representatives, either BT did not commission the analysis in the end, or it did not like the results, as it was never submitted to the regulator. This, in any event, led Ofcom to draft the statement with extra care.

Of course, in a world of scarce resources, one could also imagine that this specific statement was a fight that operators decided not pick, given that, with functional separation benefitting competitors in 2005 and de-regulation favouring BT in 2009, every organisation got a slice of the cake. Still, the impossibility of reaching a definite conclusion on this point does not diminish the relevance of the judicial-review mechanism in this case.

Concluding remarks

The regulation of fixed narrowband retail services markets is an interesting case study, not only because it is a landmark in the history of UK telecoms regulation but also for a number of reasons related to our research design and its explanatory variables.

First of all, I should mention that finding a case fitting with the explanatory variables supporting our hypothesis H1 proved much more difficult than initially foreseen. We cannot, of course, conclude that this also means that, despite all the rhetoric on the instrumental/problem-solving use of knowledge by decision-makers embedded in rational accounts of the policy process (Albæk 1995; Caplan 1979; Torgerson 1986; Weiss, C. 1979), ideal conditions, and thus this specific knowledge usage, are difficult to find in practice. However, it is certainly true that in the field of telecoms regulation, cases with a very low level of conflict are rare, because of the zero-sum-game nature of policy-making in this sector. As a result, the agency may have to resort to some 'bricolage' (Carstensen 2011) to reconcile the requirements of analytical rigour (and an instrumental use of economic analysis) with the reality of policy-making and previous regulatory choices. This also reminds us that the explanatory typology is constructed with ideal-types (Weber 1949[1904]) in mind: in reality, the walls that divide our hypotheses are porous and require us to view the collected information with a more deductive lens.

Secondly, when trying to make sense of what happened on the basis of available sources and interview transcripts, one should not forget that the contrasting depiction of events provided by the actors concerned can also be seen in dramaturgical terms (Goffman 1959; Schimmelfennig 2002) with each actor playing its part as if the regulation of fixed narrowband retail services was a long-rehearsed play. 'What else was he/she supposed to say?' was a recurrent comment in the mind of the interviewer. Yet, as Goffman (1974: 8) clearly explains 'of course, in many cases some of those who are committed to differing points of view and focus may still be willing to acknowledge that theirs is not the official or "real" one'. In our case study, both the idea of strategic use of economic analysis and the idea of instrumental use point to a common thread running through all the official positions. Specifically, it appears that, after the Undertakings, further de-regulation was expected as a logical consequence of the success of functional separation or because this was Ofcom's direction of travel because of a sort of path-dependency derived from historical choices and theoretical expectations. Also, no one really claimed that the economic analysis presented by Ofcom was flawed; it was rather its interpretation (and thus its use) that was contested. Yet, under this combination of circumstances, somehow all players seem to converge on the fact that de-regulation of the retail market was among the sensible policy outcomes from which Ofcom could have chosen. The only alternative would have been to keep the SMP finding but figures did not lend clear support to that choice either; and this would perhaps not have fully accounted for the effect of functional separation. As the real fight was not so much on the 'if' of de-regulation but rather on the 'when', our overall impression is that Ofcom's final decision was a delicate balance between strategic considerations in terms of policy appropriateness and actors' expectations and an instrumental use of evidence that would withstand judicial review. In terms of our explanatory typology, this could be a case of instrumental-strategic use of knowledge, where the amount of economic evidence that is sufficient to instrumentally support a long-awaited decision eventually materialises. In a way, Ofcom displays a rational (in the sense of politically expedient) attitude in this case, showing how an instrumental use of expertise is not the only rational way to make policies, as often assumed in the literature (Albæk 1995; Caplan 1979; Torgerson 1986; Weiss, C. 1979).

Finally, an analysis of the information collected for this case study and a comparison of the different narratives (Jones and McBeth 2010; Shanahan *et al.* 2011) with the actual unfolding of events allowed me to isolate three mechanisms that played a role in the knowledge-utilisation process under examination, and thus flesh out our explanatory variables. These are the historical evolution of the sector, the theoretical assumptions underpinning the chosen regulatory approach, and the threat of judicial review. As we will see, some of these mechanisms will also be present in other episodes, thus suggesting that they may have a more general influence on the knowledge-utilisation choices of an agency; others are limited to this particular case.

chapter six | strategic economics?

Setting the scene: a case of high conflict and high tractability

This chapter covers a case where the explanatory variables can by and large be described as a combination of high conflict in the policy arena and high problem tractability. According to the typology introduced in Chapter Three, these conditions are likely to lead an IRA towards a strategic use of knowledge (H2), either in political terms (to 'win the fight' in an adversarial policy context) or in substantiating terms (to support a preferred policy option), or both.

In real settings, things are seldom so clear cut, particularly as the nature of the chosen explanatory variables tends to vary during the decision-making process. For example, the level of conflict can change, following the entry of a new actor in the policy arena; and the degree of problem tractability can increase or decrease when new information and findings are added to the debate. Despite this caveat, this episode fits the high conflict/high tractability cell of the proposed typology and thus offers a valuable test for hypothesis H2.

In what follows, I will reconstruct the process that led to the adoption of the 2007 regulatory statement for mobile call termination rates (MTRs).[1] The statement was applicable to all operators in the UK market for mobile telephony between 2007 and 2011.[2] It is important to note that this episode is the least recent of the three case studies covered in this book, and was one of the first major dossiers that Ofcom had had to deal with since its creation in 2003. This statement was appealed to the Competition Appeals Tribunal (CAT) and is cited by several interviewees as one of the milestones in Ofcom's recent history, particularly as regards learning through judicial review, as described in Chapter Four.

After a brief illustration of the policy problem at stake, in the next section I will present the key elements of the regulatory debate by focusing in turn on procedural issues, actors and the chronology of events. Then, I will analyse the findings in light of the proposed typology and of expectations regarding the occurrence

---

1. The full text of the 2007 regulatory statement regulatory statement: Online. Available: http://ofcom.org.uk/consult/condocs/mobile_call_term/statement/statement.pdf. All the relevant Ofcom documentation for this case study can be found at/stakeholders.ofcom.org.uk/binaries/consultations/termination/summary/wholesaleprelim.pdf (first consultation); /stakeholders.ofcom.org.uk/binaries/consultations/mct/summary/mct.pdf (second consultation); and /stakeholders.ofcom.org.uk/consultations/mobile_call_term/ (third consultation, corrections, and supporting analyses); (accessed 24 September 2012).

2. The 2007 Statement was under review when I performed the interviews for this case study, as Ofcom had to adopt a new MTR rule for 2011–15. However, this recent review is not covered here.

of a strategic use of knowledge when both conflict and problem tractability are high; finally, I will offer some concluding thoughts. For this case study, I coded qualitatively the three consultation documents and all consultation responses,[3] the regulatory statement, and the transcripts of five interviews with Ofcom (three) and industry (two) performed between May and December 2009.

The regulation of mobile termination rates: key aspects

Mobile call termination rates (MTRs) are the wholesale charges that telephone operators levy to connect calls between each other's networks and between their network and fixed telephony ones. As each mobile network operator (MNO) is the only market player able to terminate calls on its own network – which in economic terms can be assimilated to a monopolistic position (de Bijl *et al.* 2005) – there is a risk of excessive MTRs being charged, with obvious consequences for competition in the mobile market and the retail prices charged to consumers of mobile services (Albon and York 2006; Armstrong 1997; Crandall and Sidak 2004; Dewenter 2005; Harbord and Pagnozzi 2008; Laffont *et al.* 1998; Littlechild 2004; Valletti and Houpis 2005; Wright 2002).[4] As a result, Ofcom has been looking into MTRs since the end of the 1990s and has imposed a progressive reduction of charges, to reflect the efficiency gains generated by the technological evolution of the sector.

The main policy objective of MTR regulation is to find the right balance between guaranteeing that mobile operators recover the costs incurred for terminating calls on their network and ensuring that they do so without charging excessive and inefficient prices, possibly damaging consumers and driving competitors out of the market. Applicable MTRs should also ensure that MNOs still have incentives and resources to invest in innovation, as this is crucial for the long-term development of mobile communications and for the type and quality of the services made available to consumers.

MTR regulation has always been controversial, as the sustained level of litigation following Ofcom's decisions clearly shows.[5] As a matter of fact, MTRs

---

3. The individual consultation responses: Online. Available: http://stakeholders.ofcom.org.uk/consultations/termination/?showResponses=true (first consultation); http://stakeholders.ofcom.org.uk/consultations/mct/?showResponses=true (second consultation); and http://stakeholders.ofcom.org.uk/consultations/mobile_call_term/?showResponses=true (third consultation); (accessed 24 September 2012).

4. This is only a limited selection of the literature on mobile termination rates. Scholars have different views on whether mobile termination should be regulated or not and, if so, how, and start from different premises/assumptions (e.g. whether the costs of the call are borne by the calling party – as in the UK – or by the receiver of the call, as in the United States). The literature also distinguishes between fixed-to-mobile termination rates and mobile-to-mobile termination rates. As we will see in the remainder of this chapter, both perspectives were reflected in the 2007 MTR, with BT being concerned with fixed-to-mobile termination charges (as BT did not have a mobile network), while mobile operators were essentially focusing on mobile-to-mobile termination.

5. An examination of the Communications Act 2003, section 192 appeals heard by the CAT (last accessed on October 29, 2012) shows that out of a total of fifty-five cases (including both telecoms and broadcasting) submitted by individual companies since Ofcom took office, fifteen

constitute a considerable source of income for UK MNOs: at the time of the 2007 statement, MTR revenues were estimated at £2.5 billion annually, about 15 per cent of the mobile sector's revenue (Ofcom, March consultation 2006c: 9). It is thus hardly surprising that, from the beginning, MNOs were clearly opposed to the regulation of MTRs. But absent the possibility of doing away with regulation altogether, because of each operator's monopolistic position in terminating charges on its network, MNOs concentrated their efforts on limiting as much as possible the erosion of MTR profits. Conversely, other market-players with no mobile network, such as the former fixed-telephony incumbent British Telecom, had a completely different set of interests to defend in the MTR debate, thus bringing to the fore other, potentially opposed, regulatory solutions.

The process leading to the 2007 regulatory statement

The process leading to the 2007 regulatory statement on MTRs was quite long and complex; it is thus worth breaking the description into stages and focusing on some preliminary background aspects before looking at the unfolding of events. Specifically, the coming sub-sections will cover the legal aspects of MTR regulation, the key players in this process, and the milestones of this particular episode.

Legal basis for action and main regulatory steps

The origin of the present regulatory approach to mobile termination rates can be traced back to the EU Regulatory Framework (RF) for electronic communications, in place since 2002. As explained in Chapter Four, Ofcom's duties, as set out in the 2003 Communications Act, also include the implementation of Community legislation in the UK market for electronic communications. In particular, Community rules require national regulators to undertake market reviews in order to establish the level of competition in home communications markets, with a view to deciding whether *ex-ante* regulation is needed in certain cases and what the most appropriate regulatory instruments are. The RF is accompanied by a Communication from the European Commission listing the markets (hence, this second act is also known as the 'list of relevant markets') that are likely to exhibit competition problems and thus could be subject to appropriate *ex-ante* regulatory intervention. This list is meant to evolve with time, along with changes in market conditions across the EU. Once a market is taken out of the list at Community level, national regulators will have to prove that *ex-ante* intervention is still necessary at home. In 2007, the list included the market for wholesale mobile termination rates,

---

cases concern mobile call termination (27%). Out of the total number of cases, mobile operators account for nineteen cases (34.5%) and BT for fourteen cases (25.4%). Adjusting these data for the telecoms sector cases only (47 out of 55), then the incidence of MTR cases is about 32% of the total, BT appeals account for about 30% of the total telecoms cases, and mobile operators for 40%.

also known as 'market 16'.[6]

As explained above, mobile termination rates had been regulated in the UK since the end of the 1990s but the first application of the Community approach to this policy problem occurred with the 2004 regulatory statement. In fact, Ofcom was the first European electronic communications regulator to perform a market analysis in line with the EU RF for market 16, thus paving the way for other regulators in the EU block. The 2007 statement was thus a review of an existing rule about to expire: in other words, it was neither a new policy issue or a surprise for concerned parties but a 'scheduled regulatory appointment' to set MTRs and their reduction pattern for a number of years.

As regards procedural requirements for the adoption of the Statement, Ofcom has the statutory duty to perform an impact assessment on its regulatory initiatives as well as to consult widely. Once adopted, Ofcom's rules may be subject to judicial review by the CAT and, for price-related matters, by the Competition Commission (CC).[7] As judicial review occurs only once a statement has been adopted, reportedly, Ofcom used to insert a 'gap year' between the expiration of a given regulatory arrangement and the entry into force of a new rule, to leave room for any changes stemming from judicial review. This did not happen for the statement under examination, which became applicable one month after the expiration of the previous rule. During the decision-making process, Ofcom is also required to notify the European Commission of the future rule, to ensure that there are no negative consequences for the EU internal market.

After this brief sketch of the formal background of the case, let us now turn to the main institutional actors in the debate.

Key players

Besides Ofcom, the key players involved in the decision-making process leading to the 2007 regulatory statement were limited to the actors directly concerned by the proposal, namely the five mobile network operators active on the UK mobile market both for 3G and 2G technology,[8] British Telecom, and Cable&Wireless.

---

6. For a theoretical discussion of the EU's approach to market definition for mobile termination, *see* de Bijl *et al.* (2005); Valletti and Houpis (2005) and, for a critical perspective (on Ofcom's approach) based on more recent theoretical and empirical analyses, Harbord and Pagnozzi (2008). The list of relevant markets and the EU RF were reviewed in 2009; however this review had no impact on the episode covered in this chapter.

7. For further details on these procedural aspects, *see* Chapter Four.

8. 2G technology refers to the second-generation mobile phone system, also known as Global System for Mobile Communications (GSM), the pan-European operating standard for mobile phones. At the time of the 2007 MTR Statement, Vodafone, Orange, T-Mobile and O2 were using this standard. Instead, 3G technology refers to third generation mobile communication systems, which feature advanced capabilities in terms of data transmission (video and multimedia). In the UK, they are based on the Universal Mobile Telecommunication System (UMTS) technology. In the context of this case study, I must add that the auction for 3G licences in the UK ended on 27 April 2000 and raised £22.5 billion. It is one of the biggest auctions so far. As mobile operators

Before I describe in detail the respective positions of the actors, let us briefly focus on who was not (at least, visibly) present in the debate but would normally have been active in policy decisions of such importance.

First of all, the role of the parent ministry was not really apparent in the decision-making process under examination. This is of course in line with Ofcom's formal independence established by the Communications Act of 2003 and is this expectation was reinforced by the fact that the 2007 regulatory statement on MTRs was a review of an already existing rule and not a new initiative.

In fact, a more visible presence of the ministry in policy debates should be expected when general policy guidelines need to be set on a given issue, as confirmed by the perception held both by the regulator and by regulatees regarding the institutional distribution of competence between the parent ministries and Ofcom. Instead, for the review of rules, policy guidelines are already set and remaining matters tend to be relatively technical, thus reducing the potential need for ministry intervention in decision-making. On the other hand, as explained below, the ministry is never completely absent from debates, given that an IRA is always aware of the policy preferences of its principal so, although these are not binding, they may nonetheless influence the final decision.

A second category of actors traditionally present in major regulatory policy debates is providers of external expertise, such as academics and specialised expert consultants. Their advice and support can be requested by the agency to increase problem tractability; they can provide additional evidence or co-operate in modelling exercises during the decision-making process. As mentioned in Chapter Four, Ofcom has a board of permanent academic advisors whose role in decision-making varies on a case-by-case basis. For the 2007 MTR Statement, the involvement of academic experts was relatively limited, as reported by all interviewees. Specifically, one of the academic advisors was consulted at a certain point but no broader debate was launched to involve the academic community further. As regards expert consultants, Ofcom co-operated with a specialised consultancy for some of the modelling work; however, most of the economic expertise used during decision-making came from the agency.

The most important actors in the 2007 MTR debate, therefore, were the five mobile operators for 2G and 3G telephony (Vodafone, O2, Orange, T-Mobile, and H3G). For 3G telephony, the only provider at the time was H3G, which ran a network using both 2G and 3G technology; the other players had acquired 3G licences but were still offering retail services on 2G frequencies.

Up to the 2007 statement, H3G had not been regulated, as the use of 3G technology was still limited and a regulation of MTRs in that case would have hampered the survival of the company. However, the market had changed since the rules imposed in 2004, with a significant take-up of 3G phones among consumers.

---

invested a considerable amount of resources in buying 3G licences, they may have expected the regulator to take this into account in future rules. This is apparent in some of the quotations included in this chapter and in part of the modelling exercise developed by Ofcom to set the final termination charges in the 2007 statement. For a first-hand account of the 3G auction, *see* Binmore and Klemperer (2002).

Hence, Ofcom had already envisaged gradually extending regulation to H3G in the 2007 Statement.

As all operators (with the exception of H3G) acknowledged (to different degrees) their monopolies on terminating calls on their own network, their main interest was to preserve revenues from MTRs as much as possible, so as to guarantee, among other things, investments and a certain range of retail offers to consumers (such as subsidised handsets and cheap pay-as-you-go contracts for marginal users).

Another key player in the debate was the former fixed-telephony incumbent, British Telecom. BT only operates in the fixed-line sector and, as illustrated in the previous chapter, had been regulated since the liberalisation of telecommunications in the 1980s; as a result, termination charges applied to fixed-line calls and the ensuing revenues were significantly lower than MTRs. This created an asymmetry between fixed-to-mobile communications and mobile-to-mobile communications that put fixed operators at a disadvantage. For instance, it was cheaper for consumers to call mobiles from a mobile telephone than from a fixed one. As a result, a reduction of MTRs would of course be favoured by BT and this locates the former telephony incumbent in a completely different position from MNOs in the MTR debate.

Other players, such as cable operators (a competing infrastructure in electronic communications, thanks to technological convergence)[9] also took part in the debate, albeit in a more limited fashion. Their position in the debate was closer to BT's, as these players do not have their own mobile networks.

This brief overview shows how Ofcom was under pressure from competing interests on the issue right at the start of the 2007 MTR debate. This was a new position for the regulator, who had previously dealt mostly with one set of views at a time.[10] Hence, the good fit with the high-conflict explanatory variable. In fact, the 2007 MTR Statement was an anticipation of the growing number of 'zero-sum' policy debates, in which the existence of several opposed views resulted in sustained levels of conflict that affected not only decision-making but also the post-regulatory phase, when judicial review came into play.

In this respect, the picture of the actors involved in the policy arena at the time would not be complete without what I could term 'the shadow' of judicial review. The UK appeal bodies for the communications sector are obviously excluded from decision-making as they can only intervene *ex-post*. However, the threat of being appealed was a serious prospect during the process and referred to quite frequently by all sides in the debate. As mentioned, this became a landmark in Ofcom's appeal track record.

---

9.   For further details, *see* Chapters Four and Seven.

10.   On this point, *see also* Chapter Four.

Key events

The debate leading to the 2007 regulatory statement had begun in June 2005, when Ofcom published a preliminary consultation document, exploring future options for regulating MTRs. This move was prompted by the cyclical review of the existing 2004 MTR regulation. It should be noted that the 2004 MTR rule was due to expire at the end of March 2006; however, Ofcom envisaged the possibility of freezing applicable charges for an additional year, until the end of March 2007, to complete the necessary analytical work for the future statement. One of the main drivers behind this initiative was the need to gather additional data and evidence on new market conditions and adapt the existing models for the calculation of MTR charges to incorporate the effects of 3G technology. The possibility of extending the previous charges until the adoption of the new statement was subject to a separate consultation. Views from the operators diverged and some were, of course, opposed to such extension. Eventually, in December 2005, Ofcom froze charges until the end of March 2007.[11]

As regards the production and use of knowledge leading to this preliminary consultation document, all research was done in-house. To that end, Ofcom put together a multidisciplinary team of economists, lawyers, financial experts and engineers. Reportedly, economists were in the driving seat, as in most cases involving the imposition of charges on operators. While internal views remained closed to the outside world, bilateral meetings with stakeholders took place and stakeholder notes were circulated. Reportedly, the majority of the knowledge used in that phase of the process was included in one form or another in the first consultation document.[12]

The preliminary consultation of June 2005 consisted of 11 questions on different technical solutions for addressing MNOs' monopolistic position in setting MTRs on their network. It also raised the issue of whether regulation of 3G should begin and, if so, how. Overall, Ofcom's position at that time appeared to be fairly open, as shown by its request for input on technical or billing alternatives that would allow a gradual phasing out of regulatory intervention.[13]

Eleven non-confidential responses were submitted, by Vodafone, O2, Orange, T-Mobile, H3G, BT, UKCTA, C&W, MCI and two private individuals, one of whom asked to remain anonymous. All views tended to converge on the fact that

---

11. *Wholesale Mobile Voice Call Termination – Statement and notification extending the charge controls*, published by Ofcom on 16 December 2005. Online. Available: http://stakeholders.ofcom. org.uk/binaries/consultations/wholesale/statement/statement.pdf, (accessed 24 September 2012).

12. This approach is in line with Ofcom's principles of consultation (2005a: 27): 'Where possible, we will hold informal talks with people and organisations before announcing a big consultation to find out whether we are thinking in the right direction. If we do not have enough time to do this, we will hold an open meeting to explain our proposals shortly after announcing the consultation.'

13. For example, Ofcom put forward the option of switching from the current regime of 'calling-party-pays' to a regime of 'receiving-party-pays', which would represent a considerable change for market-players. This reflects well known debates in the academic and policy literature and may be taken as an indicator that the regulator was trying to think outside the box.

technological alternatives to the current system were not workable solutions and thus the debate shifted towards the discussion of appropriate regulatory remedies and the need to impose them (or not) on 3G, and if so, how.

Following the results of the preliminary consultation, Ofcom complemented its analysis and published a second, more elaborated, consultation document in March 2006. This time, Ofcom's views on market structure were more defined and included a *prima facie* assessment of each operator's significant market power (SMP),[14] its potential effects and the impact of these on different categories of consumers. The consultation surveyed the following regulatory options: do nothing and rely on the *ex-post* application of competition law; impose price transparency; tie wholesale charges to retail ones; impose fair and reasonable cost-orientated charges; and, finally, retain the current approach of imposed charge controls.[15] In the document, the agency signalled its intention to adopt charge controls: this was presented as the most efficient and proportionate remedy, together with some additional obligations on non-discrimination, price transparency and network access. Ofcom also clarified its reasons for advocating the regulation of 3G technology, namely, to eliminate artificial and potentially damaging incentives in the distribution of calls across 2G and 3G networks, while preserving incentives for investment by operators.[16] Other questions, such as the assessment of countervailing buyer power (CBP),[17] the cost-modelling work, and the determination of the final amount of applicable charges were left open, as these were still being examined by the agency at the time, with the help of external consultants.[18] The second consultation consisted of eight questions on Ofcom's findings regarding market definition and SMP, on the reasons for discarding some regulatory remedies, and on the best approach for setting technologically neutral charges.

Responses to the March 2006 consultation were fewer than in the previous round (seven in total) and came mostly from fixed and mobile operators. Views were along the lines of those expressed in 2005, with BT welcoming the regulation of 3G networks and advocating the application of a unique charge control for

---

14. For further details, *see* Chapter Five and the glossary at the beginning of the book.

15. This part of the consultation was considered by Ofcom as an initial impact assessment, to be completed during the third and last round of consultation, also on the basis of the responses received (Ofcom 2006c: 63). The label 'impact assessment' fits with the description of the different types of economic analyses presented in Chapter Three.

16. In the consultation document Ofcom (2006c: 11) also notes that it was the only national regulatory authority (NRA) in the EU to set different charges for 2G and 3G, as the 2004 statement entered into force when 3G technology was not widespread. The 'technologically neutral' regulatory framework adopted at the EU level and market analyses in all the EU countries with a 3G network all concluded that 3G technology was taking off and should thus be regulated. This supported Ofcom's proposed approach.

17. As defined by Ofcom (2007: 61): 'CBP exists when a particular purchaser (or group of purchasers) of a good or service is sufficiently important to its supplier to influence the price charged for that good or service.'

18. The chosen consultants (Analysis Mason) had already assisted Ofcom and Oftel in developing the original 'long run incremental costing' (LRIC) model for calculating MTRs in the past.

both 3G and 2G networks, set at a lower rate than 2G charges, given that 3G was expected to be a more efficient and cheaper technology in the long run. While H3G kept opposing the regulation of 3G technology, most of the other MNOs conceded the need for some regulatory intervention on that point but put forward different views on the cost model used by Ofcom; and they suggested alternative approaches to setting the most appropriate MTRs. Finally, several responses argued that Ofcom was giving the impression of having already decided how to proceed, without a sound analytical basis for doing so, as key elements such as the evaluation of CBP were still absent from the analysis.

Following the responses to the March 2006 consultation, Ofcom produced a very complex economic analysis, with twelve different scenarios derived from various combinations of future demand levels and possible valuations of spectrum costs (see below). This modelling exercise was used to establish a range of possible termination rates. The text, which constitutes a full impact assessment with specific policy options to choose from, was subject to a third and last round of consultation in September 2006.[19] Ofcom also published a *Report on Market Research Findings*, illustrating the latest findings of the regulator's consumer research regarding MTRs.[20] In line with the statutory obligation set by the 2002 EU Regulatory Framework for electronic communications, Ofcom also submitted its regulatory proposal to the European Commission for review.[21] This third consultation consisted of six questions: on market definition and SMP; on the appropriateness of imposing charge controls on mobile-to-mobile communications and on fixed-to-mobile communications; in addition to a set of additional obligations such as prohibitions of undue discrimination and the publication of access contracts. The final questions are more specific and concern the possible levels of charge controls and the different glide-path[22] scenarios to be imposed on H3G and on the other MNOs.

Nine responses to this last round of consultation were submitted and included the 'usual suspects', that is, the five MNOs, Cable&Wireless, and four individual contributors, of whom three wished to remain anonymous. The European Commission also submitted its views, touching in particular on the issue of 3G spectrum valuation and suggesting it be calculated at current value on a forward-looking basis and not at the overrated historical costs paid by MNOs when spectrum licences were auctioned.

Eventually, Ofcom's Board reached a final decision on the applicable MTRs

---

19. The impact assessment covers the different technical and billing options already proposed in the previous document; however, it does not do a full cost-benefit analysis for all options, as some were deemed too uncertain or unfeasible. This approach is in line with the principle of proportionate analysis.

20. The full text of the Report. Online. Available: http://stakeholders.ofcom.org.uk/binaries/consultations/mobile_call_term/annexes/report.pdf (accessed 24 September 2012).

21. For further details on this notification procedure, *see* Directive 2002/21/EC of the European Parliament and of the Council of 7 March 2002 on a common regulatory framework for electronic communications networks and services, OJ L 108, 24.4.2002, p. 33 and above, Chapter Four.

22. A glide-path scenario is a planned path of charge-reduction to get to the target charge value.

Table 6.1: Key steps leading to the 2007 statement on MTRs

Date	Event
7 June 2005	Preliminary consultation (responses by 30 August)
30 March 2006	Second consultation: Market Review (responses by 25 May)
13 September 2006	Third consultation (responses by 22 November) & publication of *Report on Market Research Findings*
27 March 2007	Publication of the regulatory statement
1 April 2007	Entry into force of MTRs until 31 March 2011

and the last details of the rule were finalised by Ofcom's Policy Executive.[23] The result of this process is the regulatory statement of March 27, 2007, ruling that charges for 2G mobile operators should be reduced to 5.11 ppm (pence per minute) by the final year of the charge-control period (1 April 2010 to 31 March 2011), while charges for the 3G operator should be reduced to 5.9 ppm, to reflect the exogenous cost differences between the two technologies. Reduction paths were specified in the statement and differ between the two types of MNOs. Ofcom's initial approach also included the obligation that MNOs publish all contract agreements setting MTRs, but this was removed from the final Statement as too burdensome. The statement entered into force after one month, in April 2007 and was immediately appealed. The main steps leading to the 2007 statement as well as the final charges and respective glide paths per type of operator are summarised in Tables 6.1 and 6.2.

A case of strategic use of economic analysis?

According to the explanatory dimensions of the typology, the level of conflict in the 2007 MTR case can be described as high: the various stakeholders had clashing interests regarding the details of the regulation and pressured the agency with competing demands. The possibility of judicial review on the merits and thereof of blocking the whole implementation process by appealing Ofcom's decision further contributed to a sustained degree of tension. Broadly speaking, the debate was polarised between the MNOs, trying to protect the revenue stream from MTRs as much as possible, and BT, aiming to achieve greater symmetry between regulated fixed telephony termination rates and mobile ones. A third stance was taken by H3G, whose interests partially differed from those of the other MNOs because of its reliance on 3G technology but had little in common with BT's. These clashing positions did not converge at any time during the debate, as reflected by responses to the different rounds of consultation.

In terms of problem tractability, available economic models addressed rather uncontroversially one part of the problem, the identification of SMP, while greater uncertainty surrounded the analytical path leading to the identification of

---

23. For the difference between the two, *see* Chapter Four on Ofcom's organisational structure.

Table 6.2: Charge control conclusions following adjustment for notice period

	Current average regulated charges	First year target charge (nominal)	Second year % reduction (i.e. X in RPI-X)	Third & fourth year % reduction (i.e. X in RPI-X)	Final charge in 2010/11 (real 06/07 prices)
Vodafone & O2	5.6	5.7	3.2%	2.5%	5.1
T-Mobile & Orange	6.3	6.2	5.8%	5.3%	5.1
H3G Option 2 (*immediate cut + glide path*)	Not regulated	9.1	15.1%	11.8%	5.9

Source: Ofcom 2007: 182

the appropriate termination charges. To determine these, Ofcom used a model known as 'long run incremental costing' (LRIC),[24] plus a mark-up for common and externality costs. The structure of the model is generally accepted in the telecommunications sector;[25] however, calibrating the informational input for its practical application is less straightforward.

At the start of the debate, the two most difficult issues, which subsequently became the core of Ofcom's modelling, had not fully been outlined. These were forecasts of the growth of mobile broadband services and how to deal with the cost of spectrum-licensing for 3G technology.[26] Hence, the agency seemingly entered the decision-making process under relatively high problem-tractability conditions. With the passing of time, these two thorny points became central and reduced problem tractability. Yet, expectations for this case still fit in the H2 cell of the explanatory typology. Thus, I should expect a strategic use of economic analysis for all the questions for which problem tractability is rather high (H2);

24. The LRIC of voice termination is the additional cost that an MNO incurs to provide termination. It can also be seen as the cost that the firm would avoid if it decided not to provide voice termination, taking a long-run perspective. For further details, *see* Ofcom (2006e: 141, Annex 5).

25. This model is commonly used in systems where the calling party pays (e.g. UK). A receiving-party-pays regime as in the US (a policy option explicitly discarded by Ofcom, *see* above) would warrant a different modelling approach; however these considerations fall out of the scope of the book.

26. As mentioned, MNOs had just spent a significant amount in acquiring 3G licenses and held different views on how these costs were to be reflected in the modelling. MNOs believed that MTRs should take into account the investment undertaken to acquire 3G licenses and allow operators to cover their costs; conversely, fixed operators such as BT disagreed that MTRs should be used to cover these costs, as doing so would contravene the principle of auctioning spectrum-licenses in the first place.

and, possibly, a symbolic or non-use of such expertise (that is, a final decision based on other grounds) when issues became more problematic (H3). Let us now compare these hypotheses with what happened during the various stages of decision-making outlined in the previous section.

The unfolding of events and the use of economic analysis

The preliminary consultation launched in 2005 was presented by the regulator as a 'green paper' for exploring the state of play in the mobile market, outlining the core elements of potential regulatory approaches for the forthcoming statement and gathering preliminary impressions of how different options would be received by the concerned parties. There seems to have been no strategic use of knowledge in this initial phase of the debate, as confirmed by different categories of interviewees. In particular, the regulator explained that:

> In this case, there had been a sort of very green consultation where I said 'well, let's see if there are some thoughts about [...] if things have radically changed in terms of market power, or there is a completely alternative remedy that is worth exploring'. (Ofcom 1, December 2009)

The absence of a strategic use of knowledge by the agency in this initial phase is confirmed by an industry representative who, when asked to recall how the policy debate started, went as far as to claim that, in fact, this so-called 'green paper approach' was the result of the agency's disorganisation:

> Ah, you've reminded me now! They started it too late [...] and when they realized this they put out [...] in about 2006 it must have been or maybe in 2005, they put out what they called a preliminary consultation: rather than going to consultation they said 'we are going to go to a consultation, and these are things that I think we're going to be asking you.' (Industry 1, November 2009).

When probed further about whether the 'green paper' approach might have been a thought-through attempt of the agency to gather all the necessary evidence and take a comprehensive perspective on the policy issue, the interviewee went on to explain:

> I would say that it means they don't know what to do. They haven't really got an open mind. An open mind suggests that [...] I am a bit more cynical really...normally they have a view and a plan and you know, fairly they want to implement their plan and [...] they already have an idea most of the time and when they do these preliminary ones [consultations] it means they do have an idea but they are not sure they can make it stick. So [...] they love saying 'we asked people about this.' They love, obviously, protecting their backs, saying 'people were given adequate chance to comment on this.' (Industry 1, November 2009)

Despite the difference in tone, and the mention of Ofcom's intention to 'protect their backs', both interviewees seem to agree that no strategic behaviour was at work as far as knowledge-utilisation was concerned in this preliminary phase of decision-making.

In terms of knowledge-production, the necessary expertise came directly from the Ofcom team in charge of the proposal, with additional contributions from other departments, when relevant. From the published written evidence it is, of course, impossible to determine whether there was any in-house strategic selection of expert knowledge by the responsible team (in the sense of discarding evidence that would go against a preferred course of action); however, all agency interviewees claimed that, usually, most available and relevant knowledge somehow found its way into the consultation document or into other published sources (such as statistics, market reports and annexes to the main consultation). This claim seems to be substantiated by the exploratory nature of this first consultation document compared to subsequent ones and by the fact that it refers to and relies on other analyses or market studies previously published by Ofcom.

As the debate and the underlying economic analysis progressed, new knowledge became available. Gradually, economists' all-time-favourite saying that 'prediction is very difficult, especially about the future' started to seem pertinent, particularly once the two issues of growth forecasts and cost of spectrum were put on the table. While the level of conflict generated by the diverging positions of the various market-players was clear from the start and remained stable over time, the evolution of the economic analysis partially reduced problem tractability.

It is clear from official documents, responses to consultation and interviews with agency staff and regulatees that, after the preliminary consultation phase, a great amount of economic knowledge was produced by all sides. As confirmed by all interviewees, at Ofcom, the dossier was very much in the hands of the economists, given the nature of the policy issue. Hence, all the arguments put forward by stakeholders revolved around economic thinking and referred to specific aspects of the modelling or its underlying assumptions. Only for what were, arguably, weaker positions (for example, H3G's claim that 3G should not be regulated, in spite of all existing analyses across the EU supporting regulation of the new technology), were legal arguments brought to the fore. Otherwise, the main debate remained an economic battle of assumptions, modelling alternatives, different methods to calculate blended rates for 2G and 3G and so on.

What was the link between the considerable amount of economic analysis produced, and its use in decision-making?

Up to the intervention of Ofcom's Board it is somewhat difficult to fully separate the production of economic analysis from its use, as the two processes evolved in parallel and, when more knowledge became available, it was immediately fed into the analysis to produce additional evidence and to advance decision-making. This is common practice at Ofcom and is in line with formal requirements, particularly the statutory duties to perform impact assessments and consult widely. Moreover, as testified by other work on knowledge-utilisation (Sjörgen 2006), when generating knowledge, producers normally bear in mind its intended use, thus creating a close link between the two processes.

This raises the question of whether there was a discrepancy between the expected and the actual use of the produced knowledge. For example, the agency could have produced the analysis in line with statutory requirements with a view to using it instrumentally (for problem-solving purposes, as in H1 of the explanatory typology) and could have subsequently been led by certain conditions to use it strategically or symbolically. Or instead, a strategic intention to use knowledge to support a preferred policy decision could have been embedded in the production phase. Establishing the intentions of the agency is virtually impossible, unless one has the chance to do participatory observation and access internal correspondence and, where relevant, confidential documents, in order to uncover a possible decoupling of talk and actions (Brunsson 1989) within the organisation. However, the aim is not to find an indisputable truth but rather to outline the great variety of the mechanisms at work in terms of knowledge-utilisation during decision-making by an IRA. This brings us back to the explanatory power of the independent variables and the dynamic nature of regulatory policy processes, seen from the perspectives of conflict and problem tractability. A change in these two variables could indeed alter the course of (intended) knowledge-utilisation, independently of the initial intentions of the knowledge producer/user. I will come back in detail to these considerations in the concluding chapter of this book. Let us now turn to the behaviour of individual actors in the 2007 MTR episode.

The interaction between actors and knowledge

An examination of stakeholders' responses to the three consultations shows a predictable attempt by all MNOs to bring the debate on to a strategic platform, in line with the litigation culture surrounding MTRs. Hence, from the beginning, each market-player selected the best economic arguments to back its case and influence Ofcom during the decision-making process. Moreover, stakeholders, both in consultation submissions and during interviews, appear to have been fully aware of the possibility of using judicial review as a weapon and this may have reinforced their strategic behaviour more than in other cases, as also noted inside Ofcom:

> If there was no litigation, the idea would be that we [Ofcom] eventually make decisions but the process would be more cooperative; this way instead operators cooperate up to a certain point, but they always keep the litigation option open. (Ofcom 2, June 2009)

Ofcom's response to regulatees' strategies is quite interesting. When looking at the evolution of the agency's economic analysis in several published documents, one gets the impression that Ofcom tried to stick as much as possible to an instrumental use of knowledge, by trying to increase problem tractability while managing or preventing conflict, to keep the debate on an 'evidence-based' track. The statutory duty to perform an impact assessment for each policy decision was clearly respected and may have even served as a means to steer the debate away from purely strategic approaches. In other words, the initial impression is that economic knowledge was used strategically by the agency but in a slightly different manner from what the typology predicts.

Specifically, there are signs of strategic uses of economics in terms of 'presentation': in all documents, economic language is also used as a rhetorical device (McCloskey 1998) to strengthen the weight/credibility of evidence in decision-making; the intention to build an economic argument that would stand up in court is clearly visible. Stakeholders' remarks are systematically addressed and refuted where necessary, most often on the basis of evidence claims. To be sure, this approach is followed for other statements as well but Ofcom's presentational efforts in this case are particularly meticulous, as reflected by the lengths of all the relevant official documents (by way of example, the statement is over 400 pages long). This conscious attempt to substantiate each point was also confirmed during fieldwork. On the other hand, I found no immediate evidence in official sources or interview transcripts of a strategic substantiating use, in the sense of selecting some arguments over others to support a given position. Rather, knowledge appears as a valuable aid to preserve a problem-solving approach to regulation. That is, until we take into account the threat of judicial review and its potential effects on the production of knowledge.

Being caught between two and, at times, even three opposing and incompatible positions, Ofcom knew from the beginning that any decision would very likely be appealed by either one of the MNOs or BT. There was no way around it:

> It is fair to say we knew all the way through that there was a very high risk of appeal. I think we were all expecting that this statement would be appealed. And it was. So yes, that [judicial review] has quite a significant impact. (Ofcom 1, December 2009)

In other words, during the production of the supporting economic analyses, judicial review was clearly in the mind of the regulator and, even more so, the possible use of the produced knowledge in front of one of the review bodies in the case of an appeal. Could it be that this potential threat influenced the agency to the point of leading it to strategic knowledge-utilisation, in terms of content as well, under conditions of high conflict and high tractability, as foreseen by the explanatory typology; and also to a non-use or a symbolic use of knowledge when tractability decreased? Clearly, examining published analyses cannot answer this question directly.[27] A possible way to tackle this problem is to explore whether the probabilities of each of the regulatees appealing were equal and, if not, whether this had any impact on the production and use of economic analysis during decision-making.

---

27. As mentioned in Chapters One and Three, finding proof of knowledge-usages that depart from instrumental use is one of the major problems in the empirical application of knowledge-utilisation theories. This is why gaining a deep understanding of the context of each episode is crucial for this type of research question and is what makes the case-study method particularly suitable.

Because of their number, direct interest in the issue, and relatively convergent views (with the exception of H3G), the MNOs represented the biggest coalition in the MTR debate. The final rule is clearly closer to the wishes of the MNOs than to those of BT, which was hoping to achieve greater symmetry between mobile and fixed-line termination charges. And indeed, as soon as the regulatory statement was adopted, both BT and H3G appealed to the CAT.[28] This is insufficient to conclude that a strategic substantiating use of knowledge to support a preferred option occurred, even if some consultation responses claim that Ofcom seemed to have already decided half-way through what to do. The latter could simply be a rhetorical tactic to undermine the regulator's arguments when the analysis was still ongoing. Instead, it may be more helpful to focus on the content of the economic analysis underpinning the decision and see whether there is a clear continuity in the evolution of the reasoning through the three rounds of consultation as well as a visible connection with the final rule adopted by Ofcom. Given that official documents and consultation responses offer a more polished version of facts, as explained in Chapter Three, answering this question requires going behind the scenes (Goffman 1959) and letting the different actors speak.

Overall, Ofcom's final decision seems to follow logically from the preceding analysis, as explained by one regulatee:

> I think it was quite clear what decision they were going to come to, because everyone still accepts that call termination is a monopoly bottleneck, so does have to be regulated; but nevertheless they did go through the stages of analysis they need to do to come to that conclusion. (Industry 2, June 2009)

This is the opinion of one of the parties who did not appeal Ofcom's decision, as clearly stated by the same interviewee:

> [...] the final result was very much as we expected and we had thought. Obviously, as you know, it subsequently got appealed. But the decision that actually came out in March 2007 was very much what we had hoped for; I mean it was the first time though that I have seen Ofcom kind of place so much reliance – and it surprised everyone I think – on scenarios. (Industry 2, June 2009)

---

28. Specifically, H3G appealed both Ofcom's conclusion that the company held SMP in the termination market and the price control imposed by the Statement, while BT appealed against the price control only. The CAT referred all price-control matters to the Competition Commission (CC). The CAT dismissed the non-price control matters of H3G's appeal and, following the CC's deliberation, also H3G's appeal on the price control. Conversely, BT's appeal was upheld and Ofcom issued a new price-control scheme in 2009 for all operators (note that there was an error in one of the calculations made by the CC that was recognised and corrected by the CAT before the final judgement). The CAT's final decision entailed a greater reduction in the MTR charges that the mobile operators can levy to terminate calls on their networks (i.e. a tougher position than Ofcom's). The final CAT judgement of 2 April 2009. Online. Available: http://www.catribunal.org.uk/238–3720/Judgment-Disposal-of-the-Appeals.html (accessed 22 March 2013); while the revised scheme is available at: http://stakeholders.ofcom.org.uk/binaries/consultations/mobile_call_term/statement/CTMAmendment2009final.pdf. (accessed 22 March 2013). For more details on the case, see also 'Mobile group 3 fights cut in charges', Financial Times 29 May 2007.

However the same regulatee also acknowledged that:

Ofcom's decisions, as far as I can tell, really do always have an economic logic in there. But obviously there is potential sometimes for that economic logic to get slightly [...] altered by the political [...] what seems to be the political desire [...] but I guess, as far as I see, there always is an economic logic in there that does hold up. (Industry 2, June 2009)

So that could indeed indicate that there is potential for some strategic substantiating use of expertise prompted by 'political' factors, although carefully supported by relevant and sound economic reasoning. In the case at hand, the strong conflict among policy actors – coupled with a growing level of uncertainty – led the agency to undertake a complex modelling exercise, with twelve different scenarios providing an equal number of regulatory answers. It is thus in the scenario analysis, and particularly in the choice between the twelve possible solutions, that one has to look for some potential indication of a strategic use of knowledge.

The twelve scenarios envisaged by Ofcom were built on different combinations of the possible valuation of spectrum and prospective future demand for mobile services (Ofcom used three possible demand levels in the modelling: low, medium and high). These scenarios were then used to derive a range of acceptable MTR charges, distinguishing between 2G and 3G technology as shown in the horizontal axis of Figure 6.1. These scenarios and the corresponding charge range were subjected to consultation. I found no indications that this charge range was incorrect or not justifiable on the basis of Ofcom's modelling; and this was confirmed in the subsequent appeal process.[29] However, as the old saying goes, the devil (might)

29. Although covering the appeal process would fall outside the scope of this book, I have discussed it with interviewees to get additional information and clues on the production and use of economic analysis during decision-making by Ofcom. As mentioned, the final decision of the CAT is less favourable to MNOs than the one initially taken by Ofcom in the 2007 statement. One of the questions put to the CC by the CAT concerned the valuation of the cost of spectrum and how to arrive at the opportunity cost of 3G spectrum without relying on the 2000 auction fees. In theory, this should have corresponded to the value that 3G spectrum could fetch in a competitive market (and hence would be the same for each MNO). However, there was no competitive market for 3G spectrum. What follows are the most salient parts of the final judgement (Case Nos: 1083/3/3/07 and1085/3/3/07 point 2). The CAT, summarising the CC's evaluation, explains that: 'Ofcom had erred in two respects: in its approach to the inclusion of spectrum costs and in its inclusion of a network externality surcharge in the target average charge ("TAC") [...] the CC rejected the way that OFCOM had dealt with 3G spectrum costs and found in particular that OFCOM had erred in relying on the fees paid for 3G spectrum by the MNOs in the spectrum auction held in 2000. None of the parties is seeking to reinstate the way in which OFCOM valued 3G spectrum in the March 2007 Statement. Having rejected that approach, the CC then considered an alternative approach proposed by BT. This approach was referred to as the 2G cap [...]. The justification for the 2G cap approach to valuing 3G spectrum was as follows. The CC found that there is no material difference in the quality of the service that is provided when a call is terminated on a 3G network as compared to when it is terminated on a 2G network. In a competitive market, therefore, MNOs would not be able to charge a higher wholesale price for termination on the 3G network than the price charged for 2G call termination. The price for 2G voice call termination would therefore be the cap or upper bound of the amount that MNOs can charge for terminating calls using 3G spectrum. Secondly, it was accepted that 3G technology is more efficient than 2G

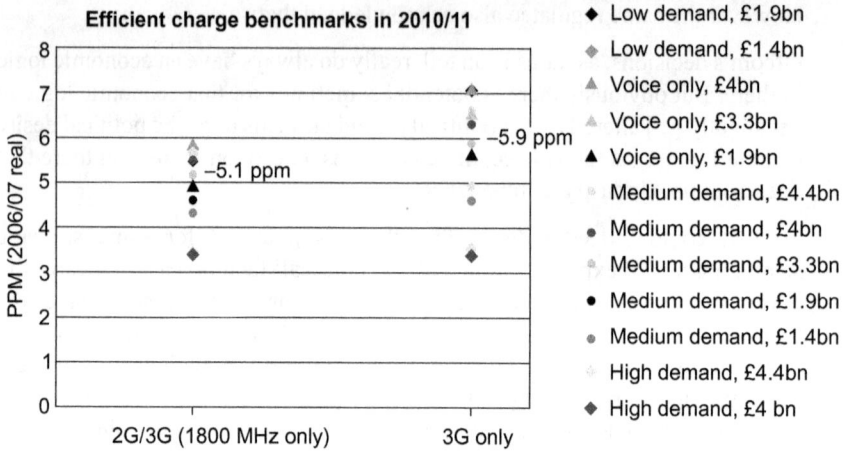

Figure 6.1: Efficient charge benchmarks derived from Ofcom's LRIC model

Source: Ofcom (2007:151 and 167)

lie in the details; hence, we have to narrow the analysis to the actual choice of the final MTR charges within the prospected range.

In this respect, one industry representative noted that the scenario analysis itself was not an easy economic exercise leading to a predictable answer:

> [...] the biggest uncertainty, by far the biggest uncertainty, was the growth of broadband mobile data traffic. For the previous price reviews, the mobile market has always been relatively predictable [...]. Mobile data, broadband data though, has completely thrown away the predictability of the market; to start with we've got relatively [...] certainly at that stage [...] relatively little idea of how many people would take up service, and even then, less idea about how much they would actually use the service. And because it was a kind of

---

for carrying voice traffic. The 2G price cap would allow the MNOs to keep any cost savings that they derived from using 3G technology for terminating voice calls. As the CC put it (paragraph 2.9.12 of the Determination) "to the extent that 3G spectrum could be said to have been acquired to save costs in the provision of voice services, efficiently incurred costs could be reimbursed by adopting the principle of the 2G cap". The CC used the medium demand scenario in its judgement and not any of the other scenarios prospected by Ofcom "They noted that OFCOM had stated that the medium-demand forecast was based on predictions towards the lower end of the range obtained from the available information and also that there will be opportunities in future price control periods to make any adjustments deemed necessary if the actual traffic outcomes differ from the forecasts. The CC therefore decided that there was no reason to adjust the medium-demand forecast [...]." The reasonableness of OFCOM's traffic forecasts had not been challenged in the appeal so it may well be, as the CC argued, that it was not open to the CC to reject the forecasts and devise new ones, particularly on the basis of information which post-dated the March 2007 Statement. But in any event, we can see nothing in the CC's discussion of the issue of 3G capacity constraint which can properly be criticised, let alone characterised as perverse or irrational [...]'.

LRIC plus contribution to common cost, the growth of the mobile broadband data was hugely important with knowing how all common costs would get allocated across the different services. So there was this huge uncertainty. So the huge uncertainty on the calling of mobile data and the huge uncertainty on [...] well not uncertainty, but [...] the different ways to value the 3G licence. So, I mean Ofcom, it really perhaps was trying to experiment with the new approach to say rather than make definite decisions and then have people trying to say 'well you just can't be certain about that decision', they kind of accepted the fact that there was uncertainty and hence went down the scenario route. (Industry 2, June 2009)

So, amidst this uncertainty, how did Ofcom choose between scenarios? And if there was indeed a strategic approach, what prompted it? Was it really the threat of being appealed? Or were other factors also relevant, for example an intervention from the parent ministry?

For another regulatee, Ofcom acted strategically by considering which party was most likely to appeal when reaching the final regulatory decision:

[...] they did a huge model, very big model [...] they got twelve answers out of this model, scenarios, and the lowest one might have been about 1 to 2 ppm, but the highest one say it was 7 ppm, and then they didn't seem to know what to do, they kind of looked at all these sighting shots they got from the model, and [...] they seemed to pick, pick some kind of area in the middle and then, which wasn't particularly the economics way of doing it, and then they seemed to write up backwards saying 'we've looked at the highs and the lows, and the intermediate cases and using our judgement we're going to go for [...] this number.' And it was a big black box, no one could understand where these 1 or 2 pence had come from, or 7 had come from, we roughly understood where it had come from, but at the end of the day, they kind of seem to all get together and say let's go for this number. It was driven by economics, except right at the very end, when someone seemed to say 'well, I think that would be a fair settlement', and my own view is that they probably looked at what the mobile operators would tolerate, and went for the lowest price they thought the mobile operators would tolerate. Because they are scared of them, scared of them appealing. (Industry 1, November 2009)

The quote above appears like a 'textbook' description of strategic knowledge-utilisation, as reflected in the reference to 'backwards writing' and to the deliberate choice of a 'tolerable number' for mobile operators, who were those most likely to appeal Ofcom's decision. In some parts instead, the description evokes a non-use of knowledge: when high uncertainty reduces problem tractability, the agency 'does not know what to do', or in other words cannot/does not rely on knowledge to decide ('It was driven by economics, except right at the very end'), in line with the expectation of H3 in the typology.[30] This reminds us of the dynamic nature of

---

30. While the typology also foresees the symbolic use of knowledge as a possible outcome, I can

knowledge-utilisation, which can be expected to follow variations in the intensity of the explanatory variables. However, since the MTR case was the review of an existing rule, many aspects of the LRIC model were fairly well accepted by most actors, and even the difficult issue of spectrum valuation was, in some respects, a matter of opinion (see the above quotation from Industry 1), this case mostly fits with the H2 hypothesis. The agency's account of the final phases of decision-making does not seem to contradict the idea that the threat of judicial review and the consideration of which side was most likely to appeal had some influence on the regulator:

> I think that what's an important consideration actually in practice is [...] on which side [...] I mean there was not a simple one side and another side here, because you had H3G, as a sort of new entrant MNO who had a different perspective from the four incumbents, who had a different perspective from BT. It's sort of three sides as it were. In a more normal situation I would have two sides. Whether there is a greater threat of appeal from one side or another can make a difference in sort of the process [...]. (Ofcom 1, November 2009)

So what led Ofcom to take this approach; was it only the threat of appeal? Digging deeper into the story two other factors come to the fore: 1) the availability of relevant data and information during the production of the economic analysis; and 2) the potential role of the parent ministry.

In terms of the availability of data and information, it is quite likely that, under conditions of uncertainty, the type of information readily accessible tilts the balance of decision-making in one direction rather than another. After all, market-players often have informational advantages over the regulator (Larouche 2008), for example, as regards some features of the market in which they operate or the detailed breakdown of their operating costs. In the MTR case, BT contributed less and at a later stage to the debate, which may have indeed worked in favour of the MNOs, as confirmed during interviews:[31]

> Another characteristic actually, and this would be very much true in the case of BT, was that they just produced far more evidence and better quality, more evidence and better quality arguments in the appeal process than they ever did during our decision-making. And frankly, if they had produced some of that evidence at the time we made our decision, we might as well have made another, a different decision that was more favourable to them. (Ofcom 1, November 2009)

---

exclude it in this case as the analysis is closely connected to the final decision. In the explanatory typology, a symbolic use of knowledge implies a decoupling between expertise and the decision.

31. Please note that I do not imply that BT withheld information on purpose. It may actually have had little interest in doing so, as providing information on time would have potentially anticipated a more favourable decision for the company in 2007 instead of their having to wait until the CAT's judgement in 2009. The impression I gathered from interviews was that, in a world of scarce resources, BT had focused its efforts on other dossiers, and only invested in the MTR case at a later stage, when the decision was well under way. In any event, this does not affect considerations on the effect of information availability at the time of decision-making.

Regarding the potential influence of the ministry, views differ and there is really no secure way to establish whether there was any interference in the decision-making: if that were the case, it would have happened behind the scenes and in an informal manner. Hence, indications of such an influence are purely speculative. For example, one industry representative explained:

They kind of were, they knew that the MNOs were quite aggressive and they would put a lot of resources there. And I would say there is a history of the UK ministry not supporting roaming reductions, and not supporting some of Viviane Reding's rules[32] in Europe, so you get the feeling that there are people in government on the side of mobile operators, so maybe that was slightly playing a part. In some way, they went soft on the decision, for whatever reason [...] So they [Ofcom] said we must lower prices, but we mustn't go too low. And I think that's what happened: so you got lots of economic work, and then a bit of kind of influence on the decision, and of course between 1 and 7 pence there is a huge range to go for. (Industry 1, November 2009)

On the other hand, the regulator explained:

They [the ministry] had no role at all in this process, there are other processes where they have a formal role, or if not a formal role, it's clear that a decision we might make might have impact or that we understand the context [...] I mean there are cases where we need to understand where they are, but that doesn't mean that we will give them what they want. (Ofcom 1, November 2009)

As indicated in the theoretical framework, the level of conflict can be generated by several factors; one is indeed the institutional balance and the relationship between the political principal and the agency. In case of conflict between the two, knowledge can be used strategically by both parties: for the principal it may become an instrument for controlling the agency (Radaelli 2009b); for the agent instead it can be a means by which to pursue a preferred policy approach that may not be fully aligned with the preferences of the principal. In the case under examination, there is no explicit sign of either of the two occurring. But even in the absence of such 'strategic games' and, specifically, of a ministerial influence on Ofcom's regulatory decision, there were enough other conflict factors (such as the clashing preferences of regulatees and the threat of judicial review) that could have potentially fostered a strategic use of economic analysis by the agency, thus diverting knowledge-utilisation away from a purely instrumental/problem-solving path. It seems indeed that, while economics played a key role in keeping the debate

32. Viviane Reding was the EU Information Society Commissioner at the time. She is known for imposing a regulation to cap roaming charges (i.e. the MTRs that mobile operators charge to consumers when they phone and receive calls abroad) within the EU, in a move to eliminate existing discrepancies between roaming within the EU internal market (e.g. charges ranged from a few Eurocents per minute to up to two Euros per minute to call from another EU member state, although the underlying cost differential in roaming services did not justify such a price gap). The UK was against this initiative.

on an instrumental track, other factors besides knowledge entered the picture when the final decision was taken. This is where the split between knowledge-production and knowledge-utilisation becomes apparent. The economic analysis produced was undoubtedly discussed by the Board in several instances, as indicated by the public minutes of the Board meetings (Ofcom 2005d 2006f, 2007b); however, these are very terse and the content of the discussion is confidential. To be sure, the MTRs chosen by Ofcom's Board are the logical result of the preceding analysis; yet, the available price range offered by the twelve scenarios left considerable room for manoeuvre.

Specifically, as regards the use of economic analysis towards the end of the decision-making process, one of Ofcom's interviewees replied in the following way when asked about the overall weight that economic expertise had in this episode:

> Let's distinguish between the weight in the decision and the [...] proportion of the resource [invested in the analysis]. There were certainly, I think it was the highest proportion of the resource, because there was a lot of economic analysis [...] In terms of weight of the decision, well the legal advice is always critical because you know [...] apart from the obvious reasons that it's the law and where there is a high probability of appeal you know it is going to be quite a legalistic process, you have to find your way, so that's important. The other reason is often that the legal framework sets up the questions that the economic analysis is trying to answer, so it's almost like they are kind of complementary or they should be complementary rather than in a sense competing for attention. And [...] taking that as given that the legal framework was there, then the economic analysis was very important in terms of lining up both the basis for regulation, and then the type of regulation, and the level of the price control, and those things where the economic answer is always important. But I mean, there are always other considerations that come into play, absolutely. And I don't want to suggest that they were not important, they were, but the foundation of all of that, we would not and did not do anything that we thought could not be justified by the economic reasoning, but I mean the nature of these cases is, economic reasoning doesn't tell the level of price control [...] the economic reasoning, well you know as an economist, it doesn't give you a single answer that that's the only right number. It says, well there is a reasonable range, for that range the arguments are quite sound, for somewhere in that range, and they might be slightly better for one point of the range, and outside the range it maybe gets a bit weaker and then comes a point where it's pretty hard to defend. So you know, in fact it's that kind of dynamic, a very interactive kind of process, but you understand, the policy-makers, sorry the decision-makers understand [...] that it needs to be within this reasonable range that is supported by the economic reasoning but within that, there are different policy choices to be made. (Ofcom 1, November 2009)

To the same question, an industry representative replied:

[...] all they did in the cost model is make a lot of assumptions, and what the Competition Commission said is 'you can't just include mutually exclusive scenarios and take an average of them. You have to decide which you believe in!' And they didn't do that, they just said there are twelve ways of looking at the world, and they were required to decide between them, which they didn't do. And economists did lots of work, but when it came to actually deciding; you know it's like you deciding how to go from Brussels to London, train or flight, or you know, ferry, but in the day you can't take an average of those, you have to decide how you are going to do it. And they didn't do that! They just took an average of the world. (Industry 1, November 2009)

Concluding remarks

Overall, it is fair to say that economic analysis played a central role in this policy episode but was not the only basis for decision-making. This is not really surprising: for any policy decision, including those in 'technical' areas like telecommunications, considerations such as the feasibility and acceptability of a rule come into play. So how did produced knowledge feed into the final decision, both in terms of weight and in terms of content? Did the conditions of high conflict and high problem tractability with some peaks of uncertainty lead to a strategic usage of economic analysis, beyond a simple 'rhetorical' make-up of the analysis?

Partially yes, not so much in terms of discarding alternative and plausible economic arguments[33] (these were extensively covered in the scenario analysis) but rather in the final choice between the several possibilities offered by the model. This is by no means to suggest that the choice was not in line with the underlying analysis but perhaps the chosen option was not the only immediately obvious choice.[34] Whether there was an explicit 'back-writing' of the analysis or a less calculated 'massaging' of available knowledge matters only to a certain extent: what is important instead is to highlight if and how the type of answers provided by the process of knowledge-production and the final usage of economics were affected by problem tractability and the level of conflict. The analysis seems to indicate that problem tractability did indeed affect the usage of economic analysis and made the agency shift between instances of strategic substantiating use for some aspects of the modelling exercise and non-use when the situation became less clear. On the other hand, the sustained level of conflict influenced the behaviour of the agency, possibly as regards its view of the most acceptable solution for market-players. In particular, the weight of judicial review in this case is a clear demonstration of the impact of high conflict on knowledge-utilisation.

---

33. This is sometimes the case in impact assessments where all options except for the chosen one are unrealistic.
34. For further details, *see* the above excerpts from the CAT judgement.

Three additional points are worth mentioning at this stage. First, the decision-making process described above shows how the link between knowledge-production and knowledge-utilisation can be very tight throughout the different phases of decision-making; however this is no guarantee that the final use of the produced economic analysis will be in line with initial expectations or that any usage will actually occur, as also foreseen by the explanatory typology. This brings us to the second point: Ofcom should not be seen as a monolithic institution in which all actors have the same approach to knowledge-production and knowledge-utilisation. As effectively described by Brunsson (1989), an organisation can decouple talk and action in an arrangement that the author calls 'hypocrisy':[35] this strategy allows the organisation to survive in an environment of competing demands. In the case of a regulatory agency this could mean distinguishing the production and the internal usage of knowledge from the production and usage presented to the outside world. While formal decision-making procedures such as impact assessment and public consultation limit the extent to which an agency can produce and use entirely different sets of knowledge for a decision, it is also clear that the same piece of evidence can have different uses and thus a different impact across the agency. In the case of Ofcom, the structure of the agency and the division between different levels of decision-making, in particular the separation between the Board, the Policy Executive, and the economic analysis department (known as the Competition Group)[36] or other relevant centres of specialised expertise within Ofcom, is relevant to this. Depending on the weight/importance of the decision, either the whole organisation or only some parts of it are involved. The more important a decision, the more active participation of the highest levels of the organisation is necessary. In the MTR debate, all three tiers of governance took part in the process; this, of course, could have affected the type of considerations driving decision-making. In particular, it seems that the involvement of the Board left room for a broader set of considerations besides the more technical ones that were present when the analysis was produced. But, as we have seen, the connection between talk and action in this case is relatively close as no decision that could not be supported by economic analysis would have been adopted. And, as confirmed by the present and former Board members I interviewed, for highly technical decisions such as the one under examination, the Board always seeks the advice of Ofcom's sectoral experts. Yet, it would be naive to conceive the usage of economic analysis as being uniform across the agency, as highlighted by one of Ofcom's interviewees when distinguishing between the weight of resources invested in economic analysis and the weight of this analysis in the final decision.

Finally, the high risk of appeal and its potential consequences on decision-making deserve some additional words. As mentioned, the MTR debate was, to a certain extent, unprecedented. It was the first time that the agency was confronted

---

35. For further details, *see also* Chapter Two.

36. For a detailed description of Ofcom's structure, *see* Chapter Four.

with such a large number of conflicting demands and this undoubtedly had a tangible effect on the way it approached and managed the MTR review and the production of knowledge, as reflected in some of the interview excerpts above. As explained in Chapter Four, this state of affairs is becoming increasingly common in electronic communications and both the regulator and regulatees reported an increase in litigation and a growing trend for using judicial review as a tactic either to delay the application of a given rule (at best) or (at worst) to tilt the balance of decision-making towards one side rather than the other.[37]

These considerations on judicial review bring to the fore an existing trade-off between the positive incentive that judicial scrutiny generates in terms of transparency, accountability and informed decision-making on the one hand[38] and potentially perverse incentives that the possibility/threat of appeal can bring to the production and use of knowledge. Clearly, judicial review has pushed the regulator to be rigorous when using evidence and to provide a logical and well documented analysis for every decision, thus improving the quality of its rulings, even when some of these efforts are also devoted to the rhetorical make-up of arguments (the additional type of strategic use I identified during fieldwork). In a world of limited resources, however, the potential abuses of judicial review by regulatees also affect quality, this time in the opposite way. In a policy-making context, there needs also to be a certain level of proportionality in terms of resources and depth of the analysis. Investing an increasing amount of money in the production of economic analyses does not always lead to better answers after a certain point. The principle of proportionate analysis, a pillar of evidence-based policy-making, becomes the first victim of one of its allies, judicial review, when the latter is misused. To put it in the words of the regulator:

> [...] it's a question of the standard we are being held by the appeal body, so clearly if you had that experience and you know that the appeal body is going to look at things in great detail and they expect high standards, you end up looking at things in greater detail. And I don't think that it may necessarily make for better decisions, and there is a definite risk to get this rather pseudo-scientific kind of [...] you know, take a price control, I don't know what the right level of this price control is, but we think this is a reasonable level, but once you are setting a price control, it's impossible to actually [...] to be honest you know, I think you could get a pretty sensible price control in reality with pretty high level analysis, you have real review of the costs, think about the other considerations, you pick a reasonable number. You can do fifty times

---

37. This point is reflected in the words of one interviewee: 'they [Ofcom] were getting very annoyed and frustrated and just said "look we can't satisfy you and X" and they just said "we might just go straight to appeal on this." And that's maybe a new thing about the UK, this kind of more, this fact that there are now two sides to issues in industry, there used to be one side, which was the regulated firm...' (Industry 1, November 2009).

38. For additional details on this point and a brief discussion of the relevant literature (e.g. Alemanno 2009; Majone 2010), *see* Chapter Eight.

more work, which is kind of probably what we did do [in the MTR case], and you end up with I suspect a slightly better answer, but probably not a huge amount better; however, it's a much more defensible answer, because on appeal you could show that you looked at this, you looked at that, you looked at the other thing [...] so this is kind of getting a bit out of control, and that's one of our challenges actually, it's to strike the right balance between the amount of time and resource, how many avenues of enquiry you get down and in what level of detail, compared to making it fit for purpose, a decision on an efficient timescale. That's always a difficult balance to strike. (Ofcom 1, November 2009)

An excessive amount of analysis can even become counterproductive, and may turn the very purpose of evidence-based policy-making into a sort of defensive checklist that risks undermining the rationale for adopting clearer and more transparent procedures in the first place. The regulator seems to be aware of that but so is the industry:

And you know, they [the mobile operators] must have really annoyed Ofcom because they [Ofcom] have to cover all their bases. And then economics becomes a huge checklist, did we consider entry barriers? Did we consider concentration? And you know, really, most people would say 'have a think about it, explain yourself, what you think is important, what you did about the important things and what answer you came to.' But that doesn't seem to be enough legally anymore. (Industry 1, November 2009)

Moreover, delaying tactics end up creating regulatory uncertainty, as decisions are dragged from one court to the other and then reviewed, suspended and eventually altered or confirmed again. This is clearly one of the paradoxes in the recent trend of evidence-based policy-making (in the UK context at least) and is a consequence of the fact that policy issues are often zero-sum games on which, no matter the decision, one or more of the parties concerned will lose something.

Ultimately, this raises the question of the future position of the regulator in increasingly complex markets characterised by intense technological change, where competition occurs within and across technological platforms featuring a growing number of market-players making irreconcilable demands. Is the regulator well equipped to survive in such a context? What are the key tools for performing its mandate in an adequate fashion? Is knowledge, and economic knowledge in particular, increasingly important or are there other resources that can be more effective in helping the regulator to perform its duties? How does the reality fit with the duties imposed by legislation on the regulator? Will this lead to more politicisation? Should we expect an increase in cases in which non-use of knowledge is the only way forward? I will turn to these questions in Chapters Seven and Eight.

chapter seven | is the road to hell paved with good intentions? from learning to other uses of economic analysis

Introduction

This third and last empirical chapter covers the 2010 regulatory statement on next-generation networks (NGNs),[1] an ideal test-bed to explore the role of economic analysis in unchartered waters. NGNs officially appeared on the policy agenda in 2004; the 2010 statement was, at the time of writing, Ofcom's latest output on the issue. From the very beginning, this dossier attracted a lot of attention in the telecoms policy community, as NGNs are among the most challenging and disruptive market changes for the regulator and the industry. There was, however, widespread agreement on the fact that NGNs would eventually deliver considerable benefits to consumers and the electronic communications sector as a whole. These expectations of the economic and commercial potential of NGNs underpinned the investment decisions and business strategies of all the parties involved during the first years of the debate. Then, around 2008, technical difficulties, the global financial crisis and a sudden political appetite for superfast broadband deployment turned NGNs into a low priority on the agenda. Whereas NGNs remain indirectly at the core of several debates currently overseen by Ofcom, the demotion of this dossier points to a series of interesting aspects of policy-making and the role of expertise in this process.

Although it focuses mostly on the 2010 statement, this case study will cover the evolution of the debate from 2004–05, when British Telecommunications (BT) first announced its intention to fully replace the existing telecoms network (the old public switched network, also known as PSTN) with a next-generation infrastructure based on the Internet Protocol (IP). The prospective change raised a set of unprecedented and complex technical, economic, commercial and legal issues for electronic communications in the UK. Since then, the debate has considerably changed and some of these challenges have been successfully met;[2] on the other

---

1. *Next Generation Networks (NGNs): Responding to recent developments to protect consumers, promote effective competition and secure efficient investment,* January 2010. The full text of the statement. Online. Available: http://stakeholders.ofcom.org.uk/consultations/ngndevelopments/statement/ (accessed 24 September 2012).

2. By way of example, one of the main technical issues in the first phase of NGN deployment was how to ensure that new and old equipment would 'talk to each other' and allow data transmission. Equipment manufacturers encountered difficulties but, through trial and error, solved the underlying issues. Nowadays, anyone investing in NGNs for the first time would not be faced with such problems.

hand, new questions emerged (for example, on the commercial arrangements to interconnect new and old networks), for which appropriate policy solutions have yet to be found.

In light of the above, in this chapter I will appraise two hypotheses: the first on instrumental learning (H4) for the period 2005-2008; the second on the symbolic or non-use of economic analysis (H3) between 2008 and the 2010 statement.[3]

In terms of the explanatory typology, problem tractability remained low throughout the period. Conversely, the disruptive nature of replacing existing infrastructures and long-standing market equilibria with a whole set of new arrangements predictably affected the level of conflict between communications providers (CPs). At first look, it seems that the tone of the debate was rather exploratory in 2004–5, given the considerable technological uncertainty surrounding the NGN project. According to the explanatory typology, around 2005, the situation was characterised by a combination of low but potentially explosive conflict and limited problem tractability, providing ideal conditions for an instrumental use of economic analysis for learning (H4). However, when the commercial interests of the different market-players became more defined, the level of conflict started to grow, seemingly shifting the NGN episode towards a combination of low problem tractability and high conflict. In the typology, this combination of variables fosters a symbolic or non-use of knowledge (H3). Analysing the evolution of the NGN debate not only allows testing of the initial hypotheses but also gives the opportunity to observe how changes in the selected explanatory variables affect knowledge usage.

As explained in Chapter Three, it is worth noting that instrumental learning (H4) and symbolic/non-use of knowledge (H3) do not automatically imply that the agency will take a regulatory decision at the end of the process (Boswell 2009). While the requirement for a specific decision to be made is necessary under the hypotheses on instrumental (H1) and strategic uses of knowledge (H2),[4] the same does not apply when symbolic usages or learning are at stake. In fact, symbolic usages and non-use of knowledge are decoupled from decision-making.[5] Decoupling can mean that, if taken, a decision is not based on relevant knowledge; but it also covers those instances where knowledge is produced but no real/substantive decision is taken. As regards the fourth hypothesis (H4), in which the agency builds knowledge instrumentally in order to learn, a decision may also be absent.

This chapter is structured as follows: the next section illustrates the features of a next-generation network in technical and economic terms and provides a description of BT's initial plan in 2004. Then, I will give an overview of the two consultations and the regulatory statement issued, up to the point at which the debate for the 2010

3. For an illustration of these hypotheses, *see* above Chapter Three and Schrefler (2010).
4. In those cases, and in line with standard regulatory-impact assessment practice, one of the possible outcomes of decision-making can also be to leave things as they are (this scenario is commonly known as the 'do nothing option'). However, this option would have to be appraised in comparison to other courses of action and adequately justified.
5. For further details, *see* Chapters Two and Three.

statement started. This concludes the first phase of the NGN episode. After this I will move on to cover the second half of the NGN debate and illustrate the content and process behind the 2010 statement. Finally, I will appraise the hypotheses on instrumental learning (H4) and the symbolic/non use of expertise (H3).

Next-generation networks: technical and economic change in uncharted waters

In the past decade, the electronic communications sector has been subject to accelerated technological change, fostered in particular by digitalisation and the development of the internet. Cost-reductions and the new possibilities offered by the digital world boosted innovation and the convergence of different technologies for the provision of services. Once operating in separate realms, cable, internet and telephony have now become competitors and consumer switching between products and the underlying supporting technology is much easier than before (Larouche 2007). New services are regularly introduced and the potential for innovation and, ultimately, for economic growth is considerable. This is reflected in several reports by international organisations such as the European Commission and the OECD (2008, 2009) also in governments' preoccupation with how well their countries are doing on key indicators such as investment, broadband penetration, the uptake of mobile telephony and so on.

In this context, concerns about how to transport data, voice, and media more efficiently become crucial, as existing infrastructure may not be fully fit for future needs, especially in view of the development of new products such as mobile-TV.[6] In very simplified terms, the prospective outcome of ongoing technological changes is an all-IP world (fully based on the Internet Protocol), where the separation between infrastructures (such as cable, telephony) as well as in the provision of services and content would disappear (Kirsch and von Hirschhausen 2008). Currently vertically independent but interconnected networks would become a horizontal structure of IP-based networks. Competition between providers would occur at different layers (for example, infrastructure, content) as shown in Figure 7.1, and would also concern the transmission of bundles of videos, data and voice (Larouche 2007: 17;[7] Renda 2008). These changes will revolutionise the communication markets and access to the internet that we experience today.

---

6. On this point *see* for example 'UK Broadband "not fit" for future', *BBC News*, 1 October 2009. Online. Available: http://news.bbc.co.uk/2/hi/technology/8282839.stm (accessed 24 September 2012).

7. While a detailed discussion of these points falls out of the scope of this book, Larouche (2007: 17–20) points to a series of elements which are crucial to understanding the context in which the NGN debate takes place. In particular, telecom operators risk seeing their networks commodified (with a consequent loss of control of the content going over their network, unless they start competing in the content layer too). They should also expect a combination of technological uncertainty and high uncertainty in future demand patterns; and rents/profits will likely move away towards providers of the content/application layers of the IP architecture, further eroding the profitability of telecoms operators.

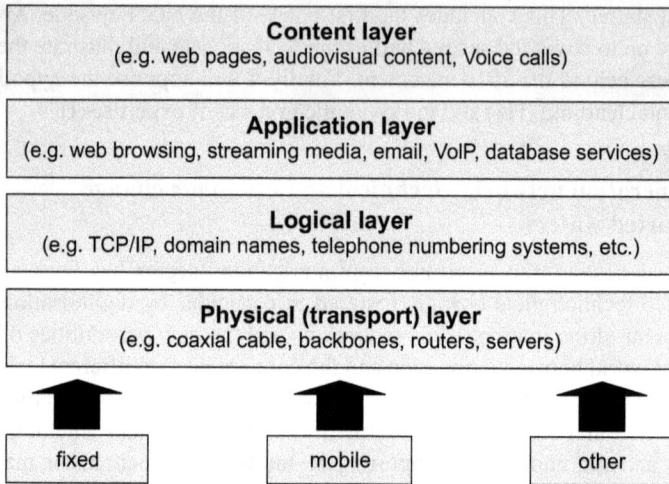

Figure 7.1: Layered architecture of an all-IP network

Source: Renda (2008:7)

Technological convergence not only affects market structures but also has considerable implications for the regulatory landscape (Kirsch and von Hirschhausen 2008;[8] McKenna 2000), as existing rules may become inadequate in an all-IP environment. For example, classical market definitions (in geographical and product terms) to establish whether a player holds significant market power (SMP) could prove inappropriate in this new context. Yet, getting the right regulatory mix in place is essential to avoid distorting incentives to investment and eventually generating negative impacts on competition if, for example, high entry barriers prevent new players from entering the market to offer new or better services. Hence, the challenges facing national regulators are quite daunting: while competition in individual markets (such as voice or data) is likely to increase because of technological convergence, it is also very possible that the horizontal integration of infrastructure, markets and services will lead to greater market-power concentration, as only a limited number of companies will be able to afford to package voice, data and video services in single bundled offers to end-users (OEDC 2008: 5). For a regulator, finding the right balance – between allowing the exploitation of economies of scale to foster infrastructure investment on the one hand and the need to protect competition and consumer choice on the

---

8. In particular, the authors discuss the three possible regulatory paths that a regulator could adopt in case of NGN deployment: unregulated competition, access regulation of integrated companies and structural separation. The theoretical discussion is then followed by an empirical assessment of the two most common regulatory patterns adopted by countries concerned by NGN deployment: promoting specific investments versus protecting competition. The UK belongs to the second group.

other – becomes quite complex, particularly as the speed and depth of potential technological and economic changes has considerably increased.

Features of a next-generation network

Next-generation networks[9] can be described as one of the telecoms sector's responses to the changes in electronic communications described above.

Traditional telecom networks use copper as the transmission medium to connect individual homes and buildings to the network (Crandall *et al.* 2012; OECD 2008: 4). With the uptake of the internet however, data (such as voice) are now transmitted in 'packets' rather than through traditional switches. NGNs are also based on the Internet Protocol (IP) and would serve as multi-purpose, networks allowing the 'packet' transmission of data.[10] In this context, copper is increasingly being replaced with fibre and while the transition from old networks to new ones implies that copper and fibre would have to coexist for some time,

9. The OECD (2008: 9) explains that 'NGNs provide the technical underpinning of convergence, representing a single transport platform on which the carriage of previously distinct service types (video, voice, and data) "converges", together with new and emerging services and applications. While different services converge at the level of digital transmission, the separation of distinct network "layers" (transport, control, service, and applications functions) provides support for competition and innovation at each horizontal level in the NGN structure. At the same time, NGNs also create strong commercial incentives for network operators to bundle, and therefore increase vertical and horizontal integration, leveraging their market power across these layers.' Ofcom defines NGN as 'an upgrade to the core or "backbone" part of the network' (Online. Available: http://stakeholders.ofcom.org.uk/consultations/nga_future_broadband/glossary) and as an 'IP network capable of being used for both voice and data, and in which there is some control over quality of service. The key features of an NGN are that it is a packet-based, multi-service network, which has a clear separation of transport and control, and where the control functions may reside on a physically separate network' (Ofcom 2009d: 84); Finally, the United Nations Agency for information and communication technologies (ITU) defines NGN as 'a packet-based network able to provide telecommunication services and able to make use of multiple broadband, Quality of Service (QoS)-enabled transport technologies and in which service-related functions are independent from underlying transport-related technologies. It enables unfettered access for users to networks and to competing service providers and/or services of their choice. It supports generalized mobility which will allow consistent and ubiquitous provision of services to users.'

10. The difference between NGNs and the internet is explained by the OECD (2008:17–18) in those terms: 'Technological developments associated with next generation networks should help combine the characteristics of the traditional telecommunication model, and of the new internet model, dissolving the current divisions and moving towards a harmonised and coherent approach across different platforms, gradually bringing to full convergence fixed and mobile networks, voice, data services, and broadcasting sectors. In short, in the future the choice of the technology used for the infrastructure or for access will no longer have an impact on the kinds and variety of services that are delivered…The telecommunications tradition emphasises the benefits of higher capacity local fibre access facilities, and powerful network intelligence [...]. On the other hand, the Internet world traditionally focuses on edge innovation and control over network use… The "Internet" still represents different things to different people, and next generation networks are seen as both a possibility for improved services or as a way to constrain the Internet into telecommunication boundaries, adding new control layers, capable of discriminating between different content, and "monetise" every single service accessed.'

eventually copper assets will become obsolete (Larouche 2007: 19). As we will see below, the choice of moving directly to fibre versus using both copper and fibre for a certain period of time depends on the position of each market-player: new market entrants that do not have any assets in the ground have strong incentives to adopt fibre immediately; incumbent and other 'legacy' operators who already own copper-based facilities may prefer a gradual move to fibre, so as to fully exploit their existing assets. The substitution between copper and fibre implies other structural changes to existing infrastructure: for example, an NGN features fewer points of interconnection between different networks (in the UK, interconnection points would decrease from circa 600 to about 30), causing a change in revenue streams when interconnecting networks belong to different companies and these have long-standing arrangements establishing who should ensure interconnection and at what price. In short, operators have different business and profit models depending on the type of technology they use.[11] Finally, the replacement of a copper-based infrastructure with fibre entails significant costs (such as civil works) and it is unlikely that a large number of market-players will have the means to undertake such investment. There is thus a risk of new monopolies, or rather oligopolies, developing,[12] a concern that any regulator would be bound to address.

The disruptive nature of the transition to NGNs can cause a considerable amount of technological and commercial uncertainty among market-players contemplating such a move, as reflected by ongoing debates in standardisation fora across the world. Initially, even the definition of NGNs could not be agreed upon internationally. Amidst such uncertainty, however, there is consensus that NGNs will affect the core/backbone of existing telecoms networks and boost their ability to carry a multitude of services such as video, voice, and data. Also, NGNs should be distinguished from next-generation access networks (NGANs), another response of the telecoms industry to technological convergence and growing competition: NGANs affect the local loop (not the core network) and are commonly associated with the development of high-speed broadband (Cave and Martin 2010) and better quality of service.[13] Policy debates on NGNs and NGANs were closely linked; however, emphasis on one or the other changed with time, as we will see in the coming sections.

To illustrate the magnitude and implications of the technological and commercial shift I have briefly outlined, the key differences between an NGN world and the traditional telecommunications environment are summarised in Table 7.1.

---

11. For a comprehensive description of alternative business models and incentives to invest in NGNs, *see* Bourreau *et al.* (2011).

12. For a legal and theoretical discussion of this concern, also in a global perspective, and a critical view of its implications for society in general, *see* McKenna (2000).

13. As explained by Ofcom, NGANs can be based on 'a number of technologies including cable, fixed wireless and mobile. Most often used to refer to networks using fibre optic technology.' Ofcom's NGN Glossary. Online. Available: http://stakeholders.ofcom.org.uk/consultations/nga_future_broadband/glossary (accessed 24 September 2012).

Table 7.1: An IP-based converged environment

Telcos environment	Next-generation converged environment
Single-purpose networks	Multi-purpose networks
PSTN, cellular, broadcast	IP network (providing voice, video and mobile services)
Narrowband	Broadband
Vertical silos	Destroys compartmentalisation, i.e. traditional boundaries between industry segments (e.g. telephony, cable, TV, broadcasting, wireless) blurring, hence need to rethink market definitions (product definition and geographic boundaries definition)
Network–service link	New services and content developed independently of the network
Operators control services to end-users	Increased consumer control

Source: OECD (2008:8)

While the core issues of the NGN debate are similar around the world, countries are likely to choose different approaches to making traditional telecom networks fit for the future, depending on the characteristics of the national market, the number of players, the geographical distribution of the population and many other factors which fall outside the scope of this book. As is often the case, the UK was among the first movers on NGNs; the debate started in 2004, when BT unveiled its 21st Century Network (21CN) project.

BT's 21st Century Network plan: initial intentions and evolution

BT expressed its intention to build an NGN (known as 21CN) for the first time in June 2004. As noted by Ofcom, this would have undoubtedly represented the biggest change in the market since privatisation and possibly one of the first experiments of this kind in the world (Ofcom 2004: 12). BT wanted to upgrade its PTSN infrastructure and systems, including an complete replacement of the TDM-based[14] voice network, to deliver a single IP-based NGN network. The move was expected to generate £1 billion savings per year by 2008–9 and the total cost of the project was estimated at around £10 billion. At that time, other communication providers had also started planning NGN investments but, given the role of BT's infrastructure for the UK electronic communications market, the company's plans immediately moved centre-stage in the debate.

---

14. Time Division Multiplexing (TDM) is defined by Ofcom in the consultation document (2009: 86) as 'technologies and methods of putting multiple data streams in a single signal by separating each signal into many segments, each having a very short duration. Each individual data stream is re-assembled at the destination based on timing'. TDM networks evolved from the analogue networks of telephone companies and are designed to deliver a steady stream of data, in particular, digitised voice.

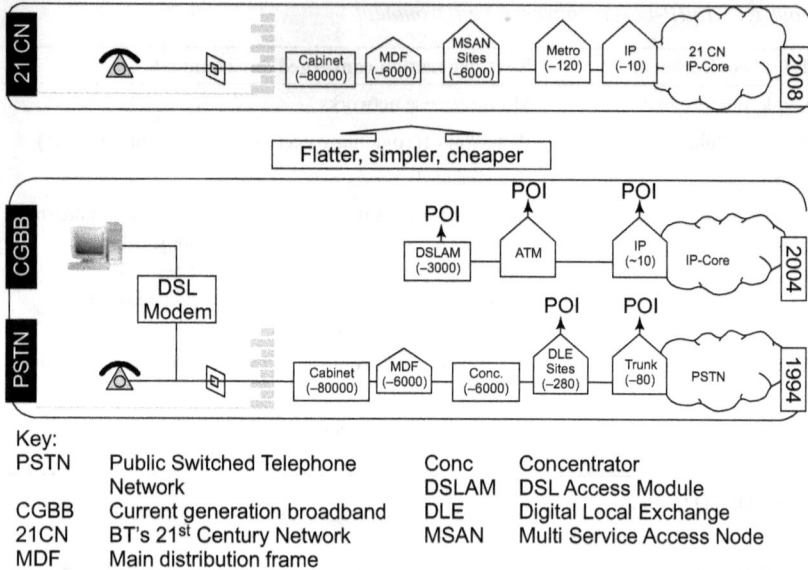

Key:
PSTN	Public Switched Telephone Network	Conc	Concentrator
CGBB	Current generation broadband	DSLAM	DSL Access Module
21CN	BT's 21st Century Network	DLE	Digital Local Exchange
MDF	Main distribution frame	MSAN	Multi Service Access Node

Figure 7.2: Comparison of existing BT and broadband networks with 21CN

Source: Ofcom (2004:12)

Initially, it was thought that the transition to 21CN would happen *en masse* through a series of customer migrations distributed over a time-span of five years or so. After each migration, that part of the old network would be 'switched off'. The milestones initially planned by BT to that effect included a trial in 2004–5 to offer NGN voice services to 1,000 customers in Wales by January 2005; delivering broadband services to 99 per cent of UK homes and businesses by the summer of the same year; and the mass migration from the legacy PTSN voice network starting in 2006 and reaching 50 per cent in 2008. Migration of the remaining customers would have taken place in the following years. The final and expected structure of the 21CN would have looked much flatter than the current PSTN, bringing about efficiencies and better services. For instance, under 21CN, broadband networks would be directly linked to the final user, as shown in Figure 7.2.

Given the prospected impact of 21CN on other communication providers (CPs) in the UK and, ultimately, on the customers of each company, BT also set up a dedicated team for its wholesale clients (other CPs), known as Consult21. This initiative aimed to provide a platform for dialogue with industry, update interested parties on the implementation of 21CN, develop a shared understanding of the implications of the NGN and grant to other communication providers the possibility of providing input and having an impact on the project.

In regulatory terms, as noted by Ofcom, BT's 21CN was also a first: for once, the issue of competition in a network industry could have been addressed from the outset when deploying the incumbent's network (Ofcom 2004: 3), rather than placing the regulator in front of a monopoly as a *fait accompli* to deal with.[15] Also, the roll-out of 21CN implied that the nature and delivery mode of many products and services available at the time both to end-users and to BT's competitors would have to change drastically. On the one hand, the new network offered many possibilities to British consumers in terms of product choice; on the other hand, it had potential incompatibilities with some existing services, such as alarms and telecare equipment. In addition, some features of the original PSTN network could not be fully replicated on an NGN. This raised the question of whether limited replicability is a sufficient reason for a regulator to mandate a faithful replication of these products on the new infrastructure whenever vulnerable users are at stake, despite the fact that this conservative approach could stifle innovation and the search for alternative and possibly better solutions. As regards other communication providers, 21CN implied that some of the SMP wholesale products currently offered by BT (under the Undertakings for example)[16] would become less relevant or possibly disappear in the new infrastructure. This could be the case of some arrangements on access and interconnection to BT's network, thanks to which several of BT's competitors have built their business models and strategies. In most cases, these arrangements are the by-product of years of regulation, commercial negotiations and disputes arbitrated by Oftel or Ofcom. 21CN would have altered those equilibria and it was initially difficult to measure whether and to what extent the final outcome of the move to NGNs would have benefitted or damaged other companies.

Despite the successful migration of the first 1,000 Welsh customers in 2005, BT soon experienced a series of (sometimes) unforeseen technical problems when deploying 21CN. This delayed the company's implementation plan. Around the same time, international benchmarking exercises showed that the UK was lagging behind other OECD countries in terms of broadband usage and deployment. Soon, the question of the country's competitiveness and the potential contribution of superfast broadband to economic growth (Cave and Martin 2010) became prominent on the national agenda. In terms of the explanatory typology, it is fair to say that while NGNs were a salient issue for the telecoms community, superfast broadband became 'the issue' for a much wider audience, leading the Prime Minister to comment:

> Consider the advent of electricity. How acceptable would it have been to say that only some people should have access to electricity? Superfast broadband is the electricity of the digital age. And I believe it must be for all – not just for some. (Digital Economy Bill 2010: 2)[17]

---

15. This is what happened, for example, in 1984, when BT was privatised and the telecoms market liberalised: what was once a public monopoly became a private one.

16. For further details, *see* Chapter Five.

17. On this point, *see also* the 'Digital Britain' report of June 2009. Online. Available: http://www.official-documents.gov.uk/document/cm76/7650/7650.pdf (accessed 23 March 2013). For the prime minister's speech, *see* http://webarchive.nationalarchives.gov.uk/20100407205403/number10.gov.uk/page22897.

This climate gradually strengthened BT's commercial and technical interest in broadband investment and the company started diverting part of its attention and funds to upgrading its access network (NGANs, rather than the core/backbone of the network as in the case of NGNs). Finally, the economic and financial crises of 2008–9 hit the economy, reducing access to funding and pushing all companies to rethink the allocation of resources across projects. This combination of factors amounted to 'the perfect storm', to put it in the words of one of the interviewees, and significantly altered the commercial incentives to invest in NGNs for BT and other legacy operators. It quickly became clear that no mass migration to NGNs would occur in the near future and that old and new networks would co-exist for a transitional period of several years. In turn, this transitional period raised a series of new technical, commercial and policy questions.

Against this background and in light of its duty to promote competition and protect consumers, what was the best course of action for Ofcom? Intervene in some way? Leave everything to market forces? And how could the regulator take such a decision amidst the uncertainty surrounding the future evolution of the 21CN project?

Different regulatory approaches would have triggered different incentives, depending on whether companies were new entrants with no networks in the ground or legacy operators with assets that were not fully depreciated. Also, the UK telecoms market is competitive in many respects (House of Lords 2007; NAO 2002, 2010). This is also due to the commercial and regulatory arrangements mentioned above, some of which could potentially cease to exist in an NGN world. Ultimately, Ofcom's choices would have had an impact on technological innovation, infrastructure investment and deployment, the type and number of market-players and, more generally, on economic growth and the competitiveness of the UK. Clearly, different types of knowledge were needed to tackle those questions and guide the regulator in addressing rather intractable policy issues with a high conflict potential. Let us see how Ofcom proceeded.

The first phase: the NGN debate between 2005 and 2008

Following BT's announcement of 21CN in June 2004, Ofcom decided to adopt an exploratory approach, as shown by the official consultation documents and the statement of that period.[18] The first consultation was published towards the end of 2004 and aimed at gaining a better understanding of the regulatory and competitive implications of BT's NGN project. Ofcom made clear that its main

---

18. *Next Generation Networks: Future arrangements for access and interconnection* (consultation, 2004). Online. Available: http://stakeholders.ofcom.org.uk/consultations/ngn/; responses available: http://stakeholders.ofcom.org.uk/consultations/ngn/?showResponses=true. *Next Generation Networks: Further consultation* (2005). Online. Available: http://stakeholders.ofcom.org.uk/consultations/nxgnfc/; responses available: http://stakeholders.ofcom.org.uk/consultations/nxgnfc/?showResponses=true. statement*Next Generation Networks: Developing the regulatory framework* (March 2006), available: http://stakeholders.ofcom.org.uk/binaries/consultations/nxgnfc/statement/ngnstatement.pdf (accessed September 25 2012).

objective was to provide clarity on the policy requirements needed to ensure competition, particularly on access and interconnection to BT's network. Without interfering in BT's and other communication providers' plans, Ofcom wanted to guarantee that market-players were aware of the constraints within which they were to design their networks. Ofcom also clarified the key policy principles it intended to apply[19] to stimulate the debate on how to implement them but stressed that it had no intention of detailing a preferred policy solution at that point. This approach was also in line with Ofcom's obligation to follow the principle of technological neutrality, which stipulates that legal rules should not favour or discriminate against a specific technological solution.[20]

The exploratory tone of the consultation[21] signals that problem tractability was quite low: many issues were technical in nature and the future evolution of BT's plan and the reaction of its competitors could not be fully apprehended. Low problem tractability is also reflected in the seventy-two questions included in the consultation, an unusually high number when compared to the other cases covered in this book. As regards the level of conflict, there were potentially clashing interests between market-players and a fear that BT could re-monopolise infrastructure. However, NGNs could have also represented a solution to existing technological bottlenecks, thus solving some persistent conflicts in the market. As explained by Ofcom:

---

19. These principles were those developed in the previous *Strategic Review of the Telecoms Market* and state that Ofcom should: 1. Promote competition at the deepest levels of infrastructure, where it will be effective and sustainable; 2. Focus regulation to deliver equality of access beyond those levels; 3. As soon as competitive conditions allow, withdraw from regulation at other levels; 4. Promote a favourable climate for efficient and timely investment and stimulate innovation, in particular by ensuring a consistent and transparent regulatory approach; 5. Accommodate varying regulatory solutions for different products and where appropriate, different geographies; 6. Create scope for market entry that could, over time, remove economic bottlenecks; and 7. In the wider communications value chain, unless there are enduring bottlenecks, adopt light-touch economic regulation based on competition law and the promotion of interoperability (Ofcom 2004: 3).

20. The principle of technological neutrality was introduced at the EU level in 1999 with the European Commission's Communication Review 'Towards a new framework for Electronic Communications infrastructure and associated services. The 1999 Communications Review', COM(1999)539 (European Commission 1999). It stipulates that 'legislation should define the objectives to be achieved, and should neither impose, or discriminate in favour of, the use of a particular type of technology to achieve those objectives'. The application of this principle has wide-ranging implications, particularly as its interpretation may vary. On this point, *see*, for instance, Reed (2007).

21. For example, Ofcom explains (2004: 14): 'The scope of this consultation is necessarily very wide. Given this wide remit, the current focus is on identifying issues, and guiding principles for their resolution, rather than on presenting particular solutions. Solutions are more likely to be effective if they are determined by industry, through a process of commercial negotiation, than if they are determined by regulatory intervention.'

Regulation of NGNs should not simply be seen as a 'zero-sum' game, where Ofcom's primary concern is to decide how the benefits of BTs investment in 21CN should be divided between BT and the rest of industry. Instead, the aim should be to promote a favourable investment climate for industry as a whole [...](Ofcom 2004: 5)

Responses were submitted by twenty-two stakeholders representing different types of organisations, ranging from industry to local government. Overall, with some exceptions, stakeholders only covered the questions that were relevant to their case and most commented on the general policy principles outlined by Ofcom. No statement was issued at the end of this process. Instead, Ofcom published a second consultation document in 2005 and commissioned an external study to investigate the possible role of a new and dedicated NGN body.[22]

The second consultation aimed to provide a response to the regulatory issues that had emerged in 2004 and to establish a regulatory framework to address them. Specifically, Ofcom put forward eighteen questions on a series of policy principles and processes. At the same time, Ofcom re-confirmed its intention to avoid micromanaging the move to NGNs, which would remain an industry-driven process. In this new document, the issues raised in the first consultation are still described as uncertain (that is, with low tractability)[23] and any specific decision by Ofcom as premature. Essentially, Ofcom's goal remained to deliver regulatory certainty to market-players wishing to embark on the NGN adventure. For each of the issues discussed in this second consultation, Ofcom specified whether they would be dealt with through the Undertakings signed with BT (*see* Chapter Five) or under the agency's existing powers. Ofcom's role in the process is summarised in Figure 7.3. As the figure shows, no regulatory decision was envisaged at that time.

The consultation also suggests a set of governance arrangements to facilitate the transition to NGNs. These are based on the co-ordinated work of a series of entities: besides the Undertakings governing access to BT's wholesale products for the company's competitors and traditional dispute procedures, discussions on the development of present and future interconnection products would take place within Consult21 (the team set up by BT to interact with industry). The development of technical standards would be the task of the Network Interoperability Consultative Committee (NICC); finally, Ofcom envisaged the creation of an independent industry-owned body (NGNCo, later known as NGNuk) 'to take ownership of the transition from existing to NGN networks, including operational planning and oversight, consumer protection, and development of new models for interconnection' (Ofcom 2005b: 7). The relationship between those bodies is illustrated in Figure 7.4.

---

22. This report, produced by Spectrum Strategy Consultants. Online. Available: http://stakeholders. ofcom.org.uk/consultations/nxgnfc/ngn/ (accessed 25 September 2012).

23. For further details on the difference between problem tractability and uncertainty, *see also* Chapter Three.

What	How
Help to identify and clarify potential regulatory issues early on	November 04 consultation, this consultation and ongoing dialogue with stakeholders
Establish clear governing policy rules to support NGN based competition	This consultation and subsequent statement in conjunction with our Enterprise Act consultation/statement on undertakings
Establish policy framework for consumer protection and information	This consultation and subsequent work on communication plan
Ensure appropriate industry led processes are established	This consultation and ongoing discussions with stakeholders
Ensure industry led processes stay on track	Ongoing informal monitoring and dialogue with BT and other providers
Resolution of competition issues when industry processes fail	Formal market reviews and *ex post* competition powers as required
Updating *ex ante* regulatory framework to take account of NGNs	Ongoing programme of market reviews (e.g. updating market definitions, remedies and de-regulating as appropriate)

Figure 7.3: Ofcom's role in the move to next-generation networks

Source: Ofcom (2005b: 10)

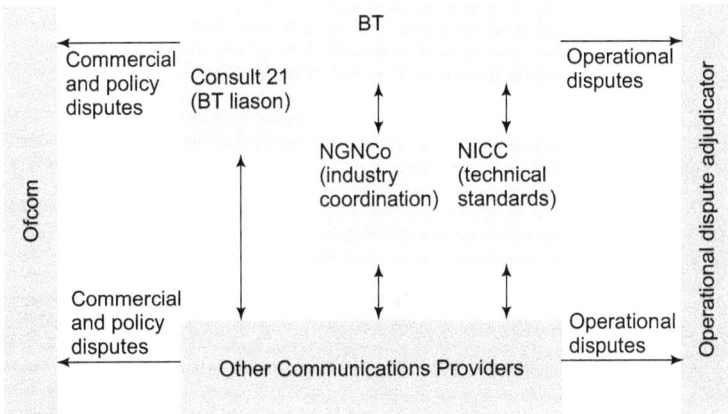

Figure 7.4: Overview of NGN process proposal

Source: Ofcom (2005b: 7)

Again, twenty-two contributions came from all sorts of stakeholders. As views diverged on the possible remit and mandate of NGNCo/NGNuk, an additional consultation was launched on that topic. Eventually, the regulatory statement *Next-Generation Networks: Developing the regulatory framework* was published in March 2006. Most of the interviewees for this case study described it as a 'high-level policy piece', establishing general and broad principles but no concrete proposal besides the creation of NGNuk. As a matter of fact, the statement did not contain a regulatory impact assessment precisely because no regulatory proposal was being considered. As regards the new industry body, the statement clarified that NGNuk should focus initially on IP interconnection architecture, the related commercial model, and issues of network intelligence interoperability. The statement also specified that NGNuk would have a limited lifespan and spelled out its governance structure and position *vis-à-vis* Ofcom. Finally, the statement listed the related policy and regulatory decisions on which Ofcom intended to act in order to develop the *ex-ante* framework for NGNs, as well as the next steps in addressing emerging consumer-protection issues. The proposed workplan for both is presented in Figure 7.5.

For the purposes of the analysis, the two consultations described above and the 2005 statement can be seen as the conclusion of the first phase of the NGN case. In a way, this view was shared by interviewees and supported by the ensuing turn of events. As mentioned, the first experiments with NGN roll-out raised a series of issues which, on the one hand, increased actors' understanding of the functioning and implications of the new network. On the other hand, practical experience generated a series of new problems. Also, this is the period in which all the factors leading to the 'perfect storm' described in the previous section came to the fore.

When asked to compare the present situation with the 2005–8 period, each and every interviewee replied something along the lines of 'things did not work out as planned': BT slowed down its 21CN roll-out programme and stated explicitly that it would not be able to provide information on its plans beyond the next eighteen months (instead of the three to five years initially envisaged when the 21CN project was launched). While two operators (TalkTalk and Sky) had already built their own NGN networks, also on the assumption that BT would complete 21CN, other players in the market had adopted different strategies and were now faced with the need to rethink their priorities.

One thing was certain, though: new and legacy networks would co-exist for a longer period of time than originally planned, opening a whole series of new issues that could alter the tractability of the problem and the level of conflict in the policy arena.

The other uncontested element in this scenario is that the combined effect of growing demand for superfast broadband, political pressure and limited access to finance after the 2008–9 crisis made investment in next-generation access networks (NGANs) the new priority for many communication providers, including BT. This move was further reinforced by a growing awareness that fibre would quickly supersede copper-based alternatives (the use of copper was still foreseen

NGN Issues	Next steps
Market and product convergence in backhaul	To be considered in converged backhaul market review starting in Spring 2006
Market and product convergence in access	To be considered in 2007 converged access review
CPS, WLR, IA and future narrowband access	To be considered in voice access and origination market review starting towards the end of 2006
Evolution of narrowband call conveyance	Issues to be addressed as part of independent study into distance gradients, converged backhaul market review and voice access and origination market review
Next generation wholesale broadband	To be considered in 2006 broadband market review
Implication of NGNs for distance gradients	Publish independent study on NGN distance gradients (March 2006)
Consumer Issues	**Ofcom's next steps**
Service disruption during NGN migration	Monitor the effectiveness of the responsible industry group (currently Consult21 Implementation and Migration Working Group) and contribute where necessary
Communication to consumers about NGN migration	Continue to participate in the industry communications working group
Management of end-to-end call quality	Work with industry to ensure there are adequate processes to manage and co-ordinate this issue
Emergency call prioritisation	Continue to monitor this issue
Text relay services	Commission a study into feasibility of alternative relay services
Emergency call location	Monitor technical work and address in VoIP consultation
Number portability	Review as part of General Conditions review
Network integrity	Withdrawal of the essential requirements guidelines in VoIP consultation in favour of relying on the reasonably practical test in General condition 3
Social alarms and telecare systems	If necessary, we will help to ensure there is adequate dialogue between NGN providers and telecare system suppliers
New NGN related consumer issues	Considered in recent consultation on VoIP services. Further research and analysis to understand future risks to consumers
Continuity for large business customers	Support pro-active engagement between affected customers and their suppliers

Figure 7.5: Ofcom's work to develop the ex-ante framework for NGNs and address consumer-protection issues

Source: Ofcom (2006a:32 and 38)

for some parts of 21CN), making a direct investment in fibre more appealing. Finally, NGANs are expected to bring return on investment within a shorter time than NGNs and tend to be less subject to demand uncertainty.[24] All in all, this sounded like a death sentence for NGNs. It is at this point that the second part of the case study starts.

The second phase: the 2010 statement

The unforeseen turn of events described in the previous section led Ofcom to launch a third consultation in July 2009, to take stock of the situation and explore the implications of BT's change of plans. The title of the consultation document *Next-Generation Networks: Responding to recent developments to protect consumers, promote effective competition and secure efficient investment* speaks for itself.[25] Starting from the premise that 'it now seems more likely that NGNs will be adopted gradually, forming part of the wider evolution of network technologies, and with many opportunities for changes in direction along the way' (Ofcom 2009d: 1), the consultation had two objectives: 1) outlining Ofcom's response to the recent changes in BT's 21CN; and 2) updating stakeholders on the agency's thinking as regards consumer-protection issues in the new circumstances. After all, in the previous documents, consumer-protection principles were developed under the assumption that a mass migration to NGNs would occur, something that is not likely to materialise in the coming years. Against this background, Ofcom identified three trends with potentially significant effects on competition and regulation: investments in NGANs; growth in mobile data services; and an increased use of software-based communications services (such as voice-over-IP). The consultation document also contains a chapter and a series of questions on the longer-term implications of a widespread adoption of NGNs and asks for feedback on whether there is anything that the regulator should do today 'to cater for this future world'. The tone of the consultation is again exploratory, as shown also in the way more technical questions (for example, interconnection arrangements) are treated. When present, economic analysis often consists of 'hypothetical' reasoning on a set of different scenarios.

The sixteen consultation questions range from general topics on the evolution

---

24. Specifically, NGNs would deliver cost savings and benefits in the long term and these may become apparent only after costs have increased for a period of time. Also, the second key ingredient in the business case for NGNs is the expected benefits stemming from the development of new services. However, the benefits brought about by these yet unidentified services will depend on future demand for them. In short, there is a high risk that, in the short term, NGN will not deliver cost savings or the expected benefits. In contrast, demand for superfast broadband (NGAN investment) is more certain, although still fraught with risk, as explained by Cave and Martin (2010). For further details, *see* Ofcom's 2009 consultation document (Ofcom 2010d).

25. The official text of the consultation. Online. Available: http://stakeholders.ofcom.org.uk/binaries/consultations/ngndevelopments/summary/main.pdf; and the consultation responses at /stakeholders.ofcom.org.uk/consultations/ngndevelopments/?showResponses=true (accessed 25 September 2012).

of competition models in the next three to five years, to general consumer-protection principles, long-term trends and more specific issues, such as interconnection arrangements between IP and TDM networks, the development of certain wholesale products and the compatibility of telecare and alarm equipment with the new NGN infrastructure.

Twenty-three stakeholders, including some individuals, submitted a contribution. The respondents are not quite the same as for the previous consultation rounds, indicating a slight change in the policy arena's composition. Rather predictably, the nature and depth of comments varies and reflect the uncertainty and broad scope of the NGN debate when compared to the other cases covered in this book. Among respondents, communication providers submitted the more comprehensive contributions and one can easily distinguish new entrants who had deployed NGNs by 2009 (TalkTalk and Sky) from others, be they legacy operators or new entrants with no infrastructure. As mentioned, given the role of BT's network in competitors' business plans, all are affected by the incumbent's projects.

Trying to summarise all the issues raised by consultation respondents would not do justice to the variety of the views expressed; however, the coding exercise allowed me to single out some recurring themes. Specifically, all respondents take BT's change of plans as the starting point of their contribution, although views on whether the move away from the 21CN project is a positive or negative development vary. Supporters of broadband deployment (for example, BBBritain) consider this change of plans as an opportunity for a more meaningful allocation of resources. Contrariwise, those who had invested in NGNs or whose business models assumed a timely roll-out of 21CN (for example, Cable&Wireless) described the current situation as a waste of time and effort. All were in agreement that the current situation was again very uncertain, although some indicated that, this time, the regulator had stronger grounds for acting than in 2004–5, as the nature of the problems was likely to remain stable for a number of years.

As explained in Chapter Three, uncertainty is a broader concept than problem tractability and, while it does sometimes overlap with the explanatory variable (that is, the degree of agreement on the knowledge for solving a policy problem and the level of certainty about the consequences of a given course of action), in other instances it refers to a different set of issues. In the case of NGNs, stakeholders often mention uncertainty in connection with technical problems linked to the deployment of the new infrastructure; or they point out that business plans were difficult to establish in the wake of the financial crisis and the short-term planning horizon provided by BT. Only Ofcom's interviewees referred to uncertainty in terms of the clarity of applicable policy principles and rules, here again pointing to a different conception of uncertainty from the one implied by my explanatory variable.

As regards stakeholder comments on the latter, there is a consensus between views in all the documents and interviews that touch upon this aspect: problem tractability is low, albeit evolving in terms of the issues to be solved. In fact, under this heading are two of the most frequently recurring themes of the consultation.

The first problematic question is whether NGN technology should be considered as 'proven' (that is, the most efficient way to deliver a given service) or not. Deciding this point is crucial as, when a technology is proven, Ofcom should use it as a basis in cost models and economic analyses underpinning regulatory decisions.[26] Conversely, if a technology is not proven, the regulator should respect the principle of technological neutrality. As we will see in the coming section, deciding on this aspect also sheds light on how Ofcom perceives its role and on the expectations of external actors in the policy arena.

In 2009, Ofcom did not consider NGN the proven or most efficient technology for voice services and thus developed a model for calculating charges to be levied between operators on the basis of the old TDM technology. As we will see, this gave different incentives to providers, depending on whether they were new entrants or owners of a legacy network. This issue is directly related to a second and, possibly, less tractable question for the consultation: interconnection between legacy and IP networks. This question can, in fact, be separated in two parts: 1) who should be responsible for physically converting, let us say, a telephone call from BT's old network to an NGN-based one or vice-versa? and 2) who should bear the cost of such an operation?

The content of the consultation responses is also closely linked to the second explanatory variable, the level of conflict in the policy arena. While one of the main points of contention is again on interconnection arrangements, conflict remains distinct from problem tractability. In the case of problem tractability, interconnection is expressed in terms of what the most appropriate regulatory strategy would be. In turn, this question is linked to the broader issue of whether Ofcom should incentivise a faster move to NGNs, or instead let the market take care of things. Conversely, when looking at interconnection from a conflict perspective, the focus moves to the different commercial strategies and business models of market-players. This distinction is further strengthened by the fact that, from the beginning of the NGN debate in 2004, Ofcom had decided to leave the design of interconnection arrangements to commercial negotiations. Whether this approach was still appropriate under the new circumstances is a question at the heart of the 2009 consultation responses and may explain the apparent convergence of the two explanatory variables: in the face of changed conditions, market-players move the object of conflict back to the regulator's table, by reframing the issue in terms of the regulator's role in promoting/not promoting NGNs. In fact, most respondents stressed that commercial negotiations were not working and asked the regulator to provide a stronger framework and guidance. Some (for example, BSIA, ENA) also requested a new forum for debating other NGN-related issues.

Another point of conflict raised in the consultation was the future development of wholesale products provided by BT to its competitors. Several respondents explained that some of the products currently purchased by BT's competitors to

---

26. This approach stems from recommendations at the EU level and from the results of recent judicial review cases in the UK.

serve their customers (such as SMPF)[27] might not be provided or improved by BT in the future, when the company would not need them for its NGN infrastructure. Among other things, Ofcom analysed the case for developing xMPF (a voice-only complement to present access products, possibly cheaper than current solutions) and concluded that, while the agency remained open to new input on the topic, it would be premature to mandate its development on the basis of current evidence. Predictably, some respondents disagreed on this point.

Finally, two respondents elaborated more broadly the significant costs of deploying an NGN and the related risk of greater market concentration and reduced competition.

After reviewing the contributions and some additional in-house work, Ofcom issued its final statement in January 2010, maintaining its views broadly unchanged. As expected, the statement did not contain any policy decisions but rather responded to the points raised during the consultation, outlined Ofcom's future work plan on key issues such as interconnection arrangements, concluded that reciprocal charging between NGNs and legacy networks remained appropriate and provided additional support to the conclusion that there was no evidence to mandate xMPF for the time being.

Shifting conditions? shifting uses of knowledge?

At the start of this chapter I explained that, *prima facie*, the NGN debate between 2004 and 2010 seemed to move from a state of low problem tractability and limited but potentially explosive conflict to a combination of low tractability and high conflict. According to the explanatory typology, these two scenarios have different implications for knowledge-utilisation, with the former being conducive to (instrumental) learning (H4), while the second is likely to foster a symbolic or a non-use of knowledge. To appraise the hypotheses more in depth, let us see whether this initial impression is confirmed by a closer analysis of the documents coded for this case study and by interview transcripts.

The dynamic nature of conflict and problem tractability in the NGN case

All actors involved in this episode shared the view that problem tractability remained low for the whole duration of the NGN debate, even after BT decided to

---

27. Shared Metallic Path Facility (SMPF) 'relies on the fact that a copper line is split to allow the use of physically separate equipment for voice and broadband' (Ofcom 2009d: 3). SMPF provides access only to the broadband part of the line and is the current basis of competition for broadband-only products offered by BT's competitors. Some communication providers push for the development of a complementary facility for voice only, known as xMPF, to support competition in the voice market. Currently, competition in the voice market is achieved thanks to the availability at the wholesale level of a product called Wholesale Line Rental (WLR), while converged broadband/voice products from BT's competitors use either WLR+ SMPF (the combination used by BT), or MPF (which is believed to be more economically attractive by competitors).

set aside the 21CN project and concentrate on NGANs and superfast broadband deployment. Coded documents and interviews also confirm that the nature of problem tractability changed with time: initially, there was little clarity on the future course of events and this led the regulator to adopt an exploratory, 'green paper' approach. Several interviewees viewed Ofcom's exploratory attitude as an appropriate choice, given the technical and commercial uncertainty surrounding the prospected transition to NGNs and the absence of knowledge/evidence pointing to a clear set of actions. In some instances, the very nature of the problems to be tackled was unclear. Once BT stepped back from rolling out 21CN and it became evident that old and new networks would co-exist for some time, a whole series of new questions on interconnection arrangements and on the appropriateness of incentivising NGN roll-out came to the fore. These issues are undoubtedly more concrete than those that surfaced in the beginning of the NGN debate. This does not make them automatically more tractable, however. As mentioned, these apparently more technical questions move the debate to a different level, raising problems about the role of the regulator in the market.

The dynamic nature of problem tractability and the expectations it placed on Ofcom are reflected in the sources coded for the 2010 statement. As always, views differed. For instance, COLT Telecommunications believed that problem tractability was further reduced, given that clarity on what constitutes an efficient operator was bound to diminish in the future.[28] For ISTPA instead, following the deployment of NGNs by TalkTalk and Sky, IP technology should be seen as proven (most efficient), hence removing doubt about what the regulator should do in terms of interconnection charges. While the question of proven technology lingered in the background, all seemed to agree that the boundaries of the problems to be addressed were better defined in 2009, as shown by the following interview excerpts:

> The issues to be sorted out are getting more concrete over time. (Industry 3, January 2011)

> What has changed over the past five years is that those concerns have become more crystallised, operators and Ofcom are starting to understand what they are in light of the lack of network evolution at some operators. As these issues progress, operators and Ofcom are showing more and more certainty about how they wish to approach those issues. There is a set of issues that are important today that are probably not the same ones or exactly the same ones as they were five years ago. (Industry 4, January 2011)

When questioned on problem tractability, Ofcom's representative focused on the regulator's intention to provide regulatory clarity and the difficulty of doing so in a changing context:

---

28. In 2005, there was widespread agreement that NGNs would be more efficient than current technical solutions. Given the envisaged co-existence of old and new networks in the coming years, COLT believes it is increasingly difficult to decide which is the proven/most efficient technology.

So we were doing this work whilst all this was changing, when all these changes were taking place, and the contentious issues that we were trying to deal with were relatively tactical, they were relatively more concerned with how does the fact that BT is now not going to move its core network to NGN, how does that affect its competitors who have moved to NGN, they have to now connect with this [...] In 2005 I think it's fair to say Ofcom foresaw a brave new world in which networks would be IP within four or five years, costs would fall, new services would be made possible, and so on and so forth, but reality didn't work out that way [...] I guess our main focus was to try and create a framework that would allow competition to [...] competitors to continue to invest and BT to continue to invest, and try and strike a balance that allows that to happen, even though the technologies were now rather mixed and the direction of network evolution was rather unclear. So we were anxious and appeared to be anxious not to say what the right answer is. Is the right way to build networks to use IP or is it to use TDM? There isn't a right answer. (Ofcom 1, December 2010)

To be quite blunt, Ofcom was faced with a 'real mess'.

As mentioned, the two explanatory variables (the level of conflict and problem tractability) revolve around similar points in the NGN case, although the issues concerned are framed differently, at least by the regulator, depending on which variable is at stake. The impression of overlap is mostly created by stakeholders' comments as, for obvious reasons, their remarks are phrased in terms of commercial interests: in the face of intractable issues that cannot be answered with traditional economic models (or other types of relevant expertise), prospective profits and losses naturally become the guiding principle to assess the situation. Moreover, conflicting demands can only be fully articulated when there is clarity on which issues actually constitute sources of conflict. This is reflected in the fact that, in this episode, the level of conflict changed more between 2005 and 2010 than did problem tractability. Initially, BT's 21CN plans were met by communication providers with some (technical and commercial) apprehension rather than with open conflict. The magnitude of the prospective change made its implications difficult to grasp in full. As a result, the positions of different market-players in the policy arena were not completely established around 2005, although it was clear that conflict would eventually emerge concerning the different ways of managing transition to an NGN world. With time, BT's change of plans and NGN deployment by Sky and TalkTalk, opposing teams started to form. According to one Ofcom interviewee (interview of September 2010), as soon as things became clearer, conflict rose as well: NGN became yet another case of a zero-sum game, despite the initial hope that in the 'brave new world' in prospect in 2005 this scenario could be avoided. The other Ofcom interviewee confirmed that there was now a lot of conflict potential between BT and TalkTalk on interconnection; however, conflict might decrease in the future because 'BT is not doing anything in this area, so issues have become much smaller' (interview of December 2010). Interestingly, the consultation document stated that, in 2009, there was less pressure on Ofcom to intervene, following BT's decision to focus on NGANs and the fact that companies which took the NGN route, regardless of the incumbent's plans, remained profitable.

In any event, the coding exercise confirms two things: 1) in 2009, conflict was high and revolved around clearly identified commercial interests; and 2) the debate on and political attention to superfast broadband and NGANs noticeably affected the case for NGNs, although comments could be more or less explicit on the nature of such impact. Specifically, all interviewees stressed that Ofcom's political principals (BSI and DCMS)[29] kept clear of the NGN debate. For some however, the case of superfast broadband was a different story. Some referred to it as a 'political priority'; others called it 'the hot potato': the underlying message is clear: commercial and/or political considerations generated pressure to focus on NGANs, for both BT and the regulator. No one claims that there was potential for institutional friction on policy priorities between Ofcom and the ministry; however, the salience of the broadband dossier was difficult to ignore, as reflected in the following quotation:

> I think there is consensus in the industry that this is not the complete picture, that there was sort of willingness by the political establishment for BT to be seen to be deploying fibre and to ensure [...] all the big political words around maintaining the competitiveness of the country in relation to other countries, you get a bit the arms raised mentality between politicians: the other countries deploy fibre and the UK has to although there is probably very little economic justification for rolling-out fibre as quickly as it's being done. But that debate [NGN] has been, gone and lost, and now we are where we are [...]. I think NGA deployment is a bigger policy issue on Ofcom's plate and presumably a commercial one for BT as well. The key objective for Ofcom is to ensure that BT continues on its fibre access deployment programme. (Industry 2, January 2011)

This is the first time that the intervening variable of issue salience has a bearing on a specific case.[30] In Chapter Three I explained that high saliency is likely to affect conflict rather than problem tractability, as it normally broadens the size of the policy arena: salient issues attract more attention, hence more actors and potentially conflicting demands in the debate (Gormley 1986; Jennings and Hall 2011; Yesilkagit and van Thiel 2011). This mechanism operated in reverse fashion for NGNs: by becoming a hot topic on the policy agenda, superfast broadband turned NGNs into a lower priority, relieving Ofcom from pressure to act immediately on a difficult dossier. In turn, this created some space for a symbolic

---

29. *See* above Chapter Four.

30. As explained in Chapter Three, my typology also features a second intervening variable, the capacity of the agency in terms of available human and financial resources. The analysis of Ofcom as an organisation and the information I have collected on the agency led me to conclude that Ofcom's capacity is high and remained so in all the episodes covered in this book. This is why this variable is not discussed in the individual case studies, although it remains a constant presence to be taken into account in the analysis. For further details on this point, *see* Chapter Four.

or even a non-use of economic expertise.

Before I turn to a more detailed appraisal of the two hypotheses on instrumental learning (H4) and a symbolic/non-use of economics (H3), let me briefly describe the type of expertise used in the debate. Our coding exercise indicates that the novelty of NGNs required a mix of technical (engineering), economic and general policy expertise. Economic expertise is intended by respondents in a broader sense and includes commercial knowledge, that is, an understanding of the business models of the different competitors on the market:

> Probably the most important thing is understanding the way the industry works, not so much in a technical sense but in the commercial sense [...] I would not describe it as economics, I would describe it as understanding the reality facing different operators, and that is a mix of the economic environment and the technical environment, and also the commercial practice. (Ofcom 1, December 2010)

This mix of competence remained stable even after BT's change of plans. While people working on the case inside Ofcom changed, the core disciplines didn't. Against this background, it is fair to say that, although the focus of this book is on the use of economic analysis, the remarks that follow apply to all the types of expertise marshalled in and outside the agency to deal with the NGN case.

Knowledge-utilisation in the NGN case

Overall, the exploratory tone of the official documents produced by Ofcom since 2004 seems to indicate that the agency was interested in learning and in improving its coping skills in the face of a rather intractable and potentially explosive issue. This fits with expectations regarding hypothesis H4 on instrumental learning. That is, until the turning point of this episode (BT's change of plans), when the internal dynamics of problem tractability and conflict changed. However, despite the new circumstances, the 2009 consultation and the 2010 statement remain fairly exploratory in nature, as if circumstances had sent Ofcom back to the drawing board. The consultation states explicitly that there was not enough evidence to justify any change in regulation; the statement confirmed that:

> Respondents offered a wide range of comments on the longer-term evolution of NGNs, whilst acknowledging that this was very uncertain. We have not identified a specific issue for us to address in relation to the longer-term evolution of NGNs following the Consultation. (Ofcom 2010a: 6)

Also, the regulator is keen to confirm that market solutions are preferable for the time being, although there is a declared intention to gather additional evidence in the near future to evaluate whether this approach remains appropriate. In other words, Ofcom's official narrative of the NGN case points to an instrumental usage of knowledge, essentially geared to learning (H4). This account matches the impressions of the interviewees for what concern the first part of the debate and Ofcom's initial approach is openly praised even by some of its most fervent critics:

They effectively adopted a 'wait and see' approach [...] I think that's how it started, and even now it is still not a very detailed policy, it's still quite high level [...] Therefore, originally at least, interconnection disputes and market definitions did not necessarily need to alter in order for the industry to function. So it was only right that Ofcom would start off with a green approach to NGNs, and try and arrive at a regime that allowed the market and technology to evolve naturally, without Ofcom pre-defining a solution, or setting some sort of regulation that would have prohibited another type of technology from developing [...](Industry 4, January 2011)

As a matter of fact, of the three episodes covered in this book, this is the only one for which learning patterns are mentioned by interviewees, not only in relation to Ofcom but also to industry. Transition to NGN was, indeed, like navigation in uncharted waters and all seem to accept a certain amount of trial and error and the fact that it would have been premature for Ofcom to take any position in 2004–5. However, appreciation for the regulator's approach gradually decreased following the progressive clarification of market-players' positions. At the time of the 2009 consultation, besides BT and FCS (which supported Ofcom's *laissez-faire* approach) and two other respondents who concurred with the regulator's claim that there was not enough evidence to take a decision, all other stakeholders believed that Ofcom was not doing enough. In this respect, the same interviewee who praised Ofcom's green approach also added:

I think that in terms of Ofcom's approach, in hindsight, they should probably on the one hand congratulate themselves that they did not weigh in too heavily in response to BT's embryonic 21CN programme because the plans ended up being dramatically scaled down. Whether they would ever acknowledge that they might be setting the incentives inappropriately for BT as well is another question entirely. (Industry 4, January 2011)

In particular, given that interconnection disputes will be on the table for the next few years and current venues for commercial negotiation do not seem to work, several respondents found Ofcom's inaction unjustified.

Under those circumstances, was *laissez-faire* still the most desirable approach, thus signalling an instrumental use of knowledge? Or was inaction driven by the fact that (political and commercial) priorities lay elsewhere, for example in superfast broadband? In that case, Ofcom's 2009 consultation and the 2010 statement could essentially have been means of keeping track of market developments and responding to mounting discontent, even though the agency had no real intention to act on the situation. If that were the case, would this be enough to conclude that we are witnessing a symbolic use of knowledge? Finally, what if Ofcom had enough evidence to act at least on some of the most pressing issues (such as interconnection), but decided to do nothing for various reasons? Would this be a case of non-use of knowledge?

In fact, when one looks at the objects of conflict in 2009 and 2010 and at the level of problem tractability, it is clear that, under the new circumstances, any decision in the NGN case would have required Ofcom to take a stance and, ultimately, either facilitate or delay the deployment of NGNs on a broader scale. Specifically, if Ofcom were to decide that IP was a proven technology, then interconnection costs would fall on BT and other legacy operators, making the use of old networks less profitable and less desirable. Conversely, keeping current charging schemes would leave the burden of interconnection between old and new networks on those who have deployed NGNs.[31] According to Ofcom's analysis, this solution worked, as new entrants such as TalkTalk and Sky are profitable and keep investing despite the fact that current interconnection arrangements do not favour them.

Does this mean that Ofcom simply does not want to alter existing equilibria because the best solution is letting the market decide who is going to get the biggest slice of the profits pie? Or could this indicate that Ofcom believes that the 'brave new world' envisaged in 2005 may not be the safest bet for the coming years, as NGANs are a more promising route (thus implicitly, choosing sides)? Both ways and in contrast to the situation in 2005 when the game was still open, any move by Ofcom in 2010 would have affected the direction of market developments. So what should have been the role of the regulator under those circumstances?

This state of affairs locates this case study on a different level from the previous ones. The last two chapters covered episodes in which conflict and tractability revolved around the best way to achieve policy objective that was generally agreed upon, placing those cases in the realm of the 'technocratic modes of settlements' described by Boswell (2009). No question about values or high-level policy goals was at stake, other than for rhetorical purposes. Here, however, in spite of apparent disagreement on the technical issue of interconnection, we are facing a much deeper question: what is the role of the regulator? Should it be a facilitator for the smooth functioning of the market, leaving the latter free to follow its course, or should it point market-players in the right direction? And would this second approach still fall within Ofcom's remit? Or would it go beyond the agency's duties? And, more importantly for this book but closely linked to this issue: how is knowledge used in those cases?

The few portions of coded text that included an explicit reference to Ofcom's use of knowledge in the 2010 statement point to either an absence of real substance in Ofcom's analysis or to the use of erroneous premises. This is not only the position of those who believed that, by stating that IP technology for voice was unproven, Ofcom's paved the way for its decision to do nothing on interconnection. One of the supporters of some of Ofcom's conclusions (BBBritain) considers that the whole analysis was based on conservative premises, which allowed Ofcom

---

31. The debate on this point was also raging in Brussels, where Commissioner Neelie Kroes launched a public consultation exploring the possibility of making copper pricing less attractive for incumbents, in order to foster greater investment in superfast broadband. Eventually, and well after the events described in this chapter, the European Commission decided not to reduce copper prices. For further details, see Commissioner's Kroes's speech of July 2012. Online. Available: http://europa.eu/rapid/press-release_SPEECH-12-552_en.htm (accessed 21 November 2012).

to ignore relevant evidence. Another consultation respondent believed Ofcom's analysis did not show enough independence of mind, as the regulator's stance seemed to follow prevalent commercial interests. TalkTalk's consultation response claimed that Ofcom was beating around the bush by addressing 'blue sky questions' instead of the pressing concerns which were obvious to everyone. For some, the salience of superfast broadband deployment seemed to have been a key driver behind Ofcom's decision not to act and, by the same token, affected the use of knowledge in connection to NGNs. Yet, salience cannot be the only factor behind the decision,[32] although it may have been convenient to enable Ofcom to postpone answering intractable questions. In fact, Ofcom is portrayed as rather passive or 'stuck' on NGNs in a more general way:

> It seems to me that the large amount of what they are doing is effectively led by industry.(Industry 4, January 2011)

> Economic analysis is never conclusive in the sense that it points to one single answer. I am not suggesting for a minute that Ofcom's policy is challengeable in the legal sense or that they have done a flawed job; it's more a policy which is [...] they have taken one approach which from our perspective is wrong but for many other operators it's the correct one, particularly from BT's perspective. It's just a matter of political or, if you like, the willingness of Ofcom to drive the change [...] Ofcom's policy work on NGNs is probably one of the largest failures of the regulator over the last five years, and it's very difficult to see what Ofcom has brought to the table if you like. (Industry 2, January 2011)

> I think you'll be familiar with the term 'laissez-faire' [laughs]. So I think that summarises Ofcom's attitude, they would say 'we would like industry to sort things out', but they don't lead it. They leave things to the market-players, and of course those with the greatest market power can get things done [...] So they expect all this to happen but they don't say how, and they do not recognise that actually it's not in some players' interest for it to be easy for customers to migrate [...] I can't think of anything where they should have done less. Where they could have done more I think is the sort of thing we put in our response, it's about co-regulatory arrangements. They do have power and duties, I think under the UK legislation, to encourage and promote what's called self-regulation under the Act [...](Industry 3, January 2011)

The disappointment of several stakeholders and the contradictory positions expressed on what Ofcom should do (as mentioned, BT and two others support the regulator's stance) bring to the fore the ambiguity of the regulator's position in groundbreaking cases. There is no perfect solution to the technical problem of interconnection facing Ofcom but this is because the answer to this question is

---

32. After all, Ofcom had already invested in this dossier, and actively engaged other bodies such ad NGNuk in the debate. Companies had also undertaken significant efforts on NGNs. Hence, all actors incurred a series of transaction specific investments (Williamson 1979) that could not easily be recouped.

linked to the decision on whether to push NGNs or not. Expert knowledge may not be sufficient to solve this dilemma, as when regulation is at stake, expertise should ultimately answer questions that are set in legal terms. And Ofcom's mandate does not provide a clear direction for action in such cases.

As reported by several interviewees during the empirical part of the research, the Communications Act establishing Ofcom's duties remains vague in many respects and, despite its costs and disadvantages, judicial review has provided direction to Ofcom (in the MTR case for example).[33] In fact, judicial review has helped Ofcom learn where boundaries lie on several issues. In the present case, too, stakeholders expected a series of disputes on interconnection to unblock the situation. This may provide additional clarity on whether Ofcom should be more or less interventionist in situations like the NGN case; or perhaps this is the sort of answer that can only come from a political principal, thus opening a different debate, namely the one on the agency's independence and on the revision of its formal mandate.

Seen in this light, Ofcom's inaction appears as a sort of temporary Pareto-efficient solution, as no amount of evidence would manage to answer the real question facing the regulator:

> In relation to their NGN policy Ofcom probably thinks: 'What's the big deal, there is no huge problem, people aren't losing money, people aren't being damaged' [...] But it sort of does imply that we are to some extent ignoring what's right from an economic policy perspective in order to concentrate elsewhere, and they are fearful [...] that disrupting the legacy operators [...]. (Industry 4, January 2011)[34]

Also, expertise becomes irrelevant when there is no regulatory decision as, when no specific course of action is proposed, there is less need to justify/support it with evidence.[35] As a result, real content can be absent (or, if present, ignored) but expertise as a general concept can still play a symbolic and legitimising function (Boswell 2009) to show that the regulator is working on the policy question under examination.

---

33. *See* Chapter Six for further details.

34. In this respect, an additional element may be added to this picture, although it was only hinted at by one or two interviewees. Leaving things as they were would have also avoided a disruption in the business models and employment choices of several legacy operators. While the innovation potential of NGNs is ultimately expected to bring growth and jobs, as mentioned, these gains will not immediately materialise, while costs, also in terms of employment, could be visible immediately. It is quite possible that the regulator considered those aspects too, especially after the financial and economic crises of 2008–9.

35. On this point, one interviewee commented: '[the statement] doesn't appear to be strongly based on economics, they maybe get some consultants to give some views, but they are just reacting to market development. And in a way, if they are not making many decisions, they don't have to have many bodies of evidence to defend them, perhaps [...]' (Interview 3, industry, January 2011).

Concluding remarks

The convergence of narratives on the unfolding of events between BT's announcement on the 21CN project in 2004 and the moment when the company decided to allocate its resources to broadband deployment indicates that the hypothesis on instrumental learning (H4) is corroborated under the conditions of low problem tractability and limited conflict. In fact, this is one of the few cases where stakeholders explicitly mentioned learning in connection to a policy dossier. The only other instance where learning was brought up in interviews concerns the benefits of judicial review in terms of clarifying Ofcom's mandate and of instilling more rigour in *ex-ante* policy analysis by the regulator (*see* Chapter Four). The intention to learn in the NGN case is also apparent in Ofcom's official documents. However, as explained in Chapter Three this – taken alone – is not a strong enough indicator, given that official texts conform to a certain narrative and it is unlikely that they would report any use of knowledge departing from learning or problem-solving. Also, official narratives do not fully account for the second part of the NGN debate. Still, the exploratory tone of NGN documents is quite different from the other statements covered in this book. The only similar episode is the set of scenarios developed for the regulation of mobile termination rates in the previous chapter, another instance where the boundaries between the different knowledge usages predicted by the explanatory typology appear blurred. In relation to this, one of the most interesting aspects of the NGN case is the observable effect that changes in the explanatory variables may also have on the agency's attitude towards knowledge. As expected, the knowledge usages outlined in Chapter Three are only ideal types, while the reality of policy-making and of knowledge-utilisation is much more dynamic and complex. Also, knowledge usages are not fixed in time and may sometimes overlap.

In the second part of the NGN story, the discrepancies between Ofcom's and stakeholders' narratives start to emerge. There is no doubt that no decision was reached in the NGN case. Nonetheless, the justification for this state of things differs, depending on who was describing the episode. For Ofcom, there was no right answer to the intractable issue of interconnection, as any choice would have implied steering the market towards one option or another and currently available evidence did not provide any uncontested direction on this point. Also, the market and policy-makers exhibited stronger preferences for focusing on NGANs, thus relieving the regulator from the pressure of solving the NGNs dilemma in the immediate future. Conversely, for several stakeholders, Ofcom failed in its duty by not taking a stronger role in leading the debate. While many recognise that Ofcom's position is not an easy one, and that, indeed, any of the potential answers would be right for one side of the debate but wrong for others, many believe that Ofcom could have provided additional steering without going as far as micromanaging the market.

Where does that leave us in terms of knowledge-utilisation in the second part of this episode? Overall, it seems that, with the growing conflict about interconnection arrangements and low tractability, knowledge did not really have a role. The analysis provided in this chapter allows us to exclude a symbolic use of knowledge in which the agency produces expertise that has no real relevance for the decision at hand. We are thus faced with three alternatives: a symbolic use in which the agency tries to buy additional time and show it is working on the dossier; a case of non-use; or, again, instrumental learning, in which the agency is still in the process of gathering additional evidence.

To conclude that we are facing a case of non-use involves believing that Ofcom had enough knowledge to proceed but decided to ignore it. There is no firm indication of that; even if Ofcom had framed the analysis and assumptions differently, there would still have been the issue of deciding what the right solution for the future direction of market development was. And available knowledge could not answer that question. Possibly, the most accurate scenario is that there was indeed insufficient evidence to take a decision that would not be challengeable in court and that this situation, coupled with the financial crisis and the high political salience of broadband deployment, created a perfect scenario for postponing action while showing that NGNs were still on Ofcom's radar. In other words, this episode appears as a mixture of instrumental learning and symbolic use of expertise.

But this is only one part of the story. As mentioned, NGNs are one of those cases in which deeper questions are at stake, in particular, issues concerning the role of the regulator. We are exiting the territory of 'technocratic modes of settlement' (Boswell 2009) and entering debates on high-level policy outcomes. This is an area in which economic analysis and, in the case of NGNs, other forms of technical expertise do not always have definite answers. And in a regulatory setting, these disciplines can only answer deeper questions when these are already phrased in legal terms, either in the mandate of the agency or through judicial review. Alternatively, the direction of travel has to be set within a higher policy framework, often at the political level.

Without entering normative debates on the 'scientification' of politics (Hassenzahl 2006) and the politicisation of knowledge and the appropriateness of both trends, the NGN case clearly shows some of the inherent difficulties of delegating powers to an independent regulator, an issue often discussed in the literature on agency independence. More importantly for this research question, it is also closely linked to the issue of how a regulator copes under those circumstances. Here, Brunsson's distinction between action and political organisations can explain the regulator's choice of a temporary 'Pareto-type' arrangement based on inaction, on the grounds that no operator would have been damaged in the short term. Given the situation in the market at the time of the 2010 statement, there was perhaps no other sensible alternative.

This episode also shows how normative assumptions about the expertise-based legitimacy of agencies are misleading, as organisations can, need to, and do use knowledge in ways that are not only instrumental, as already shown by Boswell (2009). Whether this is right or wrong may sometimes be decided by looking at the question from a legal perspective (that is, the mandate of the agency and if strategic uses of knowledge are overturned by judicial review) but different knowledge usages remain nonetheless a fact of life.

chapter eight | implications of the research and conclusions

Research questions and theoretical expectations

It is often said that research questions are born out of doubts, or from the need to solve a specific problem that prevents a discipline from advancing on a certain issue (Booth *et al.* 2008). This research question was initially prompted by curiosity.

In the face of normative debates on the role of independent regulators, depicted in policy circles as organisations staffed by 'neutral' technocrats (European Commission 2002; House of Lords 2007), and with modern governments regularly advocating evidence-based policy-making (Sanderson 2002, 2006, 2009), I wanted to know more about what really happens inside an IRA. Hence, I looked for answers in the literature and was faced with a puzzling gap, in that I found no real interaction between two literature streams that are each key to understanding the functioning of independent regulators and particularly their use of the expertise, fundamental to IRAs' purpose and legitimacy.

Specifically, with some notable exceptions (e.g. Bawn 1995; McGarity 1991; Morgenstern 1997), the literature on independent regulatory agencies surveyed in Chapter Two tends to overlook explicit research questions on the role of expertise and experts within these organisations. Conversely, the literature on knowledge-utilisation[1] has developed some very interesting hypotheses on the role of expertise in policy-making. However, the difficulty of operationalising some of its research questions has resulted in a limited number of empirical publications. Quite surprisingly, these hypotheses have not been tested for IRAs, which offer an ideal environment to observe how expertise contributes to public policies when the influence of other factors (particularly political ones) is limited.

I believe that these two streams of literature should be connected to strengthen and complement existing analyses on the functioning of such central players in the modern regulatory state (Majone 1997; Vibert 2007). Finally, although some authors (Jennings and Hall 2011; McGarity 1991; Morgenstern 1997) have already explored the role of expertise (economic or scientific) in US agencies, much less is known about their European counterparts.

Against this backdrop, initial curiosity soon turned into the following research question: how do independent regulatory agencies use economic analysis?[2]

In turn, this problem can be broken into more specific queries. For example, will I observe inside an IRA the different types of usages that are so clearly

---

1. For further details, *see* the first section of Chapter Two.
2. For further details on my decision to focus on economic knowledge, *see* Chapter One.

described in the literature on knowledge-utilisation (Boswell 2006, 2009; Weiss, C. 1979)? Or will I find, as is implicit in normative assumptions about independent regulators (Majone 1997; House of Lords 2007; Vibert 2007), that IRAs use economics only instrumentally to solve problems? And should this not be the case, what are the scope conditions that are most likely to foster a certain usage of economic analysis?

To tackle those questions, I have developed an explanatory typology (*see* Chapter Three) that connects the findings of publications on IRAs and on knowledge-utilisation and puts forward four hypotheses on the possible uses of economic analysis by an independent regulatory agency. In terms of philosophy of science, as explained in Chapter Three, the approach was informed by a pragmatic perspective that has been recently advocated by scholars such as Sil and Katzenstein (2010). This allowed me to draw on the insights of other theoretical perspectives in a sort of 'analytic eclecticism' (Sil and Katzenstein 2010: 2). In particular, I employ the insights of Erving Goffman's theories on the dramaturgical aspect of social interactions (Goffman 1959) and on the framing of events (Goffman 1974) that have already proven their value for the analysis of social organisations such as enterprises. This allowed me to better analyse the different narratives provided by the various actors in the three case studies of this book. In this approach, I follow in the footsteps of Jones and McBeth (2010; Shanahan *et al.* 2011) and their 'narrative policy framework'. As explained elsewhere in this book, the analysis is built on the complementary interaction between the deductive approach embedded in the explanatory typology and its hypotheses, and a more inductive treatment of the material collected during the fieldwork. While this choice may have led at times to less formalised and somewhat 'messy' accounts of facts, I believe that such analytic eclecticism provides a sounder basis to connect different types of research questions like those covered in the literature on IRAs and knowledge-utilisation. Moreover, this approach can offer richer explanations, and should prevent me from encountering some of the limitations and compartmentalisation of knowledge that a strict adherence to a specific paradigm may cause (Sil and Katzenstein 2010: 1–3).

The proposed explanatory typology is built around two variables – the level of conflict and the degree of problem tractability – that assume different intensities in a given context. I have thus mapped four different combinations of the two variables that I expect will lead to different usages of knowledge. Then, I appraised these hypotheses through three case studies of regulatory decisions made by Ofcom between 2005 and 2010.[3] I decided to focus on specific episodes of decision-making rather than on the general interaction between the agency, its principals and the regulatees, as I believe that individual policy cases offer the most promising level of analysis for observing the different uses of knowledge I seek to explain. This naturally limits the scope for drawing general conclusions on IRAs. On the other hand, this choice is also a safeguard against the risk of

---

3. For a more detailed discussion of case selection, *see* Chapter Three.

Level of tractability

	HIGH	LOW
LOW *Level* *of* *conflict*	*H1* Instrumental/problem-solving? **2009 Fixed narrowband**	H4 Instrumental/learning use? **NGN debate 2005–2008**
HIGH	*H2* Strategic Use? **2007 MTR**	*H3* Symbolic use/non-use? **2010 NGN Statement**

Figure 8.1: Locating the case studies in the explanatory typology

Source: elaboration on Schrefler 2010

excessively diluting the explanatory power of the variables when it comes to questions of knowledge-utilisation.

Figure 17 locates the individual case studies in the relevant cell of the explanatory typology. The position of each episode in a given cell of the matrix is determined by the corresponding intensity of the explanatory variables (Elman 2005) of conflict and problem tractability.

As explained in Chapter Three, the typology has also two control variables: the capacity of the agency in terms of human and financial resources (Jennings and Hall 2011) and the salience of the policy issue under examination (Gormley 1986). As mentioned (*see* Chapter Four), in the case of Ofcom, it is fair to assume that capacity is high and does not significantly vary across the episodes presented in this book. Before turning to a more detailed discussion of the findings, let me briefly recall the methodological choices I made to tackle the research puzzle.

Because of the elusive nature of knowledge-utilisation questions and the need to gain a precise understanding of the context and mechanisms in which the use of economic analysis takes place, I have opted for a qualitative approach. As regards the treatment of the texts gathered for each episode (official documents and interview transcripts), I excluded quantitative text analysis (automated coding) on the grounds that official documents are likely to contain only a very limited set of clues on which type of knowledge-usage occurred in a given case. Instead, I opted for a qualitative coding of texts with NVivo. As explained in Chapter Three, the coding process clearly illustrates the interaction between the deductive and the inductive that underpins the analysis. All in all, I follow the case-study method.

Finally, I have chosen Ofcom to appraise the hypotheses, as this agency appears as the paradigmatic example of an IRA possessing significant in-house economic expertise. Also, it is required by statute to base its policy decisions on evidence. This, I believe, makes Ofcom a perfect test-bed for hypotheses on the use of economic analysis by an independent regulator.

Empirical findings

At this point, it is worth specifying again that what follows should not be read as a claim to 'the ultimate truth' regarding the use of economic analysis in each episode. After all, expertise is only one of the factors (supposedly quite crucial in the case of IRAs) that affect a policy decision (Jennings and Hall 2011). Hence, what I concluded for each case study should rather be seen as a plausible reconstruction of events. The purpose of these accounts is to shed light on the mechanisms that different combinations of conflict and problem tractability set in motion in each episode. As shown below, some of these mechanisms and other factors are common to all cases; others are not. I will elaborate further on this point in the next section. Let us now turn to the first case study.

For the 2009 regulatory statement on the regulation of fixed narrowband retail services markets, Ofcom was facing a combination of high problem tractability and relatively low conflict. As explained in Chapter Four, regulatory choices in electronic communications are very often zero-sum games, in which some companies lose and others gain. Hence, situations featuring no conflict at all are all but absent. According to the explanatory typology, evidence of an instrumental use of economic analysis to solve the problem under examination (H1) would be expected.

Overall, the hypothesis is not contradicted by the recollection of events and the qualitative coding of the relevant sources. Specifically, the fact that the statement was subjected to only one round of consultation can be read as an indicator that an instrumental use of economics occurred. This signals a decision-making process that is smoother and thus closer to rational accounts of policy-making than in the other episodes covered in this book. Some of the interviewees in and outside the agency confirmed the impression.[4]

The second central indicator supporting an instrumental use of knowledge is that the 2009 statement is one of the few decisions that were not appealed to the Competition Appeal Tribunal by any of the concerned parties, despite the potentially significant economic gains in case of victory in court. Nonetheless, this episode also displays some elements that could hint at a strategic reading of the available evidence, in particular the fact that available figures could have been used by Ofcom either to support full de-regulation of the market (as established in the final decision) or a more cautious approach instead. This suspicion is reflected in the narratives of the actors located in the camp that opposed the decision. Still, had the analysis been strategically crafted to support a 'done deal' to de-regulate the market, dissatisfied regulatees would not have missed the opportunity of bringing Ofcom to court.

---

4. For instance, two interviewees (one in the agency, one from industry) explicitly described this episode as one of the few cases in which Ofcom could 'get on with the job' as it is supposed to: identify the problem; do the consultation and analysis; identify and present the solution to the problem. The latter sequence appears as the textbook description of an instrumental use of knowledge.

In the unfolding of events leading to the regulatory statement, the following factors and mechanisms played a visible role: the historical evolution of the sector and path-dependency from previous decisions (BT's Undertakings of 2005 and the removal of charge controls in 2006), the theoretical assumptions underpinning the chosen regulatory approach and the threat of judicial review. While these elements had no impact when Ofcom produced the economic analysis supporting the statement, they facilitated an interpretation of evidence leading to deregulation. Hence, I could label this episode as a case of instrumental-strategic use of economics, where the amount of evidence that is sufficient to instrumentally support a long-awaited decision eventually materialises.

The second case study covered in this book is the 2007 regulatory statement on mobile termination rates (MTRs). This episode took place under a combination of a high level of conflict and high problem tractability, leading us to expect a strategic use of economic analysis (H2). I cannot conclude that the hypothesis is fully confirmed, although I did not find elements that contradict it for what concerns the final stages of decision-making.[5] Interestingly, I also observed a different kind of strategic use, of the rhetorical type (McCloskey 1998), to craft the analysis in a manner that would withstand judicial review. While this strategic make-up of official texts is present in all episodes, Ofcom appeared particularly cautious in this case, given the likelihood of being appealed (and indeed the statement was immediately appealed and part of Ofcom's decision was eventually upheld). Still, this rhetorical make-up does not affect the actual content of the economic analysis and thus cannot be used to corroborate the hypothesis.

What I did observe, however, is that Ofcom tried as much as possible to keep the debate on an evidence-based track (sticking to an instrumental use of knowledge) and managed to do so up to a certain stage. Between the second and third rounds of consultation, however, problem tractability decreased (when the lack of agreement on some informational inputs for the LRIC economic model surfaced). It is as if the uncertainty regarding some parameters (demand forecasts and the cost of spectrum) in an uncontested economic model left some room for manoeuvre to the regulator. Despite the significant amount of resources invested in economic analysis towards the end of the decision-making process, there is no firm indication that the analysis was the main basis for setting the final mobile termination rates. For some stakeholders, other factors may have played a role, possibly the desire to protect the revenues of mobile operators.[6] Moreover, the fact that mobile operators were the ones most likely to appeal may have tilted

---

5. As mentioned elsewhere, a purely deductive and confirmatory/discomfirmatory testing of the hypotheses is limited by the very nature of knowledge-utilisation questions and was not the purpose of the research.

6. As shown in the interview excerpts in Chapter Six, interviewees did not point to a specific rationale for what one of them termed 'going soft' on mobile operators. However, some noted that, in other instances, such as the EU roaming regulation, the UK (that is, one of Ofcom's parent ministries, as only ministerial departments negotiate for the UK at the EU level) appeared to side with mobile operators.

the balance in their favour when Ofcom finally had to select a point along a range of possible mobile termination charges. Finally, as mentioned by one of Ofcom's representatives, it is also true that the evidence submitted by BT (which subsequently appealed) was far better during the CAT trial than when the statement was under preparation.

Did this indeed allow Ofcom to favour mobile operators and 'back-write' the statement, thus confirming a strategic use? I cannot state this with certainty. It is also plausible that, contrary to Ofcom's initial expectations in the beginning of the decision-making process, economic analysis and the twelve scenarios[7] of the LRIC model did not really provide a clear answer. Hence, in the presence of high conflict and decreasing problem tractability, Ofcom based its final decision on other grounds. This would partially shift this episode to the H3 cell of the matrix, in which non-use of available economic evidence is one of the possible outcomes.[8]

As explained in Chapters Two and Three, a non-use of knowledge is also a sort of strategic usage of expertise but I classified it separately, as it results in a negative action. In the MTR case, one could legitimately suspect that, at the very end of the process, Ofcom used economic analysis strategically or did not really use it to set the termination charges.

Although an examination of the subsequent judgement by the Competition Appeal Tribunal (CAT) and the Competition Commission (CC) falls outside the scope of this book, the outcome of the appeal process leads me to exclude a non-use of knowledge. The courts confirmed that Ofcom's decision was based on the modelling exercise. What was contested and eventually overturned in the final judgement are some of the assumptions in the model and Ofcom's choice between the different scenarios. This corroborates the impression that, at the end of the process, decision-making was not purely instrumental. It could, indeed, have been strategic, as expected in the typology.

Finally, the third and last case study on next-generation networks (NGNs) was selected to appraise two hypotheses on the use of economic analysis: H3 on the symbolic/non-use of knowledge and H4 on instrumental learning. This episode covers a series of events stretching from the end of 2004 (when BT announced its intention to build 21CN) until the regulatory statement on NGNs of 2010. During this time, the explanatory variables feature low problem tractability[9] and a level of conflict which goes from being relatively muted between 2005 and 2008 to potentially very explosive at the time of the 2010 statement. In terms of the explanatory typology, I would expect to find initially that economic analysis (and

7. The scenarios were obtained through different combinations of spectrum-cost valuations and three possible future demand forecasts. For further details, *see* Chapter Six.

8. The other possible use foreseen in the typology when high conflict is combined with low problem tractability is the symbolic one (H3), in which produced knowledge is decoupled from the content of the decision. I can exclude this usage in the MTR case, as the content of the analysis is closely connected to the content of the final decision.

9. Low tractability was caused by the high level of uncertainty surrounding the economic and technological implications of the NGN project.

knowledge more broadly, given the strong technical/engineering component of the NGN debate) is used to learn (H4). As soon as conflict becomes more intense, I would expect to find instances of symbolic or non-use of knowledge (H3).

I found that the first hypothesis (H4) was corroborated by the analysis and broadly confirmed by the exploratory tone of official documents and analyses produced by Ofcom up to 2008. In the face of low problem tractability and a degree of uncertainty that prevented actors from formulating precise and potentially conflicting demands to the regulator, Ofcom adopted a *laissez-faire* policy approach in the statements issued in 2005 and 2006. No regulatory decision was taken, as Ofcom did not want to influence market evolution but rather gain and facilitate a better understanding of what would happen in an NGN world. This approach was not contested by regulatees. Moreover, this is the only set of events for which actors in and outside the agency explicitly mention learning and all narratives coincide on this point.

As regards the symbolic or non-use of knowledge (H3) during the second part of the debate (between 2008 and 2010), I found some indications that symbolic usages occurred but cannot fully exclude the possibility that Ofcom was also still trying to marshal additional expertise to learn again, under a completely new set of circumstances (BT's abandonment of the 21CN project, a shift of political and commercial interests towards superfast broadband/NGANs deployment and the global economic and financial crises).

As explained in Chapter Seven, this is also the only case study in which the effect of salience (one of the control variables) is visible. In particular, the shift of (political) attention and of resources/investments from NGN deployment to superfast broadband turned NGNs into a low-priority issue. Issue salience operated in this episode, as predicted by the typology. Specifically, while conflict arose as soon as commercial interests became clearer and opposing camps took shape in the NGN debate, increased attention to superfast broadband reduced the size of the NGN policy arena.[10] As a result, Ofcom had less incentive and pressure to act on this dossier, and produced a statement described by many as a 'high-level policy piece' containing no specific decision.

It is on this point that narratives in official documents and in interviews differ as regards knowledge-utilisation: on the one hand, Ofcom and a few other stakeholders claim that the decision to keep following the *laissez-faire* approach chosen by Ofcom since the start of the NGN debate in 2005 was the most sensible course of action. These actors claim there was not sufficient evidence to support an alternative choice: their account would indicate that Ofcom was still trying to learn (H4), despite the increased level of conflict. Conversely, a second group of

---

10. As explained in Chapter Three, issue salience affects conflict by reducing or enlarging the size of the policy arena. A larger policy arena has more potential to include conflicting demands and thus lead to greater conflict. In Chapter Seven I have shown that indeed the high saliency of superfast broadband diverted attention from NGNs. On the other hand, the remaining actors involved in the NGN debate were now in a position to articulate their demands more clearly. As these were incompatible, the overall level of conflict rose.

industry stakeholders claims that Ofcom had enough evidence to take a stance in the debate and decided to partially ignore it and focus on 'blue sky' questions instead of acting. This could indicate both a non-use of evidence and a symbolic production of a high-level policy statement to signal that the agency was still doing something on NGNs.

As explained in Chapter Seven, this case is slightly different from the previous two: any decision (or lack thereof) would have obliged Ofcom to choose a side in the debate. However, in this episode the choice was not between different ways to achieve a policy goal on which there was broad agreement. Instead, the NGN dossier around 2010 called into question the very role of the regulator and put Ofcom in the difficult position of having to step beyond its comfort zone and potentially indicate the best (technical) solution for the market. Yet, for this type of question, knowledge can provide answers only up to a certain point: evidence showed that there was no right or wrong choice in the NGN case. Rather, each choice would have been right for one portion of the market and wrong for others. By preserving its *laissez-faire* approach, Ofcom chose, in a way, the side of the legacy operators. However, the statement did not really tie the agency's hands for the future. It rather bought Ofcom some additional time, until more expertise becomes available or clearer direction on how to proceed comes from elsewhere. We can thus exclude a non-use of knowledge.

The most plausible scenario is that Ofcom did not have enough evidence to take a decision that would not be challenged in court and was faced with a set of circumstances that allowed it to postpone action while still doing something about NGNs. This corresponds to the definition of symbolic knowledge-utilisation. As mentioned, I cannot exclude the possibility that the agency was also trying to gather additional evidence to prepare itself for the future. Thus, it is fair to describe the second part of the NGN episode as a case of instrumental learning coupled with a symbolic use of expertise.

Table 8.1 compares the expectations of the hypotheses with the empirical findings of the three case studies.

Table 8.1: Hypotheses on the use of economic analysis and empirical findings for each case

Case	Expected use	Empirical finding
2009 Fixed narrowband	Instrumental/problem-solving (H1)	Instrumental-strategic
2007 MTR	Strategic (H2)	Instrumental (initially); strategic at the end of decision-making
NGN debate 2005–2008	Instrumental learning (H4)	Instrumental learning
NGN debate 2009–2010	Symbolic or non-use (H3)	Instrumental learning and symbolic use

Interpretation of the findings

As shown in the previous section, the empirical findings do not fully match the expectations embedded in the hypotheses, although they do not contradict them either. In fact, what emerges from Table 8.1 is that the expected use of economic analysis is present in all cases but is coupled with another type of knowledge usage, except in the case of instrumental learning (H4).

As mentioned in other parts of the book, this is partially a result of the fact that knowledge usages are ideal-types (Weber 1949[1904]) while, in reality, the dynamic nature of the explanatory variables blurs the boundaries between the cells of the typology. In Chapter Three, I explained how I have used the explanatory typology as a sort of 'map' for navigating the empirical world, without losing sight of what I was actually looking for, among the many factors that affect policy decisions. The analysis also adopts a more inductive perspective focusing on narratives, however, as I wanted to avoid at all costs the risk of straitjacketing the findings in a purely deductive approach.

Coming back to the findings, what is more interesting is that I find instances of an instrumental use of economic analysis in all episodes but there is no episode with a purely instrumental usage of knowledge in the problem-solving sense (H1), precisely the usage that is at the core of (normative) assumptions in debates on IRAs and on evidence-based policy-making.[11]

In Chapter Five I pointed out that I had some difficulties in finding a case that would match the high problem tractability and low-conflict combination that, according to the theoretical expectations, should foster an instrumental/problem-solving use of expertise. I have also mentioned that, in the field of electronic communications, this is because most regulatory decisions are zero-sum-games, with winners and losers, hence the absence of non-conflictual situations. If, however, this zero-sum nature of policy decisions is also common in other sectors, as could be reasonably be expected for regulatory policies with their concentrated costs and diffused benefits, then this could imply that the ideal conditions for an instrumental/problem-solving use of evidence seldom exist in reality. This may have broader implications, particularly for the tenets of the evidence-based policy-making movement.

One could also argue that this finding implies that looking at instrumental usage of knowledge is of limited relevance for understanding how IRAs really function. However, this would ignore the widespread expectations surrounding IRAs as repositories of expertise isolated from political debates, as well as all existing attempts to foster an instrumental use of knowledge in decision-making, via procedures such as regulatory impact assessment and the use of specific analytical

---

11. In fact, the typology predicts the occurrence of an instrumental use of knowledge in two cases: H1 and H4. In the second case, the instrumental use is geared towards learning and has a long-term goal. In other words, the difference between the two is a question of time. Yet, the 'correct' use of knowledge normally portrayed in normative debates on evidence-based policy-making is the short-term problem-solving one, covered in H1.

tools such as cost-benefit analysis. Rather, what the findings seem to indicate is that these procedural arrangements cannot by themselves alter the zero-sum nature of policy-making. They can, however, channel conflict, if they are coupled with capacity and a set of well designed incentives for the regulator. I will come back to this point below, in discussing the normative implications of the research.

It is important to stress again[12] that Ofcom operates in what can be described as the ideal setting for fostering an instrumental use of expertise: the agency has high level of internal capacity for producing and using sophisticated economics; has the statutory duty to consult and perform regulatory impact assessments for its decisions; and, more importantly, is subject to judicial review on the merits. These three conditions are not simultaneously present in all independent regulators in this field and in other policy areas; this explains why, in several instances, the conflictual nature of regulatory policy-making tends to prevail over formal requirements and delegation arrangements, thus giving the impression that instrumental uses are impossible or even irrelevant for understanding how IRAs function.[13] Even within the same national context (the UK), other 'technical' regulators are not subject to judicial review on the merits and this may, in turn, leave more room for knowledge usages that depart from an instrumental/problem-solving one.

The empirical findings also indicate that, at least in these three episodes, Ofcom attempted to adhere as much as possible to an instrumental and evidence-based approach to decision-making. However, it managed to do so only up to a certain point in each case, depending on other elements that entered the picture, such as path-dependency from previous choices, the (un)availability of data or the threat of judicial review. In turn, this brings us back to the observation made in the beginning of this chapter, namely that some of these elements or mechanisms are present in all cases, while others are not.

In the 2009 statement on fixed narrowband retail-services markets, the legacy of previous regulatory choices, theoretical and policy expectations stemming from the 'ladder of investment' theory underpinning the regulation of narrowband markets and the threat of judicial review led to an instrumental-strategic use of economics. In the MTR case, the shadow of judicial review was omnipresent throughout decision-making. Another element that affected the decisions was the unavailability of crucial informational inputs for the economic LRIC model.

Lack of data is a classical problem for decision-makers. However, it can be more or less damaging, depending on the cause of the absence of information. When there is insufficient accumulated knowledge on a topic in the policy arena

---

12. For further details, *see* Chapter Four.

13. While providing precise figures on the frequency of each combination of the explanatory variables would require a much larger number of cases, when looking for specific episodes for this book I often came across the combination of variables underpinning H2 on strategic knowledge-utilisation. This is in line with the findings of knowledge-utilisation scholars in other policy fields and may be due to the fact that, apart from groundbreaking cases such as NGNs, regulatory decisions tend to revolve around the periodic review of existing rules or incremental changes to existing policies, thus featuring relatively high problem tractability.

(low problem tractability), an agency is more or less on an equal footing with other actors, including political principals and regulatees. If instead, the lack of data is because regulatees have information but withhold it from the regulator (McGarity 1991), we are faced with a classical problem of informational asymmetry that places the agency in a weaker position. A way to counter this risk is to provide the regulator with appropriate information-gathering powers and staff it adequately, so that it has the internal capacity to evaluate the quality of the evidence provided by external sources and make an informed judgement when using available knowledge (Jennings and Hall 2011). While there is no doubt regarding the quality of Ofcom's capacity, the MTR case also shows that, if BT had provided the same information it submitted during judicial review, Ofcom might have taken a different decision.

In terms of the explanatory typology, this point highlights the difficulty of separating the phase of knowledge-production from knowledge-usage, as the two often go hand-in-hand during the decision-making process. In all the cases covered by this book it is apparent that, at least in rhetorical terms, Ofcom kept in mind the possible usage of knowledge (during an appeal process) when producing it and anticipated the expectations and behaviour of external actors (Schillemans 2008). Yet, I cannot establish whether the intended use of knowledge by those who produced it was then used in another way at the time of decision-making. After all, Ofcom is not a monolithic organisation and has different decisional levels. We may find traces of this divergence between knowledge-production and use in the MTR case, if we believe the account of one industry representative that economic analysis was used (thus indicating an instrumental/problem-solving approach) 'except right at the very end of the process' (by the Board). Along the same lines and for the same case, one Ofcom representative clearly distinguished the weight in terms of resources invested in economic analysis from the weight of economics in the final decision.

This potential dichotomy should remind us of Brunsson's (1989) concept of 'hypocrisy' within an organisation, where talk (that is, decisions) is sometimes decoupled from action (in this case, the production of knowledge) to ensure survival in the policy environment. To put Brunsson's intuition in different terms, the 'action' part of the organisation obeys a logic of efficiency, while the 'talk' part follows a logic of appropriateness. In the case of Ofcom, the statutory duty to produce impact assessments coupled with judicial review on the merits tends to ensure that the same type of knowledge will be used inside and outside the agency. Yet, as explained in Chapter Seven, it would be naïve to assume that the usage of economic analysis is uniform across all levels of the organisation. It is clear that the Board will attribute a different value and role to economic evidence than the Competition Group does.[14] As a result, the prospected impact of economic knowledge can deviate from its intended course. Yet, because of judicial review on the merits, it can never go too far.

---

14. For a detailed description of Ofcom's structure, *see* Chapter Four.

The third and last policy episode, on NGNs, points again to the issue of the availability of evidence for deciding on a case. This episode is a clear example of low problem tractability, as both the regulator and regulatees were facing the same level of uncertainty and no information was being withheld. Secondly, the zero-sum-game nature of electronic communications surfaces again in this episode, showing that conflict could not be eliminated even when Ofcom was hoping to face a 'clean slate'.

In the absence of a real decision on NGNs, the shadow of judicial review seems to be missing in this episode. However, one should keep in mind that the lack of sufficient evidence to back any policy option would have left Ofcom very vulnerable to appeal, had it taken a stance in the NGN debate. This, in turn, highlights the intrinsic limitations of expertise as an aid to decision-making as soon as policy goals are not clearly set in the mandate of the agency or established by judicial review.[15] In the NGN case it almost seems as if Ofcom had hit the limit of the regulatory territory on which it could safely move in accordance with its statutory duties.

Having mentioned it in so many instances, let us now turn to judicial review. Undoubtedly, the possibility of being appealed on the merits plays a central role in Ofcom's life. It is fair to say that, in the majority of cases, Ofcom takes into account the possibility of being appealed from the early stages of decision-making. This positions the remarks that follow in recent debates on adversarial legalism (for example, Kagan 1997; Kelemen and Sibbitt 2004, 2005)[16] and in the literature that links (regulatory) impact assessment (RIA) to judicial review.[17]

Some authors (for example, Alemanno 2009; Majone 2010) have claimed that RIAs and evidence-based policy-making cannot really 'bite' and be effective unless their content is subject to judicial review. Otherwise, RIA risks becoming a box-ticking exercise that is correct in procedural terms but may produce evidence that has little bearing on a final decision. Also, in the case of IRAs exercising delegated powers, judicial review on the merits significantly contributes to the legitimacy of these organisations and their decisions.

---

15. Please note that I am in no way saying that expertise is not relevant for decision-making. Also I do not assume that some think or claim that expertise is the only element guiding public policy. I am simply noting that, even in the so-called technical fields, where expertise is supposed to have a greater bearing on decisions, it may reach its limits. It is those limits I am discussing here.

16. I concur with Kagan (1997) and other authors that American-style adversarial legalism is unlikely to fully take root in European countries. However, some features of adversarial legalism have been exported to Europe: the use of courts to delay regulatory processes and the subsequent reduction of trust in the system and surge of litigation costs described in the previous chapters are a case in point. It is thus worth keeping the US debate in mind, albeit with all the caveats about its applicability to a European context, when reflecting on the pros and cons of judicial review on the merits.

17. In Chapter Three, I listed the different types of documents that an IRA is likely to use to perform economic analyses. In the case of Ofcom, because of its statutory duty to perform regulatory impact assessments (RIAs) (Article 7 of the 2003 Communications Act), economic analyses were generally labeled as RIAs or consultation documents. Only in the case of NGNs could the analysis could be described as a foresight study although, again for statutory reasons, the text is labeled as an official consultation document.

This second view is confirmed by the accounts of most of the interviewees, who attribute a beneficial learning effect to judicial review. They also claimed that judicial review instilled more rigour in Ofcom's analyses and decision-making when compared to its predecessor, Oftel. Such positive effects of judicial review on the quality and usage of economic analysis (and evidence in the broader sense) are also corroborated by the findings of the National Audit Office (NAO 2007). As explained, of all the economic regulators in the UK, Ofcom is the only one whose decisions can also be appealed on the merits. And indeed its regulatory impact assessments were, at the time of writing, of better quality (NAO 2007; House of Lords 2007) than those of other regulators such as Ofwat and Ofgem.

In this respect, it seems that quality control, even from an external department (such as the NAO) is not sufficient: it is the threat of seeing a decision being overturned on the merits that is really effective in fostering an instrumental use of economic analysis. Yet, this description does not take into account the potentially perverse effects that judicial review may have (Kagan 1997; Kelemen and Sibbitt 2004, 2005). In particular, appeal on the merits does not only generate positive policy learning. As explained in Chapters Two and Six, judicial review can also be used strategically by industry to delay the application of a policy decision. As in the MTR case, the scenario of having a decision that takes two years to be adopted and then lingers another year or two in court because it has been appealed is not uncommon (NAO 2010; BIS 2010a). In other words, these procedural arrangements have quite predictably generated new coping strategies among policy actors, such as strategic/symbolic uses of expertise by regulators and a tactical use of judicial procedures by regulatees. Eventually, this creates regulatory uncertainty on the market, thus damaging the same players that are supposed to benefit from the existence of an appeal system (BIS 2010b: 17).

More closely linked to the research question, the growing climate of litigation in British electronic communications obliges Ofcom to produce longer and deeper analyses for each decision. Yet, an excessive amount of analysis can ultimately become counterproductive in terms of invested resources and does not automatically imply better quality after a certain point. In particular, it goes against the principle of proportionate analysis, a pillar of evidence-based policy-making, and risks turning analytical exercises into defensive checklists that undermine the rationale for adopting clearer and more transparent procedures in the first place.[18]

---

18. One of Ofcom's parent Ministries, the BIS is fully aware of this problem, which it described as 'armour plating [...] decisions against the risk of appeal' (BIS 2010a: 28). These tendencies are likely to be exacerbated by the new requirements set in the third EU telecoms package (BIS 2010a: 33). As a result, on the occasion of the transposition into UK legislation of the EU package, the BIS performed an impact assessment and launched a consultation suggesting the potential review of the appeals system. The two relevant consultation questions (BIS 2010b: 18) were: 1) 'The Government welcomes views on whether an enhanced form of Judicial Review (duly taking account of the merits) would: prevent the risk of regulatory gridlock under the new Framework by reducing the number and nature of appeals against Ofcom decisions; and whether there are any disadvantages in such an approach' and 2) 'We welcome views on whether there are steps the Government could take to ensure that appeals are focused on determining whether Ofcom has

Despite these negative effects, it is undeniable that judicial review provides strong if not the strongest incentive for an instrumental use of knowledge and has also helped Ofcom learn the boundaries of its mandate and the nature of its duties. Yet, the empirical findings show that there is still space for other usages of economic analysis to occur. In fact, I have observed a bit of all the four usages described in Chapter Two. It is as if Ofcom had an (induced?) preference for the instrumental use of expertise (both in a problem-solving and learning sense); however strategic, symbolic or a non-use of knowledge can still prove viable strategies. The purpose at this point, is to clarify why and when this is the case.

As regards the non-use of knowledge, it is fair to say that the presence of judicial review can only allow it in the cases where Ofcom has to deal with high-level policy issues, for which it is potentially easier to disregard available expertise, particularly when current circumstances do not open a window of opportunity (Kingdon 1995) for a certain course of action. In those instances, as the NGN case has shown, there is often no decision, hence no need to marshal knowledge to support it. Instead, for cases where policy goals are agreed upon and the agency has to decide on the best approach to implementing them, decisions that disregarded available knowledge could be easily challenged in court and would thus be a dangerous strategy. The only time when Ofcom could disregard evidence would be when regulatees hide it from the regulator: this would, however, be a tactical choice by industry players and not a deliberate action by Ofcom.

This leaves us with instances of strategic and symbolic uses of economic analysis. In this respect, I find the classical portrayal of the instrumental usage of knowledge as 'the' rational approach to decision-making misleading. As the case studies have shown, strategic and symbolic usages are also politically expedient choices for the regulator, when certain combinations of conflict and problem tractability prevent it from staying on the evidence-based track. In the case of NGN, a symbolic usage allowed Ofcom to gain some time and avoid making a challengeable mistake on a very explosive dossier for which there were no clear solutions. Symbolic usages remain a relatively safe option, although they cannot be sustained for a long period of time. As they are often driven by the need to follow a logic of appropriateness (Goffman 1959; March and Olsen 1989) and preserve the reputation of the agency by providing an aura of competence, symbolic usages of expertise must be carefully balanced with other strategies to deliver on the expected goals. As mentioned, an agency cannot pretend to be doing something for a protracted period of time.

Finally, strategic usages are riskier: high problem tractability makes substantiating analyses easier to detect and challenge, particularly in court. However, one must keep in mind that, in economic analysis, the strategic component is often hidden in the choice of assumptions or in the interpretation of information within an economic model. Hence, strategic usages of expertise

---

made a material error.' As mentioned in Chapter Four, at the time of writing, the public summary of the final consultation responses was still unavailable.

remain a viable strategy to facilitate the adoption of a solution that actively responds to the expectations of policy principals or regulatees, as in the case of deregulation in Chapter Five.

In light of these considerations, it is fair to conclude that, in the case of Ofcom, thanks to the statutory duty to perform impact assessments, coupled with judicial review and a high level of in-house capacity, the prevalent use of economic analysis will be instrumental. Other uses still exist, however, and can be complementary, under specific circumstances. In a way, on occasion, Ofcom has to resort to a certain amount of 'bricolage' (Carstensen 2011) in order to meet expectations in terms of effective and evidence-based decision-making while adapting this somewhat idealised vision to the reality of policy-making in a complex and ever-changing policy field.

Locating the findings in the literature

As explained in Chapter One, this book contributes to the literature in three respects. It is now time to complement those initial remarks in light of the empirical findings.

With the three case studies, I have managed to confirm that the types of knowledge usages described by Carol Weiss (1979) and more recently by Boswell (2006, 2009) do indeed occur. More interestingly however, I have explored the role of expertise in a type of organisation which is often left aside in the literature, perhaps because it is considered as unproblematic by knowledge-utilisation scholars. In fact, the publication that bears the strongest resemblance to this book is Boswell's (2009) study of different knowledge usages in immigration policy by the European Commission and a sample of European member states.[19] Yet, the author focuses on what can be defined as a politicised area, which is naturally more prone to symbolic/legitimising uses of expertise. While Boswell does not claim that this always happens, she does somewhat imply that an organisation in charge of a 'technical' policy field (such as Ofcom) has a limited need to use expertise symbolically (Boswell 2009: 78–80). In other words, although the knowledge-utilisation literature questions rational accounts of the policy-process, it does not really undermine the normative assumption that independent regulators dealing with technical subjects (such as telecoms, electricity, environment) will essentially use knowledge instrumentally. I had the suspicion that this might not always be the case. And indeed, although I have found that Ofcom tends overall to make an instrumental use (both in a problem-solving and learning sense) of expertise, it also resorts to symbolic and strategic usages of knowledge (economic analysis in this case) under certain circumstances.

---

19. As mentioned in several instances, I owe the taxonomy of knowledge usages of this book to Boswell. However, I do not fully follow her approach, which I do not find suitable for IRAs. McGarity (1991) and Morgenstern (1997) have also looked at the use of expertise in organisations and policy fields that are closer to electronic communications. Yet, their work can better be included in the literature on agencies than the one on knowledge-utilisation.

This book also provides a different, hopefully, fresh, way to look again at classic questions of the literature on IRAs, in particular questions about the balance between autonomy and accountability, and about the measurement of *de facto* autonomy, in turn often grounded in reputational variables (Busuioc *et al.* 2011; Wonka and Rittberger 2011). While the fact that this book focuses on a single organisation does not allow us to draw general conclusions on agency autonomy, I have, in a way, revisited these questions from the inside, showing how an agency builds (internally, via organisational processes) the foundation of its autonomy and reputation. Thus, the findings take us back to the roots of variables such as reputation and independence that have been much discussed over the last twenty years in the European literature on IRAs, but without fully explaining where they come from (the US literature is more advanced, *see* for example Carpenter 2010).

Moreover, I have contributed to the post-delegation literature by providing an additional perspective on how an independent regulator interacts with its principals and its policy environment. Several years ago, Cornelius Kerwin (2003) concluded his review of rule-making in the USA by noting that I need to add a theory of negotiation to the theory of delegation. He argued that delegation is a foundational act that establishes a contract between elected politicians and IRAs. But IRAs and principals keep re-defining the substance of the delegation contract in daily interactions, when individual rules are created. This book is very much on the same 'negotiation' wavelength, in that I see implementation of delegation contracts as constant evolution and negotiation of who does what in relation to specific episodes of rule-making.

Negotiation between the agency and the other actors in a policy arena occurs via the implementation of specific procedures and processes, including those for channelling expertise in decision-making. the three case studies illustrate how an agency and its stakeholders negotiated the use of economic analysis in rule-making. Procedures such as impact assessment and consultation are constantly re-defined by constellations of actors involved in rule-making. These procedures do not necessarily stack the deck in one direction or the other: they are somewhat malleable. In this connection, I argue that some of the bold statements made by delegation theorists about cost-benefit analysis requirements as 'stack-the-deck' devices need to be re-examined in light of what case studies of rule-making tell us.

In turn, these remarks raise a new set of research questions for scholars studying individual IRAs: is the regulator well equipped in terms of resources and powers to survive and act effectively in its policy context? Given the growing complexity of policy problems and the interdependence of policy decisions, do independent regulators need more or less in-house expertise? And can and should expertise provide an answer on intractable and highly uncertain and risky policy issues? Some of these questions, and particularly the latter, are not completely new, especially in normative debates. Yet, a balanced and pragmatic (Sanderson 2009) answer still has to be found.

Finally, the contribution of this book to general theories of the policy process is present but remains indirect. By their very nature, research questions on knowledge-utilisation require a relatively narrow focus in order to be operationalised. And indeed, the proposed typology is deliberately anchored to the level of specific episodes of policy-making. Linking the findings to more general theories in the literature would require exploring a different chain of mechanisms (Gerring 2011) from what is done in this work. Without this additional step, I risk stretching the concepts and findings beyond their intended use. Yet, by focusing on the level of conflict, the typology incorporates some of the key variables of the literature on the policy process and illustrates the possible impacts that these generate at a more 'micro' level, when specific decisions are at stake. For what concerns the role of expertise, the findings directly contribute to current debates on better/smart regulation, and evidence-based policy-making. In particular, and bearing in mind the usual caveat that expert knowledge is only one ingredient in policy decisions, the analysis of the use of economic expertise by IRAs allows us to conclude that some of the tenets and normative assumptions on the role of evidence in policy decisions are inaccurate.

This is not fully surprising, and several scholars (Hertin *et al.* 2008; Owens *et al.* 2004, Radaelli 2009a) have already criticised rational accounts of the policy process. Moreover, the literature and policy practitioners acknowledge that expertise is only one of the elements that contribute to a decision and thus cannot always be used instrumentally. Yet, while the emphasis on evidence-based policy-making has positively changed the culture and praxis of decision-making, it has also reinforced the myth of 'the rational decision-maker'. This book has shown that the ideal conditions for an instrumental/problem-solving use of knowledge are very rare: in regulatory policies, conflict is always around the corner. The zero-sum nature of policy debates puts independent regulators in a delicate position and, in some instances, an instrumental use of expertise, even when intentionally sought by the agency, may not be a viable option. This book has provided a preliminary illustration of the scope conditions that are likely to create such a situation.

Normative aspects

Where does this leave us in terms of IRAs and the use of expertise? Albeit limited to a single but paradigmatic case, the findings of this book point to two broad normative considerations.

The first concerns the position and legitimacy of independent regulators in modern states. Claiming that these organisations were created and are legitimate because they use knowledge instrumentally and not politically is somewhat incorrect. The days of the independent regulator shielded from political influence (Majone 1997; Vibert 2007) are long gone. By this, I do not necessarily imply that the image of the politically insulated regulator is wrong: rather, the complexity of current policy problems and the reality of decision-making indicate that this image is in need of some serious 'restyling'. At least, I should acknowledge that IRAs' legitimacy is not solely grounded on a neutral/impartial use of expertise.

At the same time, we can also say that the opposite and often feared scenario of unaccountable regulatory experts running out of control can and has been avoided. To be sure, concerns in this respect remain, for example in the case of EU agencies and the complex multilevel governance structure of the European Union (e.g. Busuioc *et al.* 2011; Everson 2011). Yet, the case of Ofcom has shown that there are effective procedural, institutional and organisational steps to counter the risk of a runaway bureaucracy (Bartle and Vass 2007: 898).

In fact, although it has decreasingly few supporters, the traditional dichotomy between neutral/bureaucratic and political decision-making cannot be upheld. Regulatory policy-making is better depicted as a continuum ranging from 'government by experts' and 'government by politicians'. In this context, there is no such thing as neutral policy appraisal. Nor is it realistic to conceive that a purely technical use of power exists.

It is difficult to imagine that independent regulators will not make use of the regulatory and policy-making powers they received at the time of delegation. In some instances this may imply venturing into more 'political' territory, depending on the nature of the policy problem at stake. In other words, we have to accept that a portion of regulatory decision-making is political.[20] On the other hand, claiming that policy-making is inevitably politicised and that this undermines the rationale for having independent regulators in the first place, would be incorrect.[21] Very often, Independent Regulatory Agencies possess and are developing a wealth of expertise that is crucial for modern policy-making. I concur with Vibert (2007) that having an independent but accountable locus for decision-making contributes to the success and equilibrium of today's regulatory states. In fact, one could go as far as saying that the degree of legitimacy of independent regulators is the result of the overall interplay between power and expertise used to find policy solutions that work (Sanderson 2009). What can we conclude on knowledge-utilisation by IRAs? This is the second point I wish to address here.

We already mentioned that instrumental, strategic, symbolic, and the non-use of expertise are all politically expedient choices for an actor involved in real-world policy processes. While I do not deny that an instrumental usage of expertise is the 'ideal' one, I am not fully convinced that it is always appropriate. For example, building a reputation can be vital for an organisation, and symbolic usages of knowledge become a crucial step to achieve this goal. In fact, alternative uses of expertise can be a positive complement to an instrumental use. They become 'wrong' (ineffective) when they are prevalent and when they are pathologically used, for example, if an organisation systematically ignores existing research because it goes against the wishes of its political principals.

This book has also shown that the ideal conditions for fostering an instrumental use of knowledge are seldom found in modern policy processes. Yet, as pointed out by Sanderson (2009), this is not sufficient a reason to settle for 'evidence-informed'

---

20. On this point, *see also* Meier (2008: 313).

21. In a similar vein I disagree with the view that regulators mainly serve as blame-shifting organisations for politicians. There may be blame shifting on occasion (*see* Chapter Two for further details), but focusing on this aspect provides a simplified view of reality. As this book has shown, IRAs are organisations with a life of their own, and what happens in the post-delegation stage is more articulated than what is expressed in the formal design of the organisation.

policy-making. There are solutions for creating a climate that is conducive to an instrumental use or knowledge or at least to ensure that it is distinguishable from other types of usages. In this light, expertise and, more importantly, its production and use are legitimate (and contribute to the agency's legitimacy) if they are embedded in a specific procedural, organisational and incentive-based context. It is on this context that political principals should concentrate when they delegate and monitor the usage of regulatory powers.

In procedural terms, the statutory duty to consult widely and to 'give reason' through impact assessments is a valid approach. When coupled with the incentive provided by judicial review on the merits, these tools can lead to a system in which analytical rigour, transparency and accountability are preserved. Policy-makers should, however, strive to find solutions that deliver the benefits of review on the merits without falling into the traps of adversarial legalism. Yet, these procedures are not sufficient if an agency is not adequately staffed in terms of expertise and resources. In the long run, a competent agency with a strong reputation (hence the importance of symbolic usages of knowledge) can put in motion a virtuous circle among regulatees, pushing them to use knowledge more instrumentally too. Finally, there should be indicators to facilitate the identification of an instrumental/problem-solving use of knowledge, for example, by ensuring that an agency has and allocates resources to different type of appraisals (such as impact assessments and *ex-post* evaluations) throughout the policy cycle and more broadly, by actively monitoring how procedures to foster the use of expertise in decision-making are implemented.

The balance between procedural requirements, incentives and capacity may vary depending on the policy or national/institutional context but all three are important. Actually, they are essential to build and consolidate trust in the regulatory system.

Concluding remarks

As mentioned several times, I have focused on a single organisation and have selected an ideal example for exploring whether non-instrumental usages of knowledge occur even in a setting that is the most conducive imaginable to instrumental use of expertise. While I cannot generalise the findings,[22] it is fair to expect that some of the mechanisms that lead to different usages of expertise will be at play in other regulatory agencies too. As Ofcom is characterised by a high capacity level, I could not assess the real effect of this control variable. It is very possible that it has more weight in the regulation of electronic communications than shown in the three empirical chapters of the book. Conversely, I believe the type and number of salient dossiers in this policy field was quite accurately reflected in the case selection.

---

22. On the absence of generaliseable findings on the use of expertise, *see* Sabatier (1978).

In Chapter Three I have also pointed to the fact that the proposed typology does not clarify the respective weight of the two explanatory variables, that is, the level of conflict and problem tractability. I expected, however, that both variables would have an effect in each episode. The empirical chapters of this book have indeed confirmed that both conflict and problem tractability are relevant in affecting knowledge-utilisation. I have not tested enough cases to establish whether, ultimately, one of the two is more influential.

Another limitation of the approach is that the hypotheses on knowledge-utilisation do not include a reflection on the quality of expertise. I have started from the premise that an agency can produce expertise strategically, or instrumentally, or an analysis that is decoupled from decision-making, but I have not tackled the question of whether there could be different behaviour depending on whether the quality of the knowledge at stake is good or bad. I suspect this issue is closely connected to an agency's capacity, as already pointed out by Jennings and Hall (2011) and deserves to be explored further. What would happen in an agency with limited capacity? Could we not envisage additional types of usages, including the unintentional misuse of information? And what would happen in contexts that have fewer checks and balances than the UK telecoms sector?

Finally, although I have managed to operationalise questions of knowledge-utilisation beyond what is commonly done in the literature, I believe that still-better indicators can be developed to distinguish and measure different types of usages.

In light of the above, possible suggestions to further develop the insights of this book could follow two tracks: the first on the scope of the analysis, and the second on methodology.

In the former case, one could envisage testing the hypotheses in other agencies within the same sector in different countries. The most suitable candidates are other European IRAs, as they are subject to the same EU-derived regulatory framework but operate in different political and economic contexts and may be staffed differently in terms of capacity. In this, I would follow the steps of Thatcher (2005, 2007), albeit with a different focus. However, this approach should be carefully thought through in terms of case selection, to avoid ending up with the finding that country A is different from country B, rather than understanding how the difference between country A and country B affects knowledge-utilisation.

Another option could be to focus on other independent regulators in different sectors within the UK, to isolate the differences linked to the policy questions facing each agency. In a way, this would embed this research more strongly in the literature on IRAs, by replicating common research designs to tackle a relatively new research question for this stream of literature.

Finally, this type of research can be widened beyond the case of economic analysis to other types of expertise. In fact, as already argued elsewhere (Schrefler 2010), the hypotheses can be tested on scientific knowledge in general. One way of reasoning is that results are not contingent on the type of science under scrutiny, since the hypotheses are drawn from political and organisational features and do not hinge on the type and form of scientific knowledge at hand. An alternative argument is that I should expect only instrumental and symbolic uses (for example, to establish a reputation) of 'hard science', given that the strategic construction of arguments is difficult to nest inside disciplines like physics or biology (although recent debates on the regulation of stem cells in different countries seem to suggest that this is not at all inconceivable).

Turning to methodology, there are certainly alternative ways to handle the research question. One option is discourse analysis, possibly informed by an understanding of the institutional and organisational setting in which discourse is first co-ordinated and then communicated to seek legitimacy. In political science, Vivien Schmidt has suggested a type of discourse analysis labelled discursive institutionalism (Schmidt 2008, 2010). Although she has used this approach for macro-comparisons, it is perfectly reasonable to argue that researchers could investigate how actors co-ordinate and communicate discourses concerning the use of science in IRAs at the level of policy sectors (as opposed to macro comparisons across countries).

Another, more promising, approach is participant observation. The latter is possibly the ideal method for tackling some of the issues that emerged during empirical research that I could not pursue further due to resource constraints. For instance, participant observation would allow greater access to internal and confidential documents; to acquire a deeper understanding of the potential distinction between knowledge-production and knowledge-usage; and to observe from the inside the structure of the agency and the interaction of different hierarchical levels (in line with Brunsson's distinction between action and talk within the same organisation). It would also offer the opportunity to observe how different types of expert knowledge (such as economics, law and engineering) interact. Finally, it would provide clearer insights on instances in which knowledge is not used and why. This is undoubtedly the hardest type of usage to detect and measure.

In more practical terms, ideal candidates for a participant observation exercise would be the subsequent reviews of the dossiers treated in Chapters Five to Seven, as policy problems are treated cyclically by Ofcom and are often scheduled regulatory appointments. This would also facilitate the observation of the dynamic nature of knowledge-utilisation across time and test whether, under different scope conditions, the same policy problem is being tackled in a different manner. Also, it would open avenues to explore research questions on organisational learning and the crafting/definition of an organisation's memory and *modus operandi*.

Besides its obvious technical and sectoral focus, this book also offers a more general and potentially iconoclastic reflection on the interaction between the rhetoric of policy-making and what happens in the real world. Indeed, choosing to study an independent agency and, more importantly, its use of expertise in relation to policy-making and situations of conflict, implies that we attribute a sort of neutrality and legitimacy to a social organisation that exists to produce knowledge that can be labelled as impartial. This is, after all, the common assumption on independent regulators that kick-started my research. However, this vision tends to diminish the weight of social contingencies and of the compromises involved in any policy decision. This book tries to set the record straight and to show that there are social actors who (if they are left free to use their expertise and are put in a favorable professional context) can exercise control over policy-making by providing a base of so-called 'objective' knowledge, as well as a repository of social practices and experience from which political actors can draw to legitimise decisions that are difficult to accept either socially or politically.

appendix | methodology

Potential challenges in empirical research and proposed solutions

This appendix describes the methodological obstacles and other classical field-work problems that emerged during the implementation of this research, as well as the solutions that were adopted to counter them.

Coding issues

One of the key challenges with qualitative text analysis is related to the reliability of the coding exercise itself (Miles and Huberman 1994; Krippendorff 2004), which is at greater risk of human error than automated approaches and is subject to a particular set of problems when sources are coded by a single researcher. While even quantitative text analysts have shown that, in terms of reliability, coding by several people brings to the fore a whole series of interpretative problems and different interpretations of concepts, the internal coherence of having a single coder offers greater risks of being 'carried away' with a given interpretation of findings. To solve those problems and counter those risks as much as possible, the following strategies were employed.

As suggested by Miles and Huberman (1994: 64) it is important to achieve ninety per cent reliability on the following formula for all codes:

Reliability: number of agreements/ (total number of agreements + disagreements)

In terms of time and availability of resources, recoding every single document was not possible; however, recoding the key sources was obviously a must for the validity of the study. In line with the differences in the coding outputs across the different types of sources described in Chapter Three, after an initial coding of all the documents for a given episode, re-coding was limited to interview transcripts, responses to stakeholder consultation and public hearings (when present); in other words, all the sources that were not excessively rehearsed and polished.

Another risk in coding exercises is to jump to conclusions prematurely, thus narrowing one's view of facts and eventually diminishing the validity and value of the analysis (Miles and Huberman 1994). This is why coding should be done at several stages of the research and not in one sitting; the stabilisation of the final set of codes can benefit from the feedback loops of the fieldwork, from some first ana-lytical work and, more broadly, from the learning process that takes place during any research project. On the other hand, starting the fieldwork without any coding was risky as well, as it could have led to less targeted approaches to interviewees and too much rigidity in using questionnaires. This is why official sources were always coded before each round of interviews; interview transcripts were coded only when approved in their final form by interviewees and then the re-coding (on paper and again on screen) took place at the end of the fieldwork, when all transcripts and documents were included in the database, so that all re-coded sources could be looked at with a final and stabilised set of codes. Overall, the risk of subjective interpretation was higher with interview transcripts, which are rich in terms of narratives and subjective judgements, and this is why they were re-coded several times. In contrast, polished official documents do not contain this type of input, and coding output remained fairly stable throughout the research.

Fieldwork issues

Another key issue that became apparent rather quickly was the accessibility of internal documents and informal memos/analyses/contributions such as the 'stakeholders' notes' referred to by some of the interviewees and that reportedly are submitted during bilateral meetings before the first official consultation for a policy dossier is published. Of course, for reasons of confidentiality and, often, because of the sensitivity of the data included in those documents, these were not accessible. Possibly, one could have obtained more information by focusing on a single case only but this would not have allowed the testing of the four hypotheses proposed in this book. Moreover, there would have been no guarantee of really having more access to data, as industry players were the most concerned about the potential disclosure of commercially relevant information and this would not have changed by focusing on a single case. Interestingly enough, the regulator offered the best solution to this problem as the need for accountability and the requests for greater transparency stemming from recent appeal cases has led the agency to use and publish as much as possible of the evidence that is used in a case; when figures or information are redacted this is explicitly signalled. As confirmed by several industry interviewees, the consultation process is quite transparent and, although some referred to it as a 'game' it was also clearly stated that, because of judicial review,[1] all the relevant arguments leading to a given policy conclusion must be included and discussed in a regulatory statement or put forward in the consultation in order to be taken into account. This, I believe, considerably reduces the risk that some crucial analyses or information were overlooked in the case studies.[2]

Finally, I had to face the classical problem of approaching fieldwork with an ideal list of interviewees in mind, which then turns out to be difficult to respect, as people have changed jobs, refuse to be interviewed, have no time, or cannot be traced anymore. Some of these problems occurred in this research too, although I managed to interview a representative of all the key organisations involved in

---

1.   For further details on the role and importance of judicial review, *see* Chapter Four.

2.   In addition, during interviews market-players stressed that the agency is transparent on the type of information used and the contacts made during the decision-making process; when present, criticism on transparency is linked to cases of dispute resolution, which are not covered here. This seems to confirm that if a piece of evidence had a bearing on a decision, we must have seen it, at least in a summarised form, in one of the official documents coded for this book.

each case study and gather information on the organisations I could not interview (Goldstein 2002). Very seldom was it possible to interview more than one person per organisation; in most cases, that contact (especially in the case of industry) was the only person who had followed and contributed to the whole debate for the company. In the case of the agency, each interviewee also commented on the other cases covered by this book. Interviews were always organised with high-level people in the agency, including present and former Board members, the Chief Economist, and the project managers of each case study. Contact with more junior members of staff was never provided; to check whether this was motivated by the intention of countering the risk that a junior interviewee would disclose too much information, I always started the interview with a question on the size and composition of the department in which the interviewee was located, its role in policy-making in general and some information on the team that dealt with the case under examination. Overall, it seems that I could not have obtained much more information than I did, as the number of people per organisation working on each case was indeed limited.

Because of the technicality of the subjects covered by the case studies one could credibly assume that the limited number of interviewees for each case corresponds to the key people who should have been contacted. To corroborate this assumption, each interview included a question asking suggestions for additional names of people to whom the researcher should have spoken on a given issue. As soon as this 'snowballing' technique led to the same names, I stopped pursuing additional contacts.

There are of course 'ideal candidates' who have not been interviewed. These include the external consultants who have contributed the economic modelling in our second case study (for contractual reasons, they could not disclose more than the final output of their research, which is already public) and members of the parent ministry. In the cases selected here, all interviewees inside and outside the agency firmly confirmed that, in telecoms, the regulator is fiercely independent and the ministry had little or nothing to say at all in the cases under examination. I nevertheless felt it would have been good to interview someone in the Department of Trade and Industry (now BIS) who had been dealing with the telecoms side of Ofcom and the specific cases under examination as well. The interviewee refused to be interviewed but provided a series of confidential remarks and suggestions of names of people 'that are better placed to answer those questions'. I have followed up with each of them, successfully.

| glossary[1]

21CN: Twenty-first Century Network. Name of BT's planned next generation network.

2G: second generation mobile telephones (*see also* GSM). Uses digital transmission to support voice, low-speed data communications, and short messaging services.

3G: third generation mobile telephones (*see also* UMTS). Provides high-speed data transmission and supports multimedia applications such as full-motion video, video-conferencing and internet access, alongside conventional voice services.

Access network: electronic communications network which connects end-users to a service provider; running from the end-user's premise to a local access node and supporting the provision of access based services. It is sometimes referred to as the local loop or last mile.

Backhaul: backhaul connects the access network to the core network. It is generally distinguished from local access and core by the fact that it does not perform any switching or routing function. It simply takes traffic from a number of local access nodes, possibly aggregates this together, and transports it back to the core network. It is generally made up of very high-capacity transport links, which are generally provided using Ethernet in NGNs.

Core network: the core network represents the backbone of a communications network. It tends to cover a relatively large area and carries traffic between geographically distant points. What tends to distinguish core from backhaul is that the core network contains routers and switches which can change the direction of the traffic, and ensure that it gets to the correct destination.

Communication Provider: companies which provide electronic communications services to the general public, i.e. end-users. This category includes Internet Service Providers (ISPs).

Countervailing Buyer Power: situation in which a particular purchaser (or group of purchasers) of a good or service is sufficiently important to its supplier to influence the price charged for that good or service.

Carrier Pre-Selection: mechanism that allows end-users to select, in advance, alternative CPs to carry their voice calls without having to dial a prefix or install any special equipment at their premises. The end-user subscribes to the services of one or more CPS operators and chooses the type of calls (e.g. all national calls) to be carried by them. The end-user may have a direct retail relationship with the CPS operator, or may purchase the service via a CPS Reseller. The end-user is billed for these calls by the CPS operator or CPS Reseller.

---

1. Technical definitions are taken from Ofcom's Glossary. Online. Available: http://www.ofcom. org.uk and from the former Oftel Glossary. Online. Available: http://www.ofcom.org.uk/static/ archive/oftel/publications/glossary/index.htm#Integrated_Services_Digital_Network (accessed 24 March 2013).

Equivalence of Input: concept established by the Undertakings in which BT provides, in respect of a particular product or service, the same product or service to all CPs (including BT) on the same timescales, terms and conditions (including price and service levels) by means of the same systems and processes, and includes the provision to all CPs (including BT) of the same commercial information about such products, services, systems and processes.

European Regulatory Framework: EU legislation ('telecoms package') regulating electronic communications in the EU.

Interconnection: the linking of one public electronic communications network to another for the purpose of enabling the persons using one of them to be able (a) to communicate with users of the other one; (b) to make use of services provided by means of the other one (whether by the provider of that network or by another person).

Internet Protocol: the packet data protocol used for routing and carriage of messages across the Internet and similar networks.

Integrated Services Digital Network: a network evolved from the digital PSTN which provides digital exchange lines to customers and 64kbps end to end digital connectivity between them.

Mobile Network Operator: companies offering mobile telephony products and services on the market.

Metallic Path Facility: a circuit comprising a pair of twisted metal wires between an end user's premise and a main distribution frame that employs electric, magnetic, electromagnetic, electrochemical or electromechanical energy to convey signals when connected to an electronic communications network. It enables to offer both voice and broadband services.

Mobile Termination Rates: charges levied by mobile network operators to terminate phone calls on their network.

Next Generation Access Networks: Next Generation Access Networks. New or upgraded access networks that will allow substantial improvements in broadband speeds and quality of service compared to today's services. NGAs can be based on a number of technologies including cable, fixed wireless and mobile. The phrase is most often used to refer to access networks using fibre-optic technology.

Next Generation Networks: a packet-based electronic communications network which is able to provide electronic communications services and to make use of multiple broadband and quality of service-enabled transport technologies, and in which service-related functions are independent of underlying transport-related technologies.

NGNuk: body set up by Ofcom to oversee NGN deployment in the UK.

National Regulatory Authority: indicates the IRAs in the electronic communications sector that each EU member state had to set up in order to comply with the EU requirements set in the EU RF.

Openreach: name of the division within BT that was created as a result of BT's Undertakings, the primary purpose of which is to look after the network assets which represent enduring economic bottlenecks.

Significant Market Power: term used in the European Regulatory Framework (*see also* EU RF) to describe the position of a company, which either individually or jointly with others, enjoys a position equivalent to dominance, that is to say a position of economic strength affording it the power to behave to an appreciable extent independently of competitors, customers and ultimately consumers.

Time Division Multiplexing: technologies putting multiple data streams in a single signal by separating each signal into many segments, each having a very short duration. Each individual data stream is re-assembled at the destination based on timing. TDM is used to deliver a steady stream of data, particularly digitised voice.

Universal Mobile Telecommunications System: standard for the third generation of mobile cellular technology (*see also* 3G).

Undertakings: the Undertakings refer to a set of legally binding commitments which BT proposed and Ofcom accepted that established a regulatory framework focusing on the enduring bottlenecks of competition. These Undertakings were provided in lieu of a market investigation reference to the Competition Commission under the Enterprise Act 2002, and were accepted on 22nd September 2005.

Wholesale Line Rental: service offered by BT Wholesale to other service providers allowing them to offer their own branded telephony service.

xMPF: this is the name which has been adopted to refer to a proposed voice-only passive access product from Openreach. There are many different variants of xMPF, but it is perhaps best understood as the input which Openreach implicitly consumes in order to provide WLR in situations where an end-user also takes broadband.

| bibliography

Aberbach, J. D. and Rockman, B. A. (2002) 'Conducting and coding elite interviews', *Political Science and Politics* (35) 4: 673–6.

Abraham, J. and Sheppard, J. (1999) 'Complacent and conflicting scientific expertise in British and American drug regulation: clinical risk assessment of Triazolam', *Social Studies of Science* (29) 6: 803–43.

Ackerman, F. and Heinzerling, L. (2004) *Priceless: On knowing the price of everything and the value of nothing,* New York: The New Press.

Albæk, E. (1995) 'Between knowledge and power: utilization of social science in public policy making', *Policy Sciences* (28) 1: 79–100.

Albon, R. and York, R. (2006) 'Mobile termination: market power, externalities and their policy implications', *Telecommunications Policy* 30: 368–84.

Alemanno, A. (2009) 'The better regulation initiative at the judicial gate: a Trojan horse within the Commission's walls or the way forward?' *European Law Journal* (15) 3: 382–401.

Armstrong, M. (1997) 'Mobile telephony in the UK', *Regulation Initiative Working Paper Series*, Paper 15, London Business School.

Baldwin, R. (2005) 'Is better regulation smarter regulation?' *Public Law* autumn: 485–511.

Barrett, S. M. (2004) 'Implementation studies: time for a revival? Personal reflections on 20 years of implementation studies', *Public Administration* (82) 2: 249–62.

Bartle, I. and Vass, P. (2007) 'Self-regulation within the regulatory state: towards a new regulatory paradigm?' *Public Administration* (85) 4: 885–905.

Baumgartner, F. and Jones, B. (1993) *Agendas and Instability in American Politics,* Chicago, Illinois: The University of Chicago Press.

Bawn, K. (1995) 'Political control versus expertise: congressional choices about administrative procedures', *The American Political Science Review* (89) 1: 62–73.

Bazeley, P. (2007) *Qualitative Data Analysis With NVivo,* London: Sage.

Becker, H. S. (1998) *Tricks of the Trade: How to think about your research while you're doing it,* Chicago: University of Chicago Press.

Bendor, J. *et al.* (2001) 'Theories of delegation', *Annual Review of Political Science* 4: 235–69.

Bennet, A. (2010) 'Process tracing and causal inference', in H. E. Brady and D. Collier (eds) *Rethinking Social Inquiry: Diverse tools, shared standards*, Lanham MD: Rowman and Littlefield, second edition.

Bennett, A. and Elman, C. (2006) 'Complex causal relations and case study methods: the example of path dependence', *Political Analysis* (14) 3: 250–67.

Bennett, C. J. and Howlett, M. (1992) 'The lessons of learning: reconciling theories of policy learning and policy change', *Policy Sciences* (25) 3: 275–94.

Berg, B. L. (2001) *Qualitative Research Methods for the Social Sciences*, Boston MA: Allyn & Bacon, fourth edition.

Berry, J. M. (2002) 'Validity and reliability issues in elite interviewing', *Political Science and Politics* (35) 4: 679–82.

Biegelbauer, P. (2007) 'Learning from abroad: the Austrian Competence Centre Programme Kplus', *Science and Public Policy* (34) 9: 606–18.

Binmore, K. and Klemperer, P. (2002) 'The biggest auction ever: the sale of the British 3G telecom licences', *Economic Journal* (112): 74–96. Due to a series of typos in the published version, the authors issued a corrected one. Online. Available: http://www.nuff.ox.ac.uk/users/klemperer/biggestpaper.pdf.

BIS (Department for Business, Innovation & Skills) (2009) Digital Britain. Final Report. June. Online. Available at /www.official-documents.gov.uk/document/cm76/7650/7650.pdf (accessed 25 September 2012).

—   (2010a) *Implementing the Revised EU Electronic Communications Framework. Impact Assessment.* September. Online. Available: http://www.bis.gov.uk/assets/biscore/business-sectors/docs/i/10–1133-implementing-revised-electronic-communications-framework-impact.pdf (accessed 17 September 2012).

—   (2010b) *Implementing the Revised EU Electronic Communications Framework. Overall approach and consultation on specific issues.* September. Online. Available: http://www.bis.gov.uk/assets/biscore/business-sectors/docs/i/10–1132-implementing-revised-electronic-communications-framework-consultation.pdf (accessed 17 September 2012).

Booth, W. C. *et al.* (2008) *The Craft of Research,* Chicago IL: The University of Chicago Press, third edition.

Boswell, C. (2006) *The Legitimizing Function of Expert Knowledge in the Administration,* unpublished manuscript.

—   (2009) *The Political Uses of Expert Knowledge: Immigration policy and social research*, Cambridge: Cambridge University Press.

Bourreau, M. *et al.* (2011) 'Incentives to migrate to next generation networks: from 'old' to 'new' technology'. Online. Available: http://ftp.zew.de/pub/zew-docs/veranstaltungen/ICT2011/Papers/Bourreau.pdf (accessed 23 September 2012).

Brady, H. E. (2010) 'Data-set observations versus causal-process observations: the 2000 U.S presidential election', in H. E. Brady and D. Collier (ed.) *Rethinking Social Inquiry: Diverse tools, shared standards*, Lanham MD: Rowman and Littlefield, second edition.

Brady, H. E. and Collier, D. (ed.) (2004) *Rethinking Social Inquiry: Diverse tools, shared standards*, Lanham MD: Rowman and Littlefield, first edition, 2004.

—   (2010) *Rethinking social inquiry: diverse tools, shared standards*, Rowman and Littlefield, second edition.

Brunsson, N. (1989) *The Organization Of Hypocrisy: Talk, decisions and actions in organizations*, Chichester: John Wiley & Sons.

—   (2007) *The Consequences of Decision-Making*, Oxford: Oxford University Press.

Burton, J. (1997) 'The competitive order or ordered competition? The "UK model" of utility regulation in theory and practice', *Public Administration* 75: 157–88.

Busuioc, M. *et al.* (2011) 'Agency growth between autonomy and accountability: the European Police Office as "living institution"', *Journal of European Public Policy* (18) 6: 848–67.

Caplan, N. (1979) 'The two-communities theory and knowledge utilization', *American Behavioral Scientist* (22) 3: 459–70.

Carpenter, D. (2010) *Reputation and Power. Organizational image and pharmaceutical regulation at the FDA*, Princeton NJ: Princeton University Press.

Carstensen, M. B. (2011) 'Paradigm man vs. the bricoleur: bricolage as an alternative vision of agency in ideational change', *European Political Science Review* (3)1: 147–67.

Cave, M. (2006) 'Encouraging infrastructure investment via the ladder of investment', *Telecommunications Policy* (30) 3: 223–37.

Cave, M. and Martin, I. (2010) 'Motives and means for public investment in nationwide new generation networks', *Telecommunications Policy* 34: 505–12.

Cave, M. and Williamson, P. (1996) 'Entry, competition, and regulation in UK telecommunications', *Oxford Review of Economic Policy* (12) 4: 100–21.

Cave, M. *et al.* (2001) 'The relationship between access pricing regulation and infrastructure competition', Report to OPTA and DG Telecommunications and Post by Brunel University.

Cave, M. *et al.* (2006) 'Regulating for non-price discrimination. The case of UK fixed telecoms'. Online. Available: http://papers.ssrn.com/sol3/papers.cfm?abstract_id=1973514 (accessed 17 September 2012).

Checkel, J. T. (2007) 'It's the process stupid! Tracing causal mechanisms in European and international politics'. Online. Available: http://www.sv.uio.no/arena/english/research/publications/arena-publications/workingpapers/working-papers2005/wp05_26.pdf (accessed 17 September 2012).

Christensen, J. G. (2001) 'Bureaucratic autonomy as a political asset', in G.B. Peters and J. Pierre (eds) *Politicians, Bureaucrats and Administrative Reform*, London: Routledge.

Christensen, T. and Lægreid, P. (2006) 'Agencification and regulatory reform', in T. Christensen and P. Lægreid (eds) *Autonomy and Regulation: Coping with agencies in the modern state,* Cheltenham: Edward Elgar.

—   (2007a) 'Regulatory agencies – the challenge of balancing agency autonomy and political control', *Governance* (20) 3: 499–520.

—   (2007b) 'The regulatory orthodoxy in practice', paper presented at the ECPR Conference, Pisa, 6–8 September.

Coen, D. (2005) 'Managing the political life cycle of regulation in the UK and German telecommunication sectors', *Annals of Public and Cooperative Economics* (76) 1: 59–84.

Coen, D. and Thatcher, M. (2005) 'The new governance of market and non-majoritarian regulators', *Governance* (18) 3: 329–46.

Coglianese, C. (2011) 'Process choice', *Regulation & Governance* 5: 250–61.

Coleman, J. S. (1990) *Foundations of Social Theory*, Cambridge, MA: Harvard University Press

Crandall, R. W. and Sidak, G. (2004) 'Should regulators set rates to terminate calls on mobile networks?' *Yale Journal on Regulation* 21: 261–314.

Crandall, R. W. *et al.* (2012) 'The long-run effects of copper unbundling and implications for fiber' Telecommunications policy, forthcoming. Online. Available: http://ssrn.com/abstract=2018929 or http://dx.doi.org/10.2139/ssrn.2018929.

Dassler, T. *et al.* (2006) 'Methods and trends of performance benchmarking in UK utility regulation', Utilities Policy 14: 166–74.

de Bijl, P. W. J. *et al.* (2005) 'Interconnected networks', TILEC Discussion Paper, February.

De Streel, A. (2008a) 'The relationship between competition law and sector specific regulation: the case of electronic communications', *Reflets et Perspectives*, XLVII (1): 53–70.

—   (2008b) 'Current and future European regulation of electronic communications: a critical assessment', *Telecommunications Policy* 32: 722–34.

Dewenter, R. (2005) 'The effects of regulating mobile termination rates for asymmetric networks', *European Journal of Law and Economics* 20: 185–97.

Dexter, L. A. (2006) *Elite and Specialized Interviewing,* ECPR Press, Classic Series.

Di Maggio, P. J. and Powell, W. W. (1983) 'The iron cage revisited: institutional isomorphism and collective rationality in organizational fields' *American Sociological Review* (48) 2:147–60.

Doehler, M. (2002) 'Institutional choice and bureaucratic autonomy in Germany', *West European Politics* (25) 1: 101–24.

Dunlop, C. (2009) 'Policy transfer as learning: capturing variation in what decision-makers learn from epistemic communities', *Policy Studies* (30) 3: 289–311.

—   (2010) 'The temporal dimension of knowledge and the limits of policy appraisal: biofuels policy in the UK', *Policy Sciences* (43) 4: 343–63.

Dunlop, C. *et al.* (2012) 'The many uses of regulatory impact assessment: a meta-analysis of EU and UK cases', *Regulation and Governance* 6: 23–45.

ECTA (2010) *Regulatory Scorecard 2009*. Released on 1 June. Online. Available: http://www.ectaportal.com/en/REPORTS/Regulatory-Scorecards/Regulatory-Scorecard-2009/ (accessed 17 September 2012).

Egeberg, M. (2003) 'How bureaucratic structure matters: an organizational perspective', in G. B. Peters and J. Pierre (ed.) *Handbook of Public Administration*, London: Sage.

Eisner M. A. *et al.* (2000) *Contemporary Regulatory Policy*, Lynne Rienner Publishers.

Elman, C. (2005) 'Explanatory typologies in qualitative studies of international politics', *International Organization* (59) 2: 293–326.

Eshbaugh-Soha, M. (2006) 'The conditioning effects of policy salience and complexity on American political institutions', *Policy Studies Journal* (34) 2: 223–43.

European Commission (2001) *European Governance: A White Paper*, COM(2011) 428 final. Brussels.

— (2002) *Communication from the Commission. The operating framework for the European regulatory agencies*, COM(2002) 718 final. Brussels.

— (2005) *Better Regulation for Growth and Jobs in the European Union*, COM(2005) 97 final. Brussels.

Everson, M. (2011) 'European agencies: a double paradox', presentation at the Seminar on Experts in Policy-Making, University of Rotterdam, 25 June.

Feldman, M. S. and March, J. G. (1981) 'Information in organizations as signal and symbol', *Administrative Science Quarterly* 26: 171–86.

Franchino, F. (2002) 'Efficiency or credibility? Testing the two logics of delegation to the European Commission', *Journal of European Public Policy* (9) 5: 677–94.

Freedman, D. A. (2010) 'On types of scientific inquiry: the role of qualitative reasoning', in H. E. Brady and D. Collier (eds) *Rethinking Social Inquiry: Diverse tools, shared standards*, Lanham MD: Rowman and Littlefield, second edition.

Furner, M. O. and Supple, B. (eds) (1990) *The State and Economic Knowledge. The American and British experiences,* Cambridge: Cambridge University Press.

Galli, G. and Pelkmans, J. (eds.) *Regulatory Reform and Competitiveness in Europe,* Cheltenham: Edward Elgar, 2000.

George, A. L. and Bennett, A. (2005) *Case Studies and Theory Development in the Social Sciences,* Cambridge MA: The MIT Press.

Gerring, J. (2004) 'What is a case study and what is it good for?' *American Political Science Review* (98) 2: 341–54.

— (2007) *Case Study Research: Principles and practices*, New York NY: Cambridge University Press.

— (2011) 'Causal Mechanisms: Yes, but...' *Comparative Political Studies* (44) 5. Extended version. Online. Available: http://people.bu.edu/jgerring/documents/CausalMechanisms_Extended.pdf (accessed September 17 2012).

Gibson, D. and Goodin R. E. (2000) 'The veil of vagueness: a model of institutional design', in M. Egeberg and P. Lægreid (eds) *Organising Political Institutions*, Oslo: Scandinavian University Press.

Gilardi, F. (2002a) 'Regulation through independent agencies in Western Europe: new institutionalist perspectives', paper presented at the workshop on Theories of Regulation, Nuffield College, Oxford, 25–26 May.

— (2002b) 'Policy credibility and delegation to independent regulatory agencies: a comparative empirical analysis', *Journal of European Public Policy* (9) 6: 873–93.

— (2004) 'Institutional change in regulatory policies: regulation through independent agencies and the three new institutionalisms', in Levi Faur, D. and Jordana, J. (eds) *The Politics of Regulation: Institutions and Regulatory Reforms for the Age of Governance*, Manchester: University of Manchester Centre on Regulation and Competition.

— (2007) 'The same, but different: central banks, regulatory agencies, and the politics of delegation to independent authorities', *Comparative European Politics* (5) 3: 303–27.

Goffman, E. (1959) *The Presentation of Self in Everyday Life,* New York: Doubleday Anchor Books.

— (1974) *Frame Analysis: An essay on the organization of experience,* London: Harper and Row.

Goldstein, K. (2002) 'Getting in the door. Sampling and completing elite interviews', *Political Science and Politics* (35) 4: 669–72.

Gormley, W. T. Jr. (1986) 'Regulatory issue networks in a federal system', *Polity* (18) 4: 595–20.

Haas, P. M. (1992) 'Introduction: epistemic communities and international policy coordination', *International Organization* (46) 1: 1–35.

— (2004) 'When does power listen to truth? A constructivist approach to the policy process', *Journal of European Public Policy* (11) 4: 569–92.

Hahn, R. W. (2005) *In Defence of the Economic Analysis of Regulation*, American Enterprise Institute: Washington, D.C.

Hahn, R. W. and Tetlock, P. C. (2008) 'Has economic analysis improved regulatory decisions?' *Journal of Economic Perspectives* (22) 1: 67–84.

Hall, C. *et al.* (2000) *Telecommunications Regulation: Culture, chaos and interdependence inside the regulatory process*, London: Routledge.

Hall, P. A. (1993) 'Policy paradigms, social learning and the state: the case of economic policy-making in Britain', *Comparative Politics* 25: 275–96.

— (ed.) (1989) *The Political Power of Economic Ideas: Keynesianism across nations*, Princeton NJ: Princeton University Press.

Hanretty, C. and Koop, C. (2012) 'Measuring the formal independence of regulatory agencies', *Journal of European Public Policy* (19) 2: 198–216.

Harbord, D. and Pagnozzi, M. (2008) 'On-net/off-net price discrimination and "bill-and-keep" vs. "cost based" regulation of mobile termination rates'. Online. Available: http://papers.ssrn.com/sol3/papers.cfm?abstract_id=1374851 (accessed 18 September 2012).

Hassenzahl, D. M. (2006) 'Implications of excessive precision for risk comparisons: lessons from the past four decades', *Risk Analysis* (26) 1: 265–76.

Heller, F. (ed.) (1986) *The Use and Abuse of Social Science*, London: Sage.

Hertin, J. *et al.* (2008) 'Rationalising the policy mess? Ex ante policy assessment and the utilisation of knowledge in the policy process', *Environment and Planning A* (41) 5: 1185–2100.

Hill, M. J. (2004) *The Public Policy Process,* Essex: Pearson, fourth edition.

Holburn, G. L. F. and Vanden Bergh, R. G. (2006) 'Making friends in hostile environments: political strategy in regulated industries', *Academy of Management Review* (33) 2: 521–540.

Hood, C. *et al.* (2001) *The Government of Risk: Understanding risk regulation regimes*, Oxford: Oxford University Press.

House of Commons (2002) *The Office of Communications Bill,* Research Paper 02/03, January 14.

— (2009) 'Pre-appointment hearing with the Chairman-elect of Ofcom, Dr. Colette Bowe', Business and Enterprise Select Committee. HC 119, 19 January.

House of Lords (2007) *UK Economic Regulators.* Volumes I (report) and II (evidence). HL Paper 189 I and II, First Report of Session 2006–2007, Select Committee on Regulators, 13 November.

Howlett, M. and Ramesh, M. (2003) *Studying Public Policy: Policy cycles and policy subsystems*, Oxford: Oxford University Press, second edition.

Huber, J. D. and Shipan, C. R. (2002) *Deliberate Discretion: The institutional foundations of bureaucratic autonomy,* Cambridge: Cambridge University Press.

Jennings, E. T. Jr. and Hall, J. L. (2011) 'Evidence-based practice and the use of information in state agency decision-making', *Journal of Public Administration Research and Theory.* Online. Available: http://jpart. oxfordjournals.org/content/early/2011/07/21/jopart.mur040.abstract

Jones, M. D. and McBeth, M. K. (2010) 'A narrative policy framework: clear enough to be wrong?' *Policy Studies Journal* (38) 2: 329–53.

Jordana J. and Levi-Faur D. (eds) (2004) *The Politics of Regulation: Institutions and regulatory reforms for the age of governance.* Manchester: University of Manchester Press; Centre on Regulation and Competition.

Jordana, J. and Sancho, D. (2004) 'Regulatory designs, institutional constellations, and the study of the regulatory state', in Jordana J. and Levi Faur D. (eds) *The Politics of Regulation: Institutions and regulatory reforms for the age of governance,* Manchester: University of Manchester Press; Centre on Regulation and Competition.

Kagan, R. (1997) 'Should Europe worry about adversarial legalism?' *Oxford Journal of Legal Studies* (17) 2: 165–84.

Kelemen, R. D. and Sibbitt, E. C. (2004) The globalization of American law, *International Organization* (58) 1:103–36.

— (2005) 'Lex Americana? A response to Levi-Faur', *International Organization* (59) 2: 463–72.

Kellow, A. (1988) 'Promoting elegance in policy theory: simplifying Lowi's arenas of power', *Policy Studies Journal* (16) 4: 713–24.

Kerwin, C. M. (2003) *Rulemaking. How government agencies write law and make policy*, Washington DC: CQ Press, third edition.

King, G. *et al.* (1994) *Designing Social Inquiry: Scientific inference in qualitative research*. Princeton NJ: Princeton University Press.

Kingdon, J. W. (1995) *Agendas, Alternatives, and Public Policies:* New York NY: Longman, second edition.

Kirkpatrick, C. and Parker, D. (2007) *Regulatory Impact Assessment: Towards better regulation?* Cheltenham: Edward Elgar.

Kirsch, F. and von Hirschhausen, C. (2008) 'Regulation of NGN: structural separation, access regulation, or no regulation at all?' *Communications and Strategies* (69) 1: 63–83.

Kjellberg, F. (1977) 'Do policies (really) determine politics? And eventually how?' *Policy Studies Journal* (5) 1: 554–70.

Krause, G. A. and Douglas, J. W. (2005) 'Institutional design versus reputational effects on bureaucratic performance: evidence from U.S. Government macroeconomic and fiscal projections', *Journal of Public Administration Research and Theory* 15: 281–306.

Krippendorff, K. (2004) *Content Analysis: An introduction to its methodology*, Thousand Oaks, CA: Sage, second edition.

Lægreid, P. *et al.* (2008) 'The governance, autonomy and coordination of public sector organisations', *Public Organizations Review* 8: 93–6.

Lægreid P. *et al.* (2008) 'Controlling regulatory agencies', *Scandinavian Political Studies* (31) 1: 1–26.

Laffont, J. J. *et al.* (1998) 'Network competition I: overview and nondiscriminatory pricing', *RAND Journal of Economics* 29: 1–37.

Lambright, H. W. (2008) 'Government and science: a troubled, critical relationship and what can be done about it', *Public Administration Review* January/February: 1–18.

Larouche, P. (2007) 'Europe and investment in infrastructure with emphasis on electronic communications', *TILEC Discussion Paper* DP 2007–31, October.

—— (2008) 'Regulating to foster investment in infrastructure: a critical legal appraisal of the policy options', paper presented at the first annual conference on Competition and Regulation of Network Industries, CEPS, Brussels, November 28.

Larouche, P. and Taton, X. (2011) 'Enforcement and judicial review of decisions of national regulatory authorities. Identification of best practices', *CERRE Study*. 21 April. Online. Available: http://www.cerre.eu.

Latour, B. and Woolgar, S. (1979) *Laboratory Life: The construction of scientific facts*, Princeton NJ: Princeton University Press.

Laver, M. and Garry, J. (2000) 'Estimating policy positions from political texts', *American Journal of Political Science* 44: 619–34.

Laver, M. *et al.* (2003) 'Extracting policy positions from political texts using words as data', *American Political Science Review* (97) 2: 311–31.

Leech, B. L. (2002) 'Asking questions: techniques for semistructured interviews', *Political Science and Politics*, (35) 4: 665–68.

Levi-Faur, D. (2006) 'Regulatory capitalism: the dynamics of change beyond telecoms and electricity', *Governance* (19) 3: 497–525.

Lindblom, C. E. (1959) 'The science of muddling through', *Public Administration Review* 19: 79–88.

— (1979) 'Still muddling, not yet through', *Public Administration Review* 39: 517–26.

— (1986) 'Who needs what social research for policy making?' *Science Communication* (7) 4: 345–66.

Lindblom, C. E. and Cohen, D. K. (1979) *Usable Knowledge: Social science and social problem solving*, New Haven CT: Yale University Press.

Lindquist, E. A. (1988) 'What do decision models tell us about information use?' *Knowledge, Technology and Policy* (1) 2: 86–111.

Littlechild, S. (2004) 'Mobile call termination charges: calling party pays vs. receiving party pays', *CWPE 0426*, University of Cambridge.

Loughlin, M. and Scott, C. (1997) 'The regulatory state' in P. Dunleavy *et al.* (eds) *Developments in British Politics 5*, Basingstoke: Macmillan.

Lowi, T. J. (1964) 'Review: American business, public policy, case-studies, and political theory', *World Politics* (16) 4: 677–715.

— (1972) 'Four systems of policy, politics and choice', *Public Administration Review* 4: 298–310.

— (1988) 'An assessment of Kellow's "Promoting elegance in Policy Theory"', *Policy Studies Journal* (16) 4: 725–28.

Maggetti, M. (2007) 'De facto independence after delegation: a fuzzy-set analysis', *Regulation & Governance* 1: 271–94.

— (2009) 'The role of independent regulatory agencies in policy-making: a comparative analysis', *Journal of European Public Policy* (16) 3: 450–70.

Maggetti *et al.* (2012) *Designing Research in the Social Sciences*, London: Sage.

Mahor, M. (2007) 'A scientific standard and an agency's legal independence: which of these reputation protection mechanisms is less susceptible to political moves?', *Public Administration* (85) 4: 961–78.

Majone, G. (1994) 'The rise of the regulatory state in Europe', *West European Politics* (17) 3: 77–101.

— (1996) *Regulating Europe*, London: Routledge.

— (1997) 'From the positive to the regulatory state: causes and consequences of changes in the mode of governance', *Journal of Public Policy* (17) 2: 139–67.

— (2000) 'The credibility crisis of Community regulation', *Journal of Common Market Studies* (38) 2: 273–302.

— (2001a) 'Non-majoritarian institutions and the limits of democratic governance: a political transaction-cost approach', *Journal of Institutional and Theoretical Economics* (157) 1: 57–78.

— (2001b) 'Two logics of delegation: agency and fiduciary relations in EU governance', *European Union Politics* (2) 1: 103–22.

—   (2010) 'Foundations of risk regulation: science, decision-making, policy learning and institutional reform', *European Journal of Risk Regulation* 1: 5–19.

March, J. G. and Olsen, J. P. (1989) *Rediscovering Institutions: The organizational basis of politics*, New York NY: Free Press.

May, P. (1992) 'Policy learning and failure', *Journal of Public Policy* (12) 4: 331–54.

McCloskey, D. (1998) *The Rhetoric of Economics*, Madison WI: University of Wisconsin Press.

McCubbins *et al.* (1987) 'Administrative procedure as instruments of political control', *Journal of Law, Economics, and Organization* (3) 2: 243–77.

—   (1989) 'Structure and process, politics and policy: administrative arrangements and the political control of agencies', *Virginia Law Review* (75) 2: 431–82.

McGarity, T. O. (1991) *Reinventing Rationality: The role of regulatory analysis in the federal bureaucracy,* New York NY: Cambridge University Press.

McKenna, A. (2000) 'Emerging issues surrounding the convergence of telecommunications, broadcasting and information technologies sectors', *Information & Communications Technology Law* (9) 2: 93–127.

McNamara, K. (2002) 'Rational fictions: central bank independence and the social logic of delegation', *West European Politics* (25) 1: 47–76.

Meier, H. E. (2008) 'Independent regulatory bodies and impossible jobs: the failure of German broadcasting regulation', *Public Administration* (86) 1: 133–148.

Meuwese, A. C. (2008) *Impact Assessment in EU Law-Making,* Leiden: Kluwer Law International.

Miles, M. B. and Huberman, M. (1994) *Qualitative Data Analysis: An expanded sourcebook.* Thousand Oaks, CA: Sage, second edition.

Miller, G. J. (2005) 'The political evolution of principal-agent models', *Annual Review of Political Science* 8: 203–25.

Mintzberg, H. (1979) *The Structuring of Organizations*, Englewood Cliffs NJ: Prentice Hall.

—   (1983) *Structure in Fives: Designing effective organizations*, Englewood Cliffs NJ: Prentice Hall.

Moe, T. M. (1990) 'Political institutions: the neglected side of the story', *Journal of Law, Economics, and Organisation* 6: 213–53.

Moffitt, S. L. (2010) 'Promoting agency reputation through public advice: advisory committee use in the FDA', *The Journal of Politics* 72: 880–93.

Montpetit, E. (2011) 'Scientific credibility, disagreement, and error costs in 17 biotechnology policy subsystems', *Policy Studies Journal* (39) 3: 513–33.

Morgenstern, R. D. (1997) *Economic Analysis at EPA: Assessing regulatory impact*, Washington, DC: Resources for the Future.

Munck, G. L. (2004) 'Tools for qualitative research', in H. E. Brady and D. Collier (eds), *Rethinking Social Enquiry: Diverse tools, shared standards,* Lanham MD: Rowman & Littlefield.

NAO (National Audit Office) (2002) *Pipes and Wires*, Report by the Comptroller and Auditor General, HC 723 Session 2001–2002. April.

— (2006) *The Creation of Ofcom: Wider lessons for public sector mergers of regulatory agencies*, Report by the Comptroller and Auditor General, HC 1175 Session 2005–2006, 5 July.

— (2007) *Evaluation of Regulatory Impact Assessments*, Report by the Comptroller and Auditor General, HC 606 Session 2006–2007, 11 July.

— (2010a) *Assessing the Impact of Proposed New Policies,* Report by the Comptroller and Auditor General, HC 185, Session 2010–2011, 1 July.

— (2010b) *The Effectiveness of Converged Regulation*, Report by the Comptroller and Auditor General, HC 490 Session 2010–2011, 10 November.

Neuendorf, K. A. (2002) *The Content Analysis Guidebook*, Thousand Oaks, CA: Sage.

Nilsson *et al.* (2008) 'The use and non-use of policy appraisal tools in public policy making: an analysis of three European countries and the European Union', *Policy Sciences* 41: 335–55.

Nutley, S. N. *et al.* (2007) *Using Evidence: How research can inform public services,* Bristol: The Policy Press.

OECD (1995) *Recommendations on Regulatory Quality*, Paris.

— (2002) *Regulatory Policies in OECD countries: From interventionism to regulatory governance*, Paris.

— (2005) *Guiding Principles for Regulatory Quality and Performance,* Paris.

— (2006a) 'Report on structural separation', *OECD Journal of Competition Law and Policy* (8)2.

— (2006b) *Telecommunication regulatory institutional structures and responsibilities*, Working Party on Telecommunication and Information Services Policies, DSTI/ICCP/TISP(2005)6/FINAL. Online. Available: http://www.oecd.org/internet/broadbandandtelecom/35954786.pdf (accessed 23 November 2012).

— (2008) 'Convergence and Next Generation Networks', Ministerial Background Report, DSTI/ICCP/CISP(2007)2/FINAL.

— (2009) 'The role of communication infrastructure in economic recovery', Working Party on Communication Infrastructures and Services Policy, 19 May.

Ofcom (2004) 'Next Generation Networks – Future arrangements for access and interconnection', consultation, 25 November. Online. Available: http://stakeholders.ofcom.org.uk/consultations/ngn/ (accessed 20 September 2012).

— (2005a) 'Wholesale mobile voice call termination. Preliminary consultation on future regulation', consultation, 7 June. Online. Available: http://stakeholders.ofcom.org.uk/consultations/termination/ (accessed 20 September 2012).

—   (2005b) 'Next Generation Networks: further consultation', consultation, 30 June. Online. Available: http://stakeholders.ofcom.org.uk/consultations/nxgnfc/ (accessed 20 September 2012).

—   (2005c) 'Wholesale mobile voice call termination – Statement and notification extending the charge controls', statement, 16 December. Online. Available: http://stakeholders.ofcom.org.uk/binaries/consultations/wholesale/statement/statement.pdf (accessed 20 September 2012).

—   (2005d) Minutes of the Fifty-Fourth Meeting of the Ofcom Board, Held at Ofcom, Riverside House, London on 10 May 2005. Online. Available: http://www.ofcom.org.uk/static/about/ofcomboard/minutes/54.pdf (accessed 2 April 2013).

—   (2006a) 'NextGenerationNetworks:developingtheregulatoryframework', statement, 7 March. Online. Available: http://stakeholders.ofcom.org.uk/consultations/nxgnfc/statement/ (accessed 20 September 2012).

—   (2006b) 'Ofcom proposal to deregulate BT retail phone cost controls', Press release, 21 March 2006, London. Online. Available: http://media.ofcom.org.uk/2006/03/21/ofcom-proposal-to-deregulate-bt-retail-phone-cost-controls/?lang=cy (accessed 20 September 2012).

—   (2006c) 'Mobile call termination. Market review', consultation, 30 March. Online. Available: http://stakeholders.ofcom.org.uk/binaries/consultations/mct/summary/mct.pdf (accessed 20 September 2012).

—   (2006d) 'A case study on public sector mergers and regulatory structures' April. Online. Available: http://www.ofcom.org.uk/files/2010/07/public_sector_merger_case_study.pdf (accessed 20 September 2012).

—   (2006e) 'Mobile call termination. Proposals for consultation', consultation, 13 September. Online. Available: http://stakeholders.ofcom.org.uk/binaries/consultations/mobile_call_term/summary/new_mobile.pdf (accessed 20 September 2012).

—   (2006f) Minutes of the 85th Meeting of the Ofcom Board, held in London on 25 July 2006. Online. Available: http://www.ofcom.org.uk/static/about/ofcomboard/minutes/85.pdf (accessed 2 April 2013).

—   (2007a) 'Mobile call termination', statement, 27 March. Online. Available: http://stakeholders.ofcom.org.uk/consultations/mobile_call_term/statement/ (accessed 20 September 2012).

—   (2007b) Minutes of the 97th Meeting of the Ofcom Board, held on 13 February 2007. Online. Available: http://www.ofcom.org.uk/static/about/ofcomboard/minutes/97.pdf; and Minutes of the 100th Meeting of the Ofcom Board, held on 27 March 2007. Online. Available: http://www.ofcom.org.uk/static/about/ofcomboard/minutes/100.pdf (accessed 2 April 2013).

—   (2009a) 'Consumer preferences in narrowband communications', research report, 19 March. Online. Available: http://stakeholders.ofcom.org.uk/binaries/consultations/retail_markets/annexes/consprefs.pdf (accessed 20 September 2012).

—   (2009b) 'SME preferences in narrowband communications', Research Report, 19 March. Online. Available: http://stakeholders.ofcom.org.uk/binaries/consultations/retail_markets/annexes/smeprefs.pdf (accessed 20 September 2012).

—   (2009c) 'Fixed narrowband retail services market. Consultation on the identification of markets and determination of market power', consultation, 19 March. Online. Available: http://stakeholders.ofcom.org.uk/consultations/retail_markets/ (accessed 20 September 2012).

—   (2009d) 'Next Generation Networks: responding to recent developments to protect consumers, promote effective competition and secure efficient investment', Consultation, 31 July. Online. Available: http://stakeholders.ofcom.org.uk/consultations/ngndevelopments/ (accessed 20 September 2012).

—   (2009e) 'Fixed narrowband retail services markets. Identification of markets and determination of market power', regulatory statement, 15 September. Online. Available: http://stakeholders.ofcom.org.uk/consultations/retail_markets/statement/ (accessed 20 September 2012).

—   (2010a) 'Next Generation Networks (NGNs): responding to recent developments to protect consumers, promote effective competition and secure efficient investment', statement, 28 January. Online. Available: http://stakeholders.ofcom.org.uk/binaries/consultations/ngndevelopments/statement/ngn_statement.pdf (accessed 20 September 2012).

—   (2011) 'Communications market report', research document, 4 August. Online. Available: http://stakeholders.ofcom.org.uk/market-data-research/market-data/communications-market-reports/cmr11/ (accessed 23 October 2012).

—   (2012a) 'Ofcom annual report 2010–2011', July 2012. Online. Available: http://www.ofcom.org.uk/files/2012/07/OfcomAnnualReport11–12.pdf (accessed 23 October 2012).

—   (2012b) 'Communications market report', research document, July. Online. Available: http://stakeholders.ofcom.org.uk/binaries/research/cmr/cmr12/CMR_UK_2012.pdf (accessed 23 October 2012).

Oftel (2003) 'Fixed narrowband retail services market', explanatory statement and notification, 26 August. Online. Available: http://www.ofcom.org.uk/static/archive/oftel/publications/eu_directives/2003/fix_narrow_retail0803.pdf (accessed 20 September 2012).

Owens, S. *et al.* (2004) 'New agendas for appraisal: reflections on theory, practice and research', *Environment and Planning A* (36) 11: 1943–59.

Pawson, R. (2002) 'Evidence-based policy: in search of a method', *Evaluation* (8) 2: 157–81.

Pelkmans, J. and Renda, A. (2011) 'Single eComms market? No such thing…', *CEPS Policy Brief* N.231, January. Online. Available: http://www.ceps.be/book/single-ecomms-market-no-such-thing%E2%80%A6 (accessed 20 September 2012).

Peters, G. (2000) *American Public Policy*, CQ Press, sixth edition.

Peters, G. and Pierre, J. (eds) (2001) *Politicians, Bureaucrats and Administrative Reform*, London: Routledge.

Pierre, J. and Peters, G. (2004) *Politicization of the Civil Service in a Comparative Perspective*, London: Routledge.

Pollitt, C. *et al.* (2001) 'Agency fever? Analysis of an international policy fashion', *Journal of Comparative Policy Analysis: Research and Practice* 3: 271–90.

Pollitt, C. *et al.* (2004) *Agencies: How governments do things through semi-autonomous organizations*, Basingstoke: Palgrave Macmillan.

Pollitt, C. and Bouckaert, G. (2000) *Public Management Reform: A comparative analysis*, Oxford: Oxford University Press.

Posner, E. A. (2001) 'Controlling agencies with cost-benefit analysis: a positive political theory perspective', *University of Chicago Law Review* 68.

Premfors, R. (1984) 'Research and policy-making in Swedish higher education', in T. Husén and M. Kogan (eds) *Educational Research & Policy*, Oxford: Pergamon Press.

— (1991) 'Scientific bureaucracy? Research implementation and Swedish civil servants', in M. A. Trow and T. Nybom (ed.), *University and Society. Essays on the social role of research and higher education*, London: Jessica Kingsley Publishers.

Radaelli, C. M. (1995) 'The role of knowledge in the policy process', *Journal of European Public Policy* (2) 2: 159–83.

— (2005a) 'What does regulatory impact assessment mean in Europe?' AEI- Brookings Joint Center for Regulatory Studies, Working Paper No. 05–02, January, Washington: DC.

— (2005b) 'Diffusion without convergence: how political context shapes the adoption of regulatory impact assessment', *Journal of European Public Policy* (12) 5: 924–43.

— (2007) 'Whither better regulation for the Lisbon agenda?' *Journal of European Public Policy* (14) 2: 190–207.

— (2009a) 'Measuring policy learning across Europe: regulatory impact assessment in Comparative Perspective', *Journal of European Public Policy* (16) 8: 1145–64.

— (2009b) 'The political consequences of regulatory impact assessment', paper delivered at the conference Governing the Regulatory State? Comparing Strategies and Instruments, British Academy, London, 15 January.

Radaelli, C. M. and Dente, B. (1996) 'Evaluation strategies and analysis of the policy process', *Evaluation* (2) 1: 51–66.

Radaelli, C. M. and Meuwese, A. C. (2009) 'Better regulation in Europe: between management and regulation', *Public Administration* (87) 2: 639–54.

Reed, C. (2007) 'Taking sides on technology neutrality', 4: 3*SCRIPTed* 263. Online. Available: http://www.law.ed.ac.uk/ahrc/script-ed/vol4–3/reed. asp (accessed 21 November 2012).

Renda, A. (2008) 'I own the pipes, you call the tune. The net neutrality debate and its (ir)relevance for Europe', *CEPS Working Papers*. Online. Available: http://www.ceps.be/book/i-own-pipes-you-call-tune-net-neutrality-debate-and-its-irrelevance-europe (accessed 20 September 2012).

— (2009) 'The review of the telecoms framework: tale of the anti-commons', in *Monitoring EU Telecoms Policy*, Network for Electronic Research on Electronic Communications (NEREC), Madrid.

Revesz, R. L. and Livermore, M. A. (2008) *Retaking Rationality. How cost-benefit analysis can better protect the environment and our health*, New York: Oxford University Press.

Richards, D. (1996) 'Elite interviewing: approaches and pitfalls', *Politics* (16) 3: 199–204.

Ringquist, E. *et al.* (2003) 'Salience, complexity, and the legislative direction of regulatory bureaucracies', *Journal of Public Administration Research and Theory* (13) 2: 141–64.

Sabatier, P. (1978) 'The acquisition and utilization of technical information by administrative agencies', *Administrative Science Quarterly* 23: 396–417.

— (1999) (ed.) *Theories of the Policy Process (Theoretical lenses on public policy)*, Boulder CO: Westview Press.

— (2007) (ed.) *Theories of the Policy Process (Theoretical lenses on public policy)*, Boulder CO: Westview Press, 2007.

Sabatier, P. and Jenkins-Smith H. (eds) (1993) *Policy Change and Learning: An advocacy coalition approach*, Boulder CO: Westview Press.

Sanderson, I. (2002) 'Evaluation, policy learning and evidence-based policy making', *Administration* (80) 1: 1–22.

— (2006) 'Complexity, "practical rationality" and evidence-based policy making', *Policy & Politics* (34) 1: 115–32.

— (2009) 'Intelligent policy making for a complex world: pragmatism, evidence, and learning', *Political Studies* 57: 699–719.

Schillemans, T. (2008) 'Accountability in the shadow of hierarchy: the horizontal accountability of agencies', *Public Organization Review* (8) 2: 175–94.

Schimmelfennig, F. (2002) 'Goffman meets IR: dramaturgical action in international community', *International Review of Sociology* (12) 3: 417–37.

Schmidt, V. A. (2006) *Democracy in Europe: The EU and national polities*, Oxford: Oxford University Press.

— (2008) 'Discursive institutionalism: the explanatory power of ideas and discourse', *Annual Review of Political Science* 11: 303–26.

— (2010) 'Reconciling ideas and institutions through discursive institutionalism', in D. Béland and R. H. Cox (eds), *Ideas and Politics in Social Research*, USA: Oxford University Press.

Schrefler, L. (2010) 'The usage of scientific knowledge by independent regulatory agencies', *Governance* (23) 2: 309–330.

Shanahan, E. A. *et al.* (2011) 'Policy narratives and policy processes', *Policy Studies Journal* (39) 3: 535–61.

Shapiro, M. (2002) 'Judicial delegation doctrines: the US, Britain, and France', *West European Politics* (25) 1: 173–99.

Shleifer, A. (1985) 'A theory of yardstick competition', *RAND Journal of Economics*, (16) 3: 319–27.

Shy, O. (2001) *The Economics of Network Industries*, Cambridge: Cambridge University Press.

Sil, R. and Katzenstein, P. J. (2010) *Beyond Paradigms: Analytic eclecticism in the study of world politics*, Basingstoke: Palgrave MacMillan, Political Analysis Series.

Sjörgen, E. (2006) *Reasonable Drugs: Making decisions with ambiguous knowledge,* Dissertation for the Degree of Doctor of Philosophy, Stockholm School of Economics.

Thatcher, M. (2002a) 'Delegation to independent regulatory agencies: pressures, functions and contextual mediation', *West European Politics* (25) 1: 125–47.

— (2002b) 'Regulation after delegation: independent regulatory agencies in Europe', *Journal of European Public Policy* (9) 6: 954–72.

— (2005) 'The third force? Independent regulatory agencies and elected politicians in Europe', *Governance* (18) 3: 347–73.

— (2007) 'Regulatory agencies, the state and markets: a Franco-British comparison', *Journal of European Public Policy* (14) 7: 1028–47.

— (2011) 'The creation of European regulatory agencies and its limits: a comparative analysis of European delegation', *Journal of European Public Policy* (18) 6: 790–809.

Thatcher, M. and Stone Sweet, A. (2002) 'Theory and practice of delegation to non-majoritarian institutions', *West European Politics* (25) 1: 1–22.

Torgerson, D. (1986) 'Between knowledge and politics: three faces of policy analysis', *Policy Sciences* (19) 3: 33–59.

True, J. L. *et al.* (2007) 'Punctuation-equilibrium theory: explaining stability and change in public policymaking', in P. Sabatier (ed.), *Theories of the Policy Process*, Boulder CO: Westview Press, second edition.

Turner, C. (2002) 'Strategic breakout in UK telecommunications: the case of Kingston Communications', *Strategic Change* 11: 17–24.

Valletti, T. and Houpis, G. (2005) 'Mobile termination: what is the "right" charge?', *Journal of Regulatory Economics*, (28) 3: 235–58.

Vibert, F. (2007) *The Rise of the Unelected: Democracy and the new separation of powers*, Cambridge: Cambridge University Press.

Vogel, S. K. (1996) *Freer Markets, More Rules. Regulatory reform in advanced industrial countries*, Ithaca NY: Cornell University Press.

Waterman, R. W. *et al.* (1998) 'The venues of influence: a new theory of political control of the bureaucracy', *Journal of Public Administration Research and Theory* (8) 1: 13–38.

Waverman, L. (1998) 'Telecommunications. Are the regulators killing innovations?', *Business Strategy Review* (9) 1: 21–8.

Weber, M. (1904/1949) 'Objectivity in social science and social policy', in E. A. Shils and H. A. Finch (eds/trans), *The Methodology of the Social Sciences*, New York NY: Free Press.

Weible, C. M. (2008) 'Expert-based information and policy subsystems: a review and synthesis', *Policy Studies Journal* (36) 4: 615–35.

Weick, K. E. (1995) *Sensemaking in Organizations*, Thousand Oaks, CA: Sage.

Weimer, D. L. (2008) 'Theories of and in the policy process', *Policy Studies Journal* (36) 4: 489–95.

Weiss, C. H. (1979) 'The many meanings of research utilization', *Public Administration Review* 39: 426–31.

—   (1986) 'Research and policy-making: a limited partnership', in F. Heller (ed.), *The Use and Abuse of Social Science*, Thousand Oaks, CA: Sage.

—   (1991) 'Policy research: data, ideas or arguments', in P. Wagner *et al.* (eds), *Social Science and Modern States: National experiences and theoretical crossroads,* Cambridge: Cambridge University Press.

—   (1999) 'The interface between evaluation and public policy', *Evaluation* 5: 468–86.

Weiss, J. A. (1979) 'Access to influence: some effects of policy sector on the use of social science', *American Behavioral Scientist* 22: 437–45.

Whalley, J. and Curwen, P. (2008) 'Equality of access and local loop unbundling in the UK broadband telecommunications market', *Telematics and Informatics* 25: 280–91.

Wilks, S. (2007) 'Corporate governance, boardization, accountability and the future of the Whitehall model', *International Journal of Regulation and Governance.*

Wilks, S. and Bartle, I. (2002) 'The unanticipated consequences of creating independent competition agencies', *West European Politics* (25) 1: 148–72.

Williamson, O. (1979) 'Transaction-cost economics: the governance of contractual relations', *Journal of Law and Economics* (22) 2: 233–61.

Wilsdon, J. *et al.* (2005) 'The public value of science. Or how to ensure that science really matters' *Demos*. Online. Available: http://www.demos.co.uk/files/publicvalueofscience.pdf (accessed 23 September 2012).

Wilson, C. A. (2006) *Public Policy: Continuity and change*, New York NY: McGraw-Hill.

Wilson, J. Q. (1989) *Bureaucracy: What government agencies do and why they do it,* New York NY: Free Press.

Wittrock, B. (1991) 'Social knowledge and public policy: eight models of interaction', in P. Wagner *et al.* (eds), *Social Science and Modern States: National experiences and theoretical crossroads,* Cambridge: Cambridge University Press.

Wonka, A. and Rittberger, B. (2011) 'Perspective on EU governance: an empirical assessment of the political attitudes of EU agency professionals', *Journal of European Public Policy* (18) 6: 888–908.

Wood, B. D. (1993) 'Review: *Reinventing Rationality: The Role of Regulatory Analysis in the Federal Bureaucracy*, by Thomas O. McGarity', *Journal of Politics* (55) 1: 251–54.

World Bank (2004) *Doing Business in 2004: Understanding regulation*, Washington DC: The World Bank and Oxford University Press.

Wright, J. (2002) 'Access pricing under competition: an application to cellular networks', *Journal of Industrial Economics* 50: 289–315.

Yandle, B. *et al.* (2011) 'Regulation by litigation', *Regulation & Governance* 5: 241–49.

Yesilkagit, K. and van Thiel, S. (2008) 'Political influence and bureaucratic autonomy', *Public Organization Review (8) 2:* 137–57.

— (2011) 'Autonomous agencies and perceptions of stakeholder influence in parliamentary democracies', *Journal of Public Administration Research and Theory.* Online. Available: http://jpart.oxfordjournals.org/content/early/2011/06/02/jopart.mur001.full.pdf (accessed 23 September 2012).

Zahariadis, N. (2007) 'The multiple streams framework: structure, limitations, prospects' in P. A. Sabatier (ed.) *Theories of the Policy Process*, Boulder CO: Westview Press, second edition.

| index

www.ingramcontent.com/pod-product-compliance
Lightning Source LLC
Chambersburg PA
CBHW072117020426
42334CB00018B/1631